LITERACY AND THE LIBRARY

LITERACY AND THE LIBRARY

Jeffrey L. Salter
Charles A. Salter

1991

Libraries Unlimited, Inc.
Englewood, Colorado

Printed in the United States of America

LIBRARIES UNLIMITED, INC.
P.O. Box 3988
Englewood, CO 80155-3988

Library of Congress Cataloging-in-Publication Data

Salter, Jeffrey L.
Literacy and the library / Jeffrey L. Salter, Charles A. Salter.
xxviii, 212 p. 17x25 cm.
Includes bibliographical references and index.
ISBN 0-87287-873-2
1. Public libraries--Services to the illiterate. 2. Libraries and new literates. 3. Literacy programs. I. Salter, Charles A., 1947- . II. Title.
Z716.45.S24 1991
027.6--dc20 90-24344
CIP

DEDICATION

This book is affectionately dedicated to our grandmothers

Nora Lee Daniels Robinson,
who (while in her late teens before World War I) taught in a rural Alabama one-room school and

Zanie Melvina Whitehead Salter,
who (while raising her seven children in rural Mississippi during the Great Depression) was tutored in basic literacy skills by a New England teacher working under one of Roosevelt's New Deal programs.

CONTENTS

Appendixes

BIBLIOGRAPHY *(continued)*

FOREWORD

Oxford's Bodleian Library, a three-star site on any tourist's map of England, still displays books chained to ancient desks, reminding us of a very different world. In earlier times books were few and expensive and librarians guarded their volumes with lock and key. Only selected members of the population—a tiny minority—were entitled to learn to read; the library was a tightly defended fortress of learning. Although the Bodleian now supplements its chained and unchained collection of books with sophisticated computerized catalogs and reservoirs of information, it still exists only for the already literate scholar.

But what of those for whom books and computerized information seem chained away for another reason—whose access is limited because they simply can't read? How can libraries help today's nonreaders? Charles Salter and Jeffrey Salter have written a book for modern times, when illiteracy threatens the welfare of the whole community. They have imagined a world in which libraries, no longer limited to established scholars, are partners with all who want to learn to read or to read better.

Imagination isn't enough. *Literacy and the Library* systematically presents the antecedents of illiteracy problems and realistic, careful suggestions for ways to create and sustain a partnership between libraries, literacy programs, and nonreaders. Rather than chaining this book to a desk, librarians will use it and lend it to any who want to help others become readers.

I was one of the lucky ones. I learned to read when I was very young; libraries became important points on my private map of the world. But it was not until I had finished a conventional school and college education that I began to think about the problems facing those who were less lucky. Graduate study kept the issue squarely before me. My interest deepened when I became a lecturer and the director of the writing program at the Harvard University Extension School, which is committed to opening educational opportunities to all. Libraries have been part of my life from my youngest days, and today my courses regularly include classes on library use and research. But how does one open a library to someone who cannot read?

"It is hoped that this book will help illuminate the role libraries can assume and the steps librarians should take," say the authors of *Literacy and the Library*. Chapter titles like "Removing the Roadblocks," "Materials for Adult New Readers," "Reaching Out," and "Working with Other Literacy Groups" make clear their straightforward practical approach. To draw readers methodically through the book, they start sections with careful devised introductory questions. They define and illustrate important terms—literacy levels, cataloging systems. Anticipating issues that unwary planners might forget—what to do about the standard library fines for poverty-level new readers, how to evaluate a program without terrifying the participants—they provide checklists and propose remedies. They walk us through the first three years of a new library-based literacy program, charting the difficulties of handling federal grant applications and changes in personnel, describing inventive ways a new organization can work with members of its community. Finally, they devote a full quarter of the book to references: agencies, foundations, research reports, books and articles that can add important information to what they have already presented.

We in this country have recognized the importance of literacy since the founding of the first colonies. Bernard Bailyn's *Education in the Forming of American Society* (Norton, 1972) describes the educational efforts of families, churches, towns, states, and the national government, sustained throughout more than three hundred years of history. Libraries have played an integral part in those efforts. Since the middle of the seventeenth century, individuals, educational institutions, and private groups have assembled collections of books; with the founding of the first public library in 1833, communities have insisted that this major resource be open to all members of the community.

Matching our eagerness for literacy is a pervasive anxiety about failures: doors are open but the books are still closed. Students vanish from schools, others stay and still can't read. Some newcomers have difficulty mastering the English language, some long-time inhabitants feel disenfranchised without the reading skills they need to succeed in the modern world. At one time or another we have ascribed the failures to scores of "causes." Each time a "cause" was identified a remedy was proposed that swept away earlier remedies, only to be replaced in a few years by another remedy. But our insistance in making literacy available to all has continued unabated, despite our disappointment.

Literacy and the Library does not make extravagant claims for a new diagnosis and a new cure. Rather, it places the history of illiteracy in an understandable context and then describes ways libraries can support all individuals and groups working to train new readers. Repositories of all kinds of information in a variety of forms, libraries are uniquely able to help teachers and learners in whatever way seems most appropriate. Charles and Jeffrey Salter have given librarians and non-librarians and specialists and laypersons practical advice and a new vision with which to continue unchaining the books.

—Dr. Prudence Steiner
Harvard University
1991

PREFACE

For years civic and social organizations have been fighting illiteracy with guerrilla tactics. Dedicated scouts and concerned patrols were dispatched, and modest advances were made, but costly retreats have been necessary. Without a commander, the optimistic but inexperienced volunteers did their best. The troops are overdue for reinforcements; supply channels need to be established for additional resources and updated equipment. The people they seek to liberate have waited long enough, and they do not understand the widespread apathy. The rescue efforts have been too minimal, too slow, and too scattered. In effect, so few have done so little for so many.

Attempting to affix blame for high illiteracy rates and posturing to show others we are concerned are two ineffective responses to the problem. There is too much concern and not enough involvement, too much talk and not enough action; there are too many studies and not enough programs, too many needs and not enough funding. In some areas prospective students face long waiting lists—there are not enough tutors and too few qualified trainers to equip more tutors.

The most effective force of the entire literacy movement during the last 15 years has been the dedicated volunteers. These are the people who genuinely care about others, about the nation, and who are committed to reducing illiteracy. No amount of funding can purchase a group of caring individuals willing to donate their time and effort to help others. It will take vision and leadership to stimulate more to join their ranks.

Where is the library in the literacy effort? International Literacy Year was slated for 1990: Politicians, educators, citizens—and librarians—currently list literacy as a major concern and pledge themselves to support the cause. How can they assume a meaningful role? Many libraries are barely able to keep up with the intense explosion of information, both in volume and variety, especially since automation magnified the processing speed and high-technology altered the formats. Now with smaller staffs and tighter budgets, libraries are expected to help would-be constituents *process* these mega-tons of information.

It has been relatively easy for libraries and librarians to stay out of literacy. The responsibility has been seen to lie elsewhere: society in general and education in particular. Believing libraries to be not "at fault" for causing illiteracy, most librarians were lulled into thinking that they had no obligation to contribute to its solution. Librarians have washed their hands by viewing illiteracy outside this context: libraries = books = readers. Adult nonreaders were someone else's problem.

In 1983 *A Nation at Risk: The Imperative for Educational Reform* (National Commission on Excellence in Education) caused a stir among professionals in education and other fields. This report prompted the library community to respond with *Alliance for Excellence* (Center for Libraries and Education Improvement, 1984), which called for all libraries—with emphasis on school library media centers—to become dynamic partners in the Learning Society. Academic, public, special, institutional, and state libraries also have a vital role in the sharing of resources, materials, facilities, and personnel. Academic libraries should be concerned because colleges and universities depend upon educated high school graduates to possess basic literacy skills. Private libraries, such as those in businesses, institutions, or government departments are involved because of the enormous economic impact illiteracy has upon such entities. State library agencies are expected by the state's political leaders and citizens to provide a foundation on which the other types of libraries can depend for assistance, guidance, information, or financial aid. The illiteracy crisis is pictured oversimplified as out-of-school adults who cannot read or write, with the implication that public libraries should logically bear the burden alone. Since illiterate and functionally illiterate adults either bypassed formal education or were processed through school without learning basic skills, the illiteracy cycle will probably escalate until all agencies, including libraries of all types, work together unselfishly to (1) prevent preschoolers from becoming illiterate adults, (2) increase the number of school children attaining basic skills, and (3) correct illiteracy among out-of-school adults.

Over the last 25 years many public libraries have taken on the goal of providing service to all citizens and maximizing the availability of every type and format of information. But in so doing, librarians effectively ignored the tens of millions who were not able to *use* the information that their institutions were so aggressively trying to provide. It is no wonder that citizens affected by poverty, discrimination, and lack of education are dubious of the library's ability to provide anything of actual use for them. We must face the realization that our vast resources are virtually worthless to citizens who are unable to read and write or who possess limited literacy skills.

Librarians, of course, have always espoused the practice of reading, with the unspoken assumption that most children and adults already possessed reading skills. Many in the library become recalcitrant when the subject becomes the *teaching* of reading. What about nonreading adults who have slipped through the cracks of education systems and who coexist in our society without a chance to participate fully? Who will teach them to read, and how will their children's reading skills be reinforced?

It is gratifying that the illiteracy problem is finally receiving serious attention. The second White House Conference on Library and Information Services, which highlights literacy as one of its key issues, will take place in 1991. In her landmark 1977 book, *Literacy and the Nation's Libraries*, Helen H. Lyman issued an eloquent call to battle among librarians and libraries to participate substantively in literacy efforts. Some have responded to that call, but the movement has been slow.

Libraries actually considering the illiteracy problem have usually addressed it by token involvement or other half-hearted efforts. In the early 1980s many librarians who wanted to help faced the challenge alone, without much support from their own institutions. Library administrators who recognized the problem of illiteracy often did not have time to deal with it personally and therefore assigned it as an additional duty to another employee. In some libraries, any allocation for literacy programs was among the first "luxuries" cut when budgets got tighter.

Many library professionals are waiting for a complete, standardized definition of illiteracy. At the same time others are gorging on statistical studies. Some administrators are waiting for the perfect program with complete funding before they are willing to attempt anything. A number of library professionals simply do not accept illiteracy as the library's problem.

This is not to suggest that libraries can offer the sole solution to the problems of illiteracy. For the most part, librarians are not tutors, libraries are not training facilities, and library budgets do not fund external programs. But libraries and librarians are—or should be—full partners with the other literacy efforts in their communities. Let the pundits wrestle with definitions and let the government collect statistics. We should not wait for an ideal program nor expect someone to pour extra money into our budgets. We need to break from denial and avoidance and begin—any beginning—to offer our resources toward solving the illiteracy problem. It is hoped that this book will help illumine the role libraries can assume and the steps librarians should take.

—Jeffrey L. Salter

ACKNOWLEDGMENTS

The authors would like to express appreciation to:

Sharyn M. Gilsoul, for her ideas and implementation,

Helen C. Hudson, for her concept of the library's role,

James R. Pelton, for his administrative support,

Patricia T. Bates, for her leadership and encouragement,

Lola C. Kendrick, for her dedication,

Denise W. Salter, for her bibliographic assistance,

Helen H. Lyman, for her national incentive,

Betty J. Gibbs, Jeanne S. Vince, Carlos W. Colón,
for their general support, and

the volunteer tutors, without whom the literacy effort would have been doomed.

INTRODUCTION

Most literate citizens take their ability to read and write for granted; they are lulled into thinking that everyone possesses fundamental coping skills. Even if they realize that illiteracy is a large problem, they are probably not aware of its dramatic effects on the lives of individuals. A look at the hypothetical city of Metroville will offer valuable perspective into the scope of the illiteracy problem and will set the stage for the chapters which follow.

THE METROVILLE SCENARIO

Community Characteristics

Metroville is a city on the move. It is among the top 10 most populated cities in the state and has many cultural, educational, and recreational advantages. There is a medium-sized state university, a small private college, and a community college. A well-funded public school system operates 75 sites in Metro County, and there are a few private academies and parochial schools. Citizens are proud of the symphony, the little theatre company, and the annual arts festival. There are scores of fraternal, charitable, and civic organizations in addition to a wide assortment of clubs, societies, and associations. Metro County Public Library System has a dozen branches and a downtown headquarters building that is large enough to feature a partial government documents depository and other specialized collections.

Several local plants each employ thousands of workers, and a military base boosts the local economy in many ways. Some of the banks have assets over $100 million and are large enough to serve patrons in neighboring counties as well. A large shopping mall and several smaller shopping complexes serve the area. City government employs 2,500 workers and operates a mass transit system. Construction is continual—houses in the private sector, offices in the business world, and public projects and street improvements in the municipal arena.

How typical is Metroville? How does it compare with your city's tax base? Does your community have similar educational, recreational, and cultural opportunities?

The Illiteracy Problem

With opportunities it offers in education, culture, business, and recreation, Metroville and Metro County rank high in every single category that reflects quality of life. Yet it also ranks high in illiteracy. According to census information for Metroville, over 10 percent of the adult population never entered high school and about half of that number have fewer than five years of formal education. An additional 10 percent of the total population cannot read or write well enough to be considered functionally literate. Metroville can offer something for practically all—if they possess the literacy skills to obtain the information, interpret it, and put it to use. If they do not have those essential coping skills, they are effectively cut off from participation in many of the most basic opportunities.

In an enlightened society with multifaceted educational opportunities, how is it possible for such a significant percentage of the population to remain illiterate? Why do so many drop out of formal education? What is the cost to the community of such widespread illiteracy?

Early Literacy Efforts

In the early 1980s individuals in Metroville formed a local chapter of Literacy Volunteers of America (LVA). As time went on, a few churches began small tutoring centers, and philanthropic organizations made modest donations that allowed programs to start in the county jail. This small core of dedicated individuals kept working, mostly one-on-one, to reduce illiteracy in Metroville. But during the 1980s the number of new illiterates increased far more quickly than the number of new adult readers—amplifying the scope of the illiteracy problem dramatically.

Why was the literacy effort so slow to get started in Metroville? Why didn't it grow more quickly? How could the number of illiterates grow faster than the number of people receiving assistance?

Stumbling Blocks

The general public in Metroville seems largely unaware of the scope and seriousness of the illiteracy problem. There have not been enough volunteer tutors and not enough qualified trainers to equip the tutors. Practically no funding has been available to pay additional trainers or obtain certification. Few suitable sites exist for tutoring sessions, and these are mostly in locations that are psychologically threatening to tutors, students, or both. The list of students waiting for tutors is nearly as large as the total number currently enrolled. Students are easily disillusioned because of the slow pace and seeming lack of measurable progress; most struggle with problems in transportation, child care, and low self-esteem. The student drop-out rate discourages many tutors, and some of them quit teaching after a few disappointments.

Why is there a shortage of trainers and tutors? What accounts for the high drop-out rate among literacy students? Why are students and tutors so easily discouraged? What could be done to make these situations more acceptable?

The Literacy Coalition's Activity

The Metroville Literacy Coalition, which was formed back in the early days of the local efforts, later lost its focus and meetings became infrequent. Whenever a new leader emerged willing to make an effort, it took so much effort to reactivate the Coalition that the impetus would practically vanish by the time the necessary meetings could be held. Some members became disenchanted because there was too much structure and not enough action. Others believed there could never be effective activity without strong organization. Movement leaders with good ideas quickly realized that no one was available to implement those activities. To accomplish goals, they had to do the work themselves. Others who might help were already overcommitted, understaffed, and poorly funded. The few successful efforts went largely unnoticed because of minimal media involvement and general public apathy.

Why was the Coalition so loosely formed? How could the members allow it to lapse periodically? What accounts for the dichotomy between the "action" and the "organization" factions? Why didn't the successful efforts get more media support? What other factors contributed to the public's lack of awareness?

Program Isolation

Metroville's active literacy providers were largely unaware of what, if anything, the other programs were doing. This stemmed largely from the polarity between the two main methods of tutoring: Laubach and LVA. Purists in each group were resistant to interaction with one another. A third major effort, allied with a national program called Assault on Illiteracy, was tied closely to racial lines; its coordinators made a conscious effort to eliminate non-Black influence and seemed reluctant to release information about its various activities.

Why are individual programs operating so independently, with so much isolation from each other? What are the major differences between Laubach and LVA methods and materials? Why does one program consciously limit involvement from non-Blacks?

Politics, Business, and Media

The political leaders, businesses, and media in Metro County had all but ignored the illiteracy problem until a national advertising campaign in the middle 1980s made their neglect painfully obvious. The chief reaction from politicians was to express concern without offering assistance. The media presented occasional feature stories, primarily about literacy tutors, as part of their public service quotas. Most business leaders were curiously silent, even though they were expending substantial amounts on job applicant testing, on-the-job training, and classes in remedial skills for their workers.

During the same period, a state association began to gather information on literacy programs to publish directories of those activities. But by the time the directory project was conceived, approved, finalized, printed, distributed, and publicized, the information was already more than two years old and woefully incomplete.

Why didn't the leaders responsible for the public's welfare take a stronger role in the literacy solution? Why did the media treat the problem as feature material instead of news? What accounts for the silence from the business community? Why was the state directory effort so ponderously slow?

Emphasis on Education

State government began to put more emphasis on education in the middle 1980s. Admission standards for universities were raised, high schools began having exit examinations prior to graduation, and teachers were required to pass the National Teacher Examination (NTE) with certain minimum scores. Voters in Metroville and Metro County approved additional taxes for the public school system, and the media focused on the area's educational standing compared to the rest of the state. While all this would seemingly help raise the educational levels of the students in school, it had absolutely no effect on the adults already out of school, and it did not improve the drop-out rate. No one seemed to notice that the generation of adults that was unserved by the old educational system was still unserved by improvements to that system. Twenty percent of Metro County's adults were either illiterate or functionally illiterate, and the existing education process was not reaching them. Almost 35 percent of the adults over age 25 never completed high school. Furthermore, the public college and university were alarmed by the increasing number of entering students who required remedial courses.

Why didn't the public demand more effective educational programs? Why did the state and local efforts to improve education come so late, and why did they ignore adults already out of the system? What can be done to assist the out-of-school, adult nonreader, and what role can the local library play in this effort? If secondary schools had exit examinations, why were more beginning college students being enrolled in remedial courses?

Falling through the Cracks

When television viewers responded to a national advertising campaign by calling a toll-free number, they were referred to a local number that supposedly offered literacy information and assistance. Metroville did not really have such a mechanism in place, so the number given by the national clearinghouse was actually the office phone of a Coalition member. He did what he could when called, but he had neither the staff, funding, nor time to handle these calls. Most of the callers who had already taken the extra step of calling the second (local) number were not inclined to make a third contact, and their inquiries usually stopped at that frustrating point.

Would no referral have been better than a referral to a local Coalition member who did not have the resources to handle the calls? What could the Coalition have done to respond to the inquiries from the national advertisement? What kind of local referrals could have been possible?

Public Library Involvement

In the late 1960s Metro County Public Library System joined a national movement that expressed urgency about social concerns and the relevance of libraries to potential users who were disadvantaged because of poverty, discrimination, or education. The resulting outreach programs dwindled largely because they offered only traditional library services while the would-be constituents actually needed assistance with reading skills and coping skills. In the middle 1970s the library launched an information and referral service with the intention of helping connect people with the information they needed. Subsequent studies, however, indicated that the information and referral services were devoted to information, with very little actual referral. Those who could not read were still effectively locked out of the information cycle. By the middle 1980s the library's main contributions to literacy efforts were providing meeting space for tutoring and offering a handful of very general books on the subject.

Why weren't traditional library services helpful to nonreaders? What happened to the library's 1960s outreach program? Why did its 1970s information and referral service fail to help illiterates? Why wasn't the library doing more in the 1980s?

Other Types of Libraries

During this time period, school libraries and media centers struggled to keep up with curriculum demands of teachers and service to their K-12 clientele. Although federal funds from the Elementary and Secondary Education Act (ESEA) and supplementary state allocations were available for purchasing books, the main concern at those levels was the ratio of books per pupil. At that time, many school administrators saw the library as a requirement for certification more than a resource center for the community. The school libraries were closed evenings and weekends, so use by out-of-school adults was not likely in any case.

Academic libraries faced diminished funding from their parent institutions, which were experiencing significant losses of state funding and dwindling enrollments. Many colleges and universities were forced to cut programs, and some experienced freezes on hiring. Libraries were fortunate if they could maintain serial subscriptions and purchase books in enough subject areas to satisfy department heads. There was no obvious space, time, staff, or funding to focus on the needs of adult illiterates.

What are the costs and problems for school libraries to be open for the community's adults? Would there be any material or assistance for them if the facilities were open? Since academic libraries are in the business of supporting higher education, does that prevent them from helping adults who need "lower" education? What kinds of programs could they provide?

The Information Society

Metroville has a counterpart in every state of the country. Even though the configuration may vary, each of these municipalities offers a wide range of opportunities for personal enrichment, and each has a significant population that is effectively blocked from participating in these opportunities by its lack of fundamental reading skills. The information society has widened the gulf between those who are able to participate in educational and cultural advantages and those who lack basic coping skills. Without help, the latter are doomed to a perpetual status of incomplete citizenship.

THE CHANGING SCENE

This ends the tour of the fictional Metroville and begins an investigation of illiteracy, society, individuals, and libraries in the real world. As America turns the corner into the 1990s, there is evidence on many fronts that people, organizations, business, media, and government have become serious about improving literacy. There is more and more good news about the future of literacy, and here are some of the highlights:

- The Adult Literacy and Employability Act of 1990 (i.e., the Sawyer bill) made significant progress in Congress. It is widely regarded as the best and most comprehensive proposal ever submitted on behalf of adult literacy in the United States. Among its components are planning, research, and coordination; investment in adult literacy; and work-force literacy. It proposes significant funding for the period 1991 through 1995.

- The National Literacy Act of 1990 (i.e., the Simon bill) was passed by the Senate 99-0 in February 1990. Among its components are literacy coordination, work-force literacy, families for literacy, books for families, students for literacy, and volunteers for literacy. It proposes significant funding through 1993.

- On Sunday evening prime time (March 18, 1990), there was a one-hour ABC-TV special, "To Be Free: The National Literacy Honors from the White House." Hosted by President George Bush and his wife, Barbara Bush, the program honored several new adult learners, tutors, and national spokespersons.

- The successful Kenan Trust Family Literacy Project received national television coverage on "Good Morning, America" in March 1990.

- A family-centered education program called Even Start is being administered by the U.S. Department of Education through local school districts. Focusing on families with children aged one to seven, the program specifically targets the parents for literacy training. Although funded in its first year (fiscal 1989) at less than one-third of its authorization, it was recommended by the Southport Institute's report *Jump Start: The Federal Role in Adult Literacy* to be fully funded. It is also strengthened in the Simon bill.

- The Family Support Act of 1988 contains a far-reaching overhaul of the nation's welfare system. The act would make education, training, or work available to destitute young parents and would help provide child care and transportation. It would require most able-bodied parents to take part in the programs in order to be eligible to receive welfare benefits.

- Literacy is one of the three focal points of the second White House Conference on Libraries and Information Services, which is scheduled for July 1991.

- Patricia Berger, 1990 American Library Association President, emphasized the association's role in literacy in major programs during both the midwinter and annual conferences.

- In the middle of 1989, *Library Journal* began featuring a regular column sponsored by Baker & Taylor called "Literacy Clearinghouse," which provides significant and useful information on literacy efforts and progress.

- Library Outreach Reporter Publications has begun a quarterly library newsletter called "The Lit Page—The Magazine for Library Literacy." It is edited by Debra W. Johnson and Carol L. Sheffer and provides current information on literacy programs and services. The premier issue (Spring 1990) included a full page of state literacy hotline numbers.

- Under the leadership of Harold W. McGraw, Jr., the Business Council for Effective Literacy (BCEL) publishes the quarterly "Newsletter for the Business & Literacy Communities." It features news briefs, legislative updates, information on literacy materials, and examples of corporate literacy activities. It has already published over two dozen quarterly issues.

These are just some of the more prominent national developments that are positive signals among the shocking statistics and gloomy forecasts. These and other positive steps will increase public awareness and create demand for literacy funding and for literacy services at the local level. The public will call upon all logical service agencies, including libraries, to participate in the literacy solution.

THE PLAN OF THE BOOK

Written by a librarian/educator team, this book answers the questions raised in the Metroville scenario and takes a fresh look at the unique role libraries can play in reducing illiteracy. Part 1 deals with the problems, causes, and effects of illiteracy; a brief history of literacy and relevant theories; removing the road-blocks and solving problems in the library; how libraries can become involved; what materials are available; and how they can be selected, organized, and presented. Part 2 addresses the obstacles between illiterate adults and literacy providers, working with other agencies and organizations, evaluating literacy programs, and a detailed case study of an actual library literacy program. The appendixes include a list of programs and agencies that deal with literacy; samples of writing on various grade levels; and an extensive bibliography divided by major topical areas.

Libraries can and should become more involved in the literacy effort; all librarians can play an important part. This text will put the illiteracy problem into perspective and will offer practical guidance for librarians and their institutions to become a vital part of the literacy solution.

PART 1
Libraries Accepting the Challenge

1

THE PROBLEM OF FUNCTIONAL ILLITERACY

In the struggle to eradicate illiteracy, much time and effort have been expended in an attempt to define it—to identify the people needing help and to estimate their number.

WHAT IS ILLITERACY?

If you are reading these words then you are basically literate. Webster's dictionary gives the following as its most straightforward definition of literacy: "the ability to read and write." In other words, the literate person is able both to receive and transmit communications in the written language of the culture. But is this a simple all-or-none matter, where an individual has complete competence on the one hand or absolutely zero literacy on the other? Aren't there infinite gradations between total competence and complete incompetence? If so, where does one draw the line?

Which of the following paragraphs (each reproduced with its original errors) would you consider to be literate and which illiterate? Why?

1. "Tension seen to drain energy from most people body. Sometime tension is so high the individual hand become sweat, proceeding by a funny taste in your mouth. Something tension reach the upmost. One of my friend explain that tension cause him to have Hypnosis, like of sleep cause his Hypnosis."

2. "My opinion is that I think man is not determined solely by environment but by predisternation of his own will, I think that each man maps out his own life, and determines how he is going to lead it. Each person has their own mind and no one can determine what the other person is thinking."

3. "if Solely Environment and Heredity Determined man, then man determined Solely. by man Determined Solely by the Environment by human mined of the person, the person mined are not together. it is easily to be determined, by the Environment and very easily Heredity by the man."

4. "Well man is not Free but some thing or free and Heredity, man in-heredity the earth and his environment to search for new idea + knowledge of what going on in other Place Man Heredity have can a long ways, for little time he had."

5. "Tension seems to drain energy from the body. Tension may be so great that the hands sweat and one gets a funny taste in the mouth."

Some readers may be surprised to learn that the first four of the above paragraphs were written by college students, young people who had graduated from high school and been accepted into institutions of higher learning. The middle three samples were taken from essays written for a freshman psychology class in response to the topic: "Is man determined solely by the environment and heredity, or does he have free will?" Number two has poor grammar, misspellings, and poor logical development, but most people can gather some sense of what the author is trying to communicate. Numbers three and four are hopelessly muddled and rambling—each author seems incapable of communicating thoughts linguistically.

Paragraph one was the introduction to a term paper on stress. Although full of grammatical and syntactical errors, some sense of the author's intention comes through. Paragraph five is an edited version of the beginning of one.

Where does one draw the line on illiteracy? If three and four are clearly illiterate, and five is literate, how about the first two? And even in three and four, each writer is able to write some individual words correctly, so the lack of literacy is not absolute. An all-or-none definition of literacy needs to shift to the concept of various levels of illiteracy.

LEVELS OF ILLITERACY

The most meaningful way to define illiteracy for practical purposes is to distinguish among different levels of the problem. But even then, there is considerable dispute about the lines between adjacent categories. The following are levels or degrees of the problem that are most often agreed upon as being major variations.

Total Illiteracy

Such persons are unable to read even the simplest children's picture books, advertisements, signs, and instructions. They may be able to recognize a few common words encountered frequently (e.g., *Exit* or *Entrance*) but do not so much read them as recognize them as symbols. They may be able to write and recognize their own names. But again, this reflects not a beginning literacy but a little manual trick they have learned, much as one might learn to draw a symbol. In terms of school grade levels, basic illiteracy translates into a competency of between 0 and 4.9 grade level.

Functional Illiteracy

Functional illiteracy refers to competency at the 5 to 8.9 grade level. These persons can read and write at a primitive level and have usually completed several years of school. As the previous examples show, they may even have graduated from high school and attended college, although actually functioning at a much lower level than that. As adults, they may be able to read simple instructions, manuals, want ads, and common signs. But for all practical purposes, they cannot communicate in written language in a mature way. They cannot write a clear and comprehensible business letter on any but the most simple of topics. Those at the lower end cannot comprehend textbooks, major instructional manuals, and serious newspaper articles. In most job settings, they must be shown what to do because they cannot learn it from written directives. The opportunities for career advancement, even for those in the upper range of functional illiteracy, are extremely limited by their linguistic ineptitude. They simply lack the skill to compete successfully in today's increasingly complex society.

A-literacy

Persons at this level may have achieved enough literacy skills in school to read books, manuals, newspapers, and so forth. But they choose as adults not to use these skills. It is not that they lack the capacity so much as the motivation to read and write. Such people may actually brag that they have not read a book in all their adult lives since high school.

Other Literacies

Basic literacy refers to the ability to read and write. But as our society grows more complex, there is an expanding need for other types of literacies as well. The following are some other types of literacies.

Cultural Literacy

Fully functioning adults in our society need to know something about the history of Western civilization, the great political, philosophical, religious, and scientific trends that helped to shape our society (Hirsch 1987). They need to know about current news and trends that are shaping our future. The cultural illiterate can hardly be a well-informed citizen or a responsible voter.

Mathematical Literacy

Functioning adults need to reach a certain fundamental level of competence in arithmetic and elementary algebra if they are to fill out income surveys or tax forms, or make meaningful decisions about purchasing the best buys in groceries, car loans, or home mortgages. For instance, an 8-ounce package of candy may cost quite a bit more (or less) than two 4-ounce packages of the same candy. The person who is mathematically illiterate may continuously waste money by basing decisions on emotional or perceptual factors rather than the best value.

Computer Literacy

More and more jobs are incorporating mainframe computers, desktop computers, lap-top or hand-held computers, and pocket calculators. The person who seeks a job or wishes to keep a job in a company with such equipment must learn how to use it. The person who fears computers or finds them an indecipherable mystery will be cut off from an ever-increasing number and variety of jobs.

Scientific Literacy

Almost daily, science creates breakthroughs in an expanding variety of fields. To comprehend these developments and put them to their best use, adults need to have a grasp of basic scientific concepts and the scientific method for gaining new knowledge. Otherwise, they are susceptible to all manner of myths and quacks. The scientifically illiterate person, for example, may shun proper medical treatment for cancer, preferring instead some magical approach touted in the latest supermarket tabloid. Every year people actually die this way. Millions more waste time and money on inefficient or useless items while unnecessarily avoiding new things that could prove helpful to them.

Informational Literacy

Even as the total amount of information keeps expanding at an accelerating rate, more people than ever seem unable to know how to find the information they need. As a recent American Library Association report put it, "To be information literate, a person must be able to recognize when information is needed and have the ability to locate, evaluate, and use effectively the needed information" (Brevik 1989, 1). Clearly the library can play a major role in fostering this type of literacy.

These types of literacies are certainly important, but most of this book will dwell on the fundamental literacy question of reading and writing. The person who masters that type of literacy finds that it opens the doors to all the other types as well. On the other hand, the person who remains functionally illiterate on the key skills of reading and writing probably will find literacies in computers, science, and so forth elusive.

HOW SERIOUS IS THE PROBLEM OF ILLITERACY?

Depending upon how the problem is defined, statistics vary considerably in describing the extent of total and functional illiteracy. But virtually all experts agree that it is serious and growing worse rather than better. The following are some indicators of the severity of the problem.

Overall Illiteracy

McGraw (1987) estimates that 25 million adult Americans are functionally illiterate, reading, at best, to fourth-grade level. Another 45 million adult Americans possess only marginal or limited literacy with few reading above eighth-grade level. Combining these figures results in a total of 70 million American adults—almost 50 percent—with substandard literacy skills. In other words, one out of every two adult Americans could use improvement in literacy skills!

Illiteracy Is a Growing Problem

According to the U.S. Department of Education, each year the number of illiterates in the United States grows by more than two million. Of this number, 1.2 million are immigrants (only one-third of them legal), 840,000 are high school dropouts, 150,000 are refugees, and about 15,000 are high school graduates with severely deficient skills (Reagan kicks off literacy program 1983). The number of people who are helped--taught to read--each year is significantly lower than the number of new illiterates, so the problem keeps growing worse.

Illiteracy among the Poor and Minorities

Although illiteracy can be found in virtually all segments of society, the most severe forms are concentrated largely among the poor and minorities. For instance, among poor adults with incomes less than $5,000 annually, 40 percent are functionally illiterate. Among mothers in the Aid for Dependent Children program, more than one-third are illiterate. And of all minority youth, about 40 percent are functionally illiterate (Strong 1984). The problem is most severe among those for whom English is a second language. They have an illiteracy rate of about 48 percent, as opposed to only 9 percent among those for whom English is their primary language (When mom and dad can't read 1986).

Illiteracy in International Perspective

In 1980 the United States had an illiteracy rate of approximately 15 to 20 percent, depending upon how the problem was measured. By comparison, the overall world illiteracy rate was 28.6 percent that year. At the high end was Africa, with 60.3 percent of its population illiterate. In Asia 37.4 percent and in

Latin America 20.2 percent of the adult populations were illiterate (Unesco and the struggle against illiteracy 1984). In general, the developed world has lower rates than Third World countries. For example, at the low end is Sweden with an illiteracy rate of only about 1 percent.

Illiteracy in the Business World

American businesses are confronting a major problem of illiteracy among applicants and even among employees, as the following examples indicate:

- The New York Telephone Company gives an entrance examination to all job applicants. During a six-month period in 1987, 84 percent of applicants failed to pass this test (Berney 1988).
- For AT & T nationwide, 43 percent of applicants for clerical jobs failed the screening test (Pascarella 1987).
- In California, the Greater Avenues for Independence (GAIN) program was introduced to help welfare clients obtain jobs. Between 40 and 50 percent lacked the literacy skills to read want ads and job application forms. They had to have remedial training even to apply for work (Pipho 1988).
- Screening out functional illiterates at the application stage does not solve the problem, for there are not enough adequately trained workers to fill all the positions that already exist.

All told, American businesses must spend about $25 billion a year teaching remedial literacy to their employees (Pipho 1988). These costs are passed on to the consumer in the form of higher prices for goods and services.

CAUSES OF THE ILLITERACY PROBLEM

Many experts have speculated on the causes of illiteracy. Unfortunately, there is no one cause. In fact, there is not total agreement on the complete list of possible causes. Some experts stress one or two factors while downplaying factors that other experts focus on as major causes. The following paragraphs describe some of the major factors that have been proposed as contributing to the problem as well as some evidence showing how much of a role each might play. Further research may add or delete items from this list. Future research also may clarify how much some of these factors contribute to illiteracy and the mechanisms by which they do so.

Television

Television has been available in this society for only about 40 years. The average number of television sets in use has continued to grow throughout that time. Even more significant, the average daily television use in each household has continued to increase. In 1986 the average preschooler watched 28 hours and 6 minutes per week while the average 6 to 11 year old watched 23 hours and 31 minutes per week (*World Almanac* 1988). In other words, the average American child spends more time per year with television than in school, reading, or in athletic pursuits.

According to the traditional argument, television impairs cognitive growth by displacing time from activities more beneficial to mental development, e.g., study, reading, artistic or creative activities, hobbies, and imaginative play (Neuman 1988). For years, many have blamed increasing TV use for declining Scholastic Aptitude Test (SAT) scores (Can't anyone here speak English? 1975). The SAT is a standardized examination that millions of graduating high school students have taken over the past few decades as part of the college admissions process. For many years, the average national scores did show a continuing decline, although that has leveled off recently.

But is TV to blame? A recent study by Gortmaker, Salter, Walker, and Dietz (1990) examined a nationally representative sample of 1,745 children aged 6 to 11 over a 4-year period. Simple tests of statistical association did suggest that more TV watching was related to lower scores on a variety of mental tests. However, when sophisticated statistical controls were entered into the analyses, it turned out that the association was most likely minimal, and that TV did not actually cause the lower test scores. In other words, watching more TV does not really deaden the intellect, regardless of the hype. If anything, children already achieving at a lower level for a variety of reasons (economic class, poor parenting, and so forth) simply watched more TV.

This is not to suggest that excess TV watching has no ill effects, but only that it cannot be assigned a major portion of blame for the illiteracy problem. In fact, high quality and educational television shows may foster overall knowledge and learning.

Poverty

It is hardly surprising that poverty could affect literacy. Children raised in poor homes may have little exposure to books or to parents who read. Their career aspirations may be directed more at blue collar jobs requiring little literacy rather than white collar ones which depend more on reading and writing. Children born into poverty are not doomed to illiteracy but may have a more difficult time avoiding it than a child from a more well-to-do home.

Parents as Models

One of the factors revealed in the Gortmaker, Salter, Walker, and Dietz (1990) study for poor student performance on mental aptitude tests was parents having low levels of education. The role of parents as models may mediate between poverty as a causative factor and illiteracy as an outcome. High illiteracy rates among poverty-stricken parents means their children miss the early stimulation toward good literacy which is provided by literate parents who read to their children and provide literacy role models by being regular readers.

Modern Schooling

The public education system poses a two-fold problem. First, many experts believe that the educational system in this country is not doing as good a job as it could and should do. Second, an alarming proportion of students drops out before finishing high school and thus does not take full advantage of what educational opportunities do exist.

How good is American public education? David Kearns, the chief executive officer of Xerox Corporation, has said, "Public education has put this country at a terrible competitive disadvantage ... the American workforce is running out of qualified people" (Pipho 1988). And as Perry Pascarella, the editor-in-chief of *Industry Week* magazine, has written, "Our educational system is falling short of preparing people for working and living in this technological society" (Pascarella 1987). Allan Bloom's bestselling book, *The Closing of the American Mind* (1987), argues persuasively that American education lies in ruins, that "most high-school graduates nowadays have difficulty reading and writing" (341).

These assertions are supported by the Carnegie Forum on Education and the Economy (1986). According to the report, teachers themselves are often poorly trained and qualified. Salaries are too low to attract and retain many of the best qualified teachers, who have left the profession in droves. Standards of classroom discipline and performance have grown increasingly lax in recent decades. To reverse this situation, the report continues, we must restructure teacher education, create a more professional environment for teaching, implement and reward new standards for teaching excellence, and provide new teacher incentives, salaries, and benefits (Carnegie Forum on Education and the Economy 1986).

How bad is the drop-out problem in the United States? The average drop-out rate is about 30 percent prior to high school graduation (McGraw 1987). This means that about one out of three American students does not take full advantage of the opportunity for free education. It seems clear that both poor quality education and lack of persistence on the part of many youth are, in part, responsible for the United States' current problem of illiteracy.

Cultural Values

But why has education been allowed to deteriorate to such an extent? And why do so many students not care to derive the greatest benefit from education which they can? Much of the blame for the illiteracy problem rests on society at large for transmitting anti-education values to its young. A society that pays a sports figure or rock star millions of dollars a year but grants most teachers a rather modest salary drives potentially good teachers out of the system. Worse, it transmits the not-so-subtle message that education has little value and is, in fact, virtually irrelevant. As Guerra put it, "Strong incentives are needed to provide adults with the motivation to undertake and persist in the considerable effort required to achieve literacy. Such incentives may take a variety of forms: cultural, religious, economic or political" (1984, 7). To a very large extent, such incentives for education are lacking in this society. In fact, there are many disincentives for learning, the appearance of too many rewards for those who snub the educational process. Dropouts may believe for example, that they can make far more money dealing drugs or, with a bit of talent or luck, getting into sports or music.

By contrast, in cultures which are thriving, there is always a very strong cultural emphasis on the value of education. In Japan, for instance, there is "an omnivorous desire for knowledge, a regard for learning, and a belief that effort devoted to education will be rewarded" (Carnegie Forum on Education and the Economy 1986, 12). This is one of the main reasons that Japan is excelling in the world's marketplace (Carnegie Forum on Education and the Economy 1986).

Changing Definitions of Illiteracy

Illiteracy has increased, in part, because the standards by which illiteracy is measured have been raised. As Irwin Kirsch of the Educational Testing Service put it, "It's not that people are becoming less literate. It's that we keep raising the standards" (Gorman 1988). These standards have become more stringent for good reason. Years ago, one illiteracy criterion was the number of adults with fewer than six years of schooling. By that measure, in 1982 America had only 5.2 million illiterates (When mom and dad can't read 1986)—only about one-fifth the number now considered more accurate. However, many high school and even college graduates are functionally illiterate, for they have been processed through the educational system without meeting basic standards. On the other hand, a person with a good fifth- or sixth-grade education may be more literate than many high school graduates of a poor system. Therefore, definitions of illiteracy should focus on demonstrated competence and not an arbitrary standard like the number of years of schooling.

Standards for defining literacy must grow stricter in our increasingly complex world because higher and higher levels of skills are required to continue to compete successfully. As Bernardon put it, "Nearly all of the fastest growing job categories will require some type of post-high school training" (1989, 30). This means achieving a level of proficiency commensurate with post-high school training, whether college or technical/vocational schooling.

The U.S. Department of Labor sponsored a study by the Hudson Institute, a private research organization. This study estimated that 58 percent of current jobs require completion of high school or less. Only 42 percent of current jobs require some college training or a college degree. But it is estimated that by the year 2000 only 48 percent of new jobs will be filled by persons with a high school education or less, a decline of 10 percent over a 15-year span. College training will be required for the majority—52 percent—of these new jobs, an increase of 10 percent (Bernardon 1989). The trend is likely to continue into the next century. More and more literacy will be required simply to keep pace with the rapid developments occurring around the globe. Those who fail to keep up cannot even retain an inferior position; instead, they will continue to slip further and further behind.

Changing Demographics

Segments of the population that tend toward higher literacy are declining as a percent of the total population. Conversely, the segments with the lowest literacy rates are increasing as a proportion of the total population. The Hudson

Institute study (Bernardon 1989) reports that in 1985 only 10 percent of the labor force comprised native minority persons and only 7 percent were immigrants. Because of differing child-bearing rates and immigration, it is expected that by the year 2000 native minorities will account for 20 percent and immigrants for 22 percent of new entrants into the labor force.

The Self-Fulfilling Prophecy

In an ironic paradox, illiteracy can be exacerbated by the excessive attention given to the situation and its causes. Here is how that can work: A student moves to a new school and initially does not exhibit the expected level of literacy skills (due perhaps to an inferior previous school, dyslexia, or some other problem). The teacher may peg that student as an illiterate and treat him or her differently than other students. Soon the student develops the self-image of a potential illiterate. In time, the self-image is realized (Smith 1989) as the student loses motivation and eventually leaves school as an illiterate.

To overcome that self-fulfilling prophecy, parents, teachers, and others must express high expectations for students in a warm, positive way. Adults should never peg students as losers and give up on them. Research has shown that this "expectancy effect" can make significant differences in actual student performance over time (Rosenthal and Jacobsen 1968). Unfortunately, students who know they are expected to do poorly tend to perform poorly. Fortunately, the converse is also true: students who know they are expected to do well tend to perform better. Until all adults get this message, however, adult expectations of inferior performance will continue to contribute to the problem of illiteracy.

Whatever the causes of illiteracy in any given case, the fact remains that the problem is increasing despite current efforts designed to alleviate it. The vast problem of illiteracy hurts all of society, although each person may not be aware of it. The educated person who spends most of the time among other literate persons may not realize how much they all are affected by illiteracy throughout the rest of the community and nation. The following paragraphs discuss the effects of illiteracy on the individuals who suffer from it directly. A later section will consider the effects of illiteracy on society at large.

EFFECTS OF ILLITERACY ON THE INDIVIDUAL

In centuries past, the illiterate individual was more the norm and suffered few disadvantages compared to the rest of the citizenry. There were few books and few educational opportunities to be missed. There were no written job applications, and few contracts required more than an "X" on the dotted line. The illiterate could earn a living through manual labor and make legal arrangements mostly with handshakes, spoken agreements, and oral contracts. But times have certainly changed – life is far more complicated today. Now the illiterate is at great risk economically, socially, and psychologically.

Effects of Illiteracy on the Career

Consider the plight of the illiterate, blue-collar factory worker who has been on the job for 10, 20, or more years. On the few occasions when reading and writing were required, the inability to do so could be covered up by taking home forms to be filled out by others, by asking a friend to translate, or by pretending to have lost a pair of glasses. Because literacy skills were infrequently called for, it took only a little cleverness to hide illiteracy. When it came to operating a machine or performing a manual procedure, the skill could be learned by watching others or asking for oral instructions rather than reading a manual (Ross 1986).

What does this worker do when management decides to modernize the factory with automated equipment and introduces a training program that involves extensive study of instruction manuals? Such a person is in a terrifying bind, unless the company adopts an enlightened policy of training rather than firing the illiterates on its staff.

Sometimes, when companies try to introduce remedial training programs, their efforts are alarmingly inappropriate. For instance, General Motors once administered a questionnaire to 10,000 employees at a plant in Ypsilanti, Michigan, to determine the kinds of remedial training the employees felt they needed. Ironically, many of the workers lacked the literacy skills needed to read and respond to the questionnaire (Ross 1986). When conducting needs assessments, it is wise not to assume that a minimum level of literacy exists in the group to be evaluated.

The number of jobs for illiterates is continually shrinking. Conversely, the number of jobs requiring fairly advanced skills is constantly increasing. The person who remains illiterate, therefore, is increasingly at risk for becoming or remaining unemployed or failing to advance in a career.

Effects of Illiteracy on Societal Adjustment

Full participation in society requires extensive reading and writing. People with functional illiteracy miss out on many things that the literate take for granted. For example, the Adult Performance Level study at the University of Texas found that an astonishing percentage of adult Americans could not do simple tasks that the literate depend on every day. For instance, 38 percent were unable fully to comprehend help wanted ads of relevance to their own qualifications, 26 percent were unable to identify key components on their monthly wage statements, and 14 percent could not write an ordinary bank check (Ross 1986).

On the other hand, one of the great motives for adults to enter literacy programs is so that they can finally participate more fully in their culture. As Steven D. Peck put it, "A new world opens up when an individual can obtain a driver's license, can go to the polls to vote, and can apply for a bank loan. These are important first steps toward full citizenship" (1988, 56). Many adults find that the greatest satisfaction of new literacy is being able to study religious material or read stories to their children.

Effects of Illiteracy on Cognitive Development

The diligent reader increasingly develops cognitive skills, including the abilities to comprehend logical progressions of thought, to entertain novel points of view, to apply personal perspectives in evaluating concepts and propositions. In short, compared to the nonreader, the experienced reader learns to think independently and achieves a higher degree of psychological autonomy. Literacy helps cultures and individuals rise above the primitive.

Effects of Illiteracy on the Personality

If illiteracy has such potent effects on one's socioeconomic status, standing in society, and cognitive development, it should come as no surprise that it tends to affect the entire personality. A person's whole self-concept may be seriously hindered by being unable to read and write, being unable to fit into the mainstream of society. Kurt L. Schmoke, mayor of Baltimore, who introduced a major new literacy program there, said, "Becoming an adult reader will unlock doors and create opportunities. It is the key to self-respect, self-worth and human dignity" (Prete 1989, 71).

The late psychologist Abraham Maslow developed a theory that helps explain how differing classes of motivation can dominate in various types of personalities. Maslow posits that humans not only have diverse needs but that these needs constitute a distinct hierarchy. As the lower needs are satisfied, a person is able to move to more advanced needs. A brief description of Maslow's theory follows here; more details can be found in chapter 2.

These are the major levels in Maslow's need hierarchy, in progressive order, with the lowest, most basic need listed first.

- physiological (food, drink, sleep, and so on);
- safety (shelter and protection);
- belongingness and love;
- self-esteem; and
- self-actualization (to reach one's full potential) (Maslow 1959).

In Maslow's hierarchy, no one is situated securely at one level of need. A person may achieve a certain level only to have it threatened or disrupted. This necessarily interferes with attempts to reach or remain at higher levels. For example, the self-esteem a student may gain by regularly attending a literacy tutoring program may crumble if transportation or marital problems force him or her out of the program.

Literacy can help more firmly establish a person at any of Maslow's levels. It is particularly difficult to imagine the illiterate person reaching Maslow's higher stages.

EFFECTS OF ILLITERACY ON SOCIETY

If approximately half of American adults suffer impaired literacy skills, then the remainder, no matter how literate they may be, will pay the cost. The sections that follow present many alarming examples.

The Impact on American Business

Many businesses are inculcating basic skills in reading, writing, and mathematics, which should have been learned in public schools. Consider these examples:

- More than 50 percent of America's top companies (the Fortune 500) have remedial education programs of various sorts for their employees (Gorman 1988).
- The cost of remedial instruction for a major company can run as high as $200 million per year. That is how much General Motors has paid (Ross 1986), and the cost is passed on to consumers in the form of higher prices for cars and trucks.
- American businesses as a whole train approximately one million illiterate new employees each year at a combined cost of about $25 billion (Pipho 1988).
- In addition to the cost of literacy training, the lack of adequate literary skills among employees costs businesses about $25 to $30 billion more per year in "low productivity, workplace accidents, absenteeism, poor product quality and lost managerial and supervisory time" (Berney 1988).

When business costs are raised, the extra expense is passed on to the consumer via higher prices.

Effects on the American Economy

The total dollar value of the various costs of illiteracy is staggering. Lost productivity hurts business profitability. Those illiterate people who cannot find work not only detract from the potential gross national product but add to welfare or unemployment insurance costs. Some chronically unemployed may turn to crime (Glaser and Rice 1959), leading not only to the cost of the crimes themselves, but adding to the financial burden of the judicial system and prisons. According to one estimate, the United States loses an estimated $225 billion annually to adult illiteracy (Business fights illiteracy 1988).

Such a heavy economic burden detracts from America's competitiveness in the world economy. Incredible as this would have seemed a few decades ago, the "U.S. work force is one of the most illiterate in the industrialized world" (Business fights illiteracy 1988, 50). As other countries gain ground compared to the United States both in literacy and economic growth, the United States continues to slide backward. Higher costs for American goods, lower quality control, and delays and mistakes in filling orders due to illiteracy generates more customer dissatisfaction and ultimately a further loss of contracts. Without improvement in the literacy situation, the United States will face "a steady erosion in the American standard of living" (Carnegie Forum on Education and the Economy 1986, 11). According to a report by the National Assessment of Educational Progress (NAEP), "The very survival of the United States is at stake" due to the literacy crisis (NAEP 1987, 711).

Effects on the Children of Illiterates

Illiteracy tends to propagate itself in the next generation. The children of illiterates can, with good schooling, surpass their own parents in literacy skills, but to do so is more difficult for them than for children of educated parents. Literate parents can provide good role models for their children and can help children with school and homework problems in a way that illiterates cannot. As Senator Clairborne Pell said at a meeting of an education subcommittee, "Illiteracy is a hereditary condition ... in the sense that illiterate parents tend to raise illiterate children" (although not in a genetic sense) (Fields 1987, 18). Therefore, improvements in adult literacy help adults and their children.

Effects of Illiteracy on Politics

"Literacy is power ... it can transform the world" (Smith 1989, 357). Literacy translates into economic might and into political clout as well. A person needs the capacity to read and write, plus the motivation to stay reasonably informed, in order to make sound political decisions as a voter. To play a politically active role in the community, state, region, or nation, a person needs sophisticated literacy skills. The higher the political level, the greater facility with language is required (Gintis 1984). The individual with literacy, then, possesses a degree of personal political power.

For a political system to survive very long in a competitive world, it must have an informed and largely literate citizenry. As President Ronald Reagan said when proclaiming 1987 as the Year of the Reader, "Our history demonstrates that literacy and real political freedom go hand in hand" (Nelson 1987, 29). As Fred Hechinger warned more than a decade ago, "America is in headlong retreat from its commitment to education ... education is in a decline that threatens the survival of American democracy" (Hechinger 1976, 11). Since then, the illiteracy problem has only grown worse.

Effects of Illiteracy on the Educational System

Illiteracy spawns a vicious cycle that perpetuates itself. Yesterday's students graduated with impaired literacy and became today's parents and teachers. Many graduates and aspiring teachers do not realize how inferior their academic skills are because the rampant grade inflation of recent years has given them good marks for substandard work (Scully 1975). The education system is also affected by students who remain illiterate after several years of school and who ultimately give up and drop out.

The educational psychologist Benjamin Bloom developed a theory that educational objectives can best be described as constituting a hierarchy with six levels (Bloom 1956). Success at reaching various levels is markedly affected by the degree of literacy skills one possesses. As in the case of Maslow's hierarchy, a person must succeed at each lower level before reaching the next higher one. A brief description of Bloom's theory is given here; more details can be found in chapter 2.

The following are the six levels in Bloom's taxonomy, in ascending order.

- basic knowledge (simple facts),
- comprehension (understanding),
- application to real-life situations,
- analysis (recognizing underlying structure),
- objective synthesis (developing original perspectives), and
- objective evaluation (the ability to judge one's own ideas).

By interacting purely on an oral level, the illiterate could reach the first two stages—basic knowledge and comprehension. The illiterate could make some progress in application by demonstrating knowledge through producing something with his hands, but an illiterate could make little if any progress in the three higher levels. In short, deficient literacy skills impact negatively on all levels of educational objectives and make it impossible to fulfill the highest ones.

From personal health to national health, from private finance to public commerce, from individual cognitive development to cultural intellectual growth, literacy is essential.

REFERENCES

Bernardon, N. L. 1989. Let's erase illiteracy from the workplace. *Personnel* 66 (January): 29-32.

Berney, K. 1988. Can your workers read? *Nation's Business* 76 (October): 26-34.

Bloom A. 1987. *The closing of the American mind.* New York: Simon & Schuster.

Bloom, B., ed. 1956. *Taxonomy of educational objectives, handbook 1: Cognitive domain.* New York: McKay.

Brevik, P., ed. 1989. *American Library Association presidential committee on information literacy final report.* Chicago: American Library Association.

Business fights illiteracy. May-June 1988. *The Futurist* 22: 50.

Can't anyone here speak English? 1975. *Time* 106 (25 August): 34-36.

Carnegie Forum on Education and the Economy. 1986. Restructuring American education: A time of ferment. *Current* 14 (October): 9-22.

Fields, H. 1987. Pell and McGraw ask for more money to fight illiteracy. *Publishers Weekly* 232 (28 August): 18.

Gintis, H. 1984. The political economy of literacy training. *Unesco Courier* 37 (February): 15-16.

Gorman, C. 1988. The literacy gap. *Time* 132 (19 December): 56-57.

Gortmaker, S. L.; Salter, C. A.; Walker, D. K.; and Dietz, W. H., Jr. 1990. The impact of television viewing on mental aptitude and achievement: A longitudinal study. *Public Opinion Quarterly* 54: 594-604.

Guerra, M. 1984. The cultural roots of literacy. *Unesco Courier* 32 (February): 6-8.

Hechinger, F. M. 1976. Murder in academe: The demise of education. *Saturday Review* (20 March): 11-18.

Hirsch, E. D., Jr. 1987. *Cultural literacy: What every American needs to know.* Boston: Houghton Mifflin.

Maslow, A. H. 1959. Psychological data and value theory. In *New knowledge in human values*, edited by A. H. Maslow. New York: Harper & Row.

McGraw, H. W., Jr. 1987. Adult functional illiteracy: What to do about it. *Personnel* 64 (October): 38-42.

National Assessment of Educational Progress. Improving literacy level is crucial. 1987. *Phi Delta Kappan* 68 (May): 711-714.

Nelson, D. 1987. Reagan proclaims year of the reader. *Wilson Library Bulletin* 61 (February): 29.

Neuman, S. G. 1988. The displacement effect: Assessing the relation between television viewing and reading performance. *Reading Research Quarterly* 23: 414-440.

Pascarella, P. 1987. Skills gap threatens our competitiveness. *Industry Week* 235: (19 October): 7.

Peck, S. D. 1988. Teaching literacy training. *Library Journal* 56 (15 April): 113.

Pipho, C. 1988. Sorting out the data on adult literacy. *Phi Delta Kappan* 69 (May): 630-631.

Prete, B. 1989. Baltimore, the city that reads. *Publishers Weekly* 236 (4 August): 71-72.

Reagan kicks off literacy program. 1983. *Publishers Weekly* 224 (23 September): 18.

Rosenthal, R., and Jacobsen, L. 1968. *Pygmalion in the classroom.* New York: Holt, Rinehart & Winston.

Ross, I. 1986. Corporations taking aim at illiteracy. *Fortune* 114 (29 September): 48-54.

Scully, M. G. 1975. Inflated grades worrying more and more colleges. *The Chronicle of Higher Education* 10 (19 May): 1, 7.

Smith, F. 1989. Overselling literacy. *Phi Delta Kappan* 70 (January): 353-359.

Strong, G. 1984. Public libraries and literacy: A new role to play. *Wilson Library Bulletin* 59 (November): 179-182.

Unesco and the struggle against illiteracy. 1984. *Unesco Courier* 37 (February): 33.

When mom and dad can't read: Illiteracy survey. 1986. *U.S. News & World Report* 100 (5 May): 9.

World Almanac. 1988. New York: Newspaper Enterprise Association.

2

LITERACY

A Brief History and Relevant Theories

This chapter, while helpful in providing a historical context and two psycho/educational theories pertinent to literacy, may be bypassed by readers who are interested in moving on to the practicalities of solving illiteracy, which begin with chapter 3. A review of the successes and failures of previous literacy programs helps frame expectations for what can be achieved in the present. It also helps prevent efforts to reinvent the wheel in the context of literacy efforts. This discussion is divided into two time phases: prior to 1900 and the twentieth century.

HISTORY

Prior to the settlement of America, literacy in Europe was prevalent primarily among the clergy. The Church had a monopoly on education and resisted early efforts to make learning and reading more widespread. In the sixteenth century all that began to change.

The invention of the printing press made the mass publication of books and other materials possible. But it was "the Protestant Reformation and the Protestant insistence that every man have free access to the Word, without priestly interference, that finally broke the Church's monopoly on literacy" (Brandt 1980, 7). The Puritans, in particular, encouraged education and literacy from about 1540 to 1640. This produced a literacy rate of about 30 percent in England overall, with the rate among adult males in London perhaps twice that high (Brandt 1980).

Fortunately for American literacy, the most literate people in England—the Puritans—settled New England. By the end of the seventeenth century, the literacy rate among males throughout New England was perhaps 60 percent (Brandt 1980). Over the next century, literacy in New England continued to rise, both among males and females. By the end of the eighteenth century, males had a literacy rate of about 90 percent and females of around 50 percent (Brandt 1980). In colonies without substantial numbers of Puritans, particularly in the South, rates were much lower.

As religious motivations for encouraging literacy declined in many regions, political motivations rose to take their place. Thomas Jefferson, for example, realized that a responsible electorate that could preserve democracy had to be literate. During the first century of American independence, there were many political moves to develop state-supported schooling. The individual states, more than the federal government, took the lead in promoting schooling and literacy (Arnove and Graff 1987). As early as 1830, the role of the library in particular in fostering education for adults was discussed (Coleman 1986). By 1850 the literacy rate in the United States was incredibly high: about 90 percent for both males and females (Brandt 1980). Of course, the definition of literacy at that time was considerably lower than that required in modern society. A century ago, everyone who could write their names might be considered literate in the eyes of some surveyors.

The United States began the twentieth century with fairly high literacy rates. Ironically, as we approach the final years of this century, literacy has dropped and continues to decline.

Many other countries began this century with low literacy rates and struggled to improve them. Not all of these foreign attempts proved successful. Knowledge of some of the successes and failures, abroad and at home, may prove useful.

Literacy Efforts in Other Countries

In 1919 the USSR declared war on illiteracy in its Decree on Illiteracy. All illiterates between age 8 and 50 were required to study. Local People's Commissariats of Enlightenment had the power to draft literate citizens as tutors. People refusing to study or help teach were considered in criminal violation of the decree. Did the state's intimidation and stridency help? Ten years later, none of the programs had been implemented. In fact, peasants sometimes organized their own schools, using non-Communist reading materials, and attacked teachers sent in by the state (Arnove and Graff 1987).

Communist China instituted a nationally organized literacy movement but did not retain central control. The national government left to local communities much discretion on how best to implement their portions of the program. This approach proved quite successful. Despite the poverty of its citizens, China was able to mobilize over 137 million people and achieve widespread improvement in literacy rates (Arnove and Graff 1987).

At the fall of Saigon in 1975, it was estimated that some four million Vietnamese were illiterate. The new government implemented a massive education program. In addition to formal lessons in reading, leaders developed creative ways to implement literacy reminders. For example, alphabet letters were printed on the hats of laborers, so that the alphabet could be seen as people worked together. Within one year, it was claimed that 20 percent of the illiterates in Saigon had been taught to read (Bethell 1983).

Ethiopia long suffered from one of the lowest literacy rates in the world—only 7 percent of its 32 million people were literate in the mid-1970s. After an 18-month war on illiteracy ending in 1980, which involved almost a quarter of a million tutors at more than 34,600 learning centers, the government claimed that seven million—or about 22 percent—of its population had achieved at least second-grade level literacy (War on illiteracy wins applause for Ethiopia 1981).

So much improvement in such a short time is commendable, but a person with second-grade reading skills would be considered basically illiterate in most cultures.

The General Conference of the United Nations' Educational, Scientific, and Cultural Organization (UNESCO) in 1980 decided that the illiteracy problem had become so serious that efforts to reduce it would receive the highest priority. It was decided that tactics should focus both on initial education to prevent illiteracy and on adult education to reduce it. Of course, UNESCO's effort involves planning strategy and establishing goals in conjunction with other countries more than becoming involved in grass-roots training programs (Unesco and the struggle against illiteracy 1984). Therefore, it is hard to attribute any specific success to this new emphasis.

The United States: ALA, Library and Literacy Efforts

In the 1920s the public library community began in earnest to focus its energies on so-called adult education. Early efforts usually took the form of reading and study courses in which participants read from ALA-published book lists. Ultimately, these packaged courses did not reach very many adults, and the ones who did participate were typically already quite literate to begin with. William S. Learned, an employee of the Carnegie Foundation, maintained that while children had access to the public school system, the adult community had been overlooked. He suggested a community intelligence service be established by the public library (Williams 1988, 43). Through his 1924 book, *The American Public Library and the Diffusion of Knowledge*, Learned inspired many librarians to join the adult education movement.

In 1924 the Carnegie Foundation funded a study of adult education under the direction of an ALA commission. Although the study took nearly two years to complete and see print, the basic finding was prematurely announced by ALA president Judson T. Jennings at the 1924 conference: "The library is logically ordained as the direct and primary agency of adult education" (Williams 1988, 43). Jennings's view was somewhat more conservative than Learned's, but both clearly believed the library had a primary responsibility to adult education.

The commission's final report, published in 1926, specifically included "the teaching of reading to illiterates" as one component of the library's adult education program (American Library Association 1926, 13). The report also recommended libraries get involved in such activities as providing information on local adult education programs and providing better library service to other organizations involved with adult education. There is little evidence that many libraries complied with the literacy aspects of that report.

To supplement the reading and study courses, reader's advisory services (used in a different sense than the term now connotes) were established "to provide reading courses tailored to the individual" (Williams 1988, 42). Librarians were expected to have read most or all of the books, to keep detailed records on the clients, and to make follow-up contacts. Even though these concentrated and personalized services seemed to embody the library's commitment to adult education, it was realized as early as 1928 that they were much too costly, in terms of time and money, for most libraries. In spite of heavy promotional efforts, the service was ultimately offered by only a few libraries throughout the country. By the middle 1930s, when the Great Depression hit hardest, it was difficult to justify such expensive services available to so few people (Williams 1988, 46).

The ALA commission that produced the landmark 1926 report was dissolved immediately afterward. But from 1926 to 1937, the ALA retained a Board on Library and Adult Education. In 1934 the ALA created A National Plan for Libraries, which called for a federal library agency and, rather unrealistically, requested between $50 million and $100 million in federal aid. A few years later, the library community weathered Alvin Johnson's attack, expressed in *The Public Library—A People's University* (1938), that librarians were indifferent to adult education. During World War II and in a few subsequent years, public libraries found themselves patriotically enmeshed first in the Victory Book campaign and then in demobilization efforts. Little extra attention was focused on the civilian population, and hardly a thought went to individuals without reading skills.

After the war, a National Plan for Public Library Service was produced, and the Public Library Service Demonstration Bill was introduced in Congress. The Great Books Program, begun in Chicago, promised to be the solution to the library adult education problem. It was followed by ALA's Great Issues Program and Four-Year Goals. All of these fell short of their potential, however, and the relative success of library adult education was deemed to be "very, very slight" (Williams 1988, 59).

The ALA's Board on Library and Adult Education, which survived from 1926 to 1937, was replaced by the ALA Education Board, which lasted from 1937 to 1955. With the Public Library Inquiry of 1949, the most extensive and competent study ever conducted, librarians expected to receive guidance on how "to make the public library the instrument of popular education" it could and should be (Williams 1988, 66). The library community was shocked when the principal findings indicated "the public library could never be an instrument of popular education ... [and libraries should] abandon the attempt" (Williams 1988, 66). Among the alarming findings of the inquiry: Only 25 to 30 percent of American adults regularly read books, and the library supplied only one-fourth of those books; less than 10 percent visited the library frequently; and 5 percent of the users borrowed 40 percent of the books circulated, while 20 percent of the users borrowed 70 percent of the books. The report concluded that nonfiction borrowing was "concentrated among a small group of students and well-educated adults" (Williams 1988, 66). The public was "barely aware" of the library as a source of information; more than 60 percent did not recognize the need for a public library. Other implications of the inquiry were that libraries could never adequately serve the entire community and therefore should not endeavor to do so; they should serve the people who were naturally drawn to their services in the first place. Libraries were geared to readers, to the literate populace—to the middle class. Realizing that, librarians stared hopelessly at the majority, which was not being served. Little thought was given to citizens without any reading skills.

Although many librarians ignored the findings, the inquiry (and subsequent studies) clearly showed that most libraries did not serve the needs of the disadvantaged—a euphemism for the poor, the uneducated, and the minorities. In 1957 the Adult Services Division of the ALA was created. In the 1960s the national library community expressed an urgency about social concerns and the relevance of libraries. With efforts termed *outreach*, libraries tried to deliver traditional services and materials to those who would not or could not come into the library itself. Most outreach programs merely extended traditional library services, which were largely irrelevant to the problems faced by the disadvantaged people in the target groups (Williams 1988, 102-103).

The Adult Services Division of the ALA, created in 1957, had a Committee on Reading Improvement for Adults, which in 1964 obtained a grant to examine the library's role in helping functional illiterates. The grant was used to study literacy programs already in existence to determine what contribution libraries were making and could make (Coleman 1986).

During the outreach efforts, the operating premise seemed to be that providing a variety of quality reading materials to people who were not using libraries would extend library services to them. The fact that many of those disadvantaged people were not able to read was largely ignored, and there is little evidence of significant library efforts to help teach them. This kind of outreach was of value to literate people living in relative isolation, but useless to those who still remained truly illiterate.

If it was unfeasible to educate adults, too costly to provide an intensive personalized readers' advisory service, and impossible to reach nonusers, the library community would try another tack. In the middle 1970s many libraries launched an information and referral service that was intended to assist people in finding the information they needed. Subsequent studies indicated that most information and referral services were devoted to information, with very little actual referral assistance (Williams 1988, 106). Public libraries had taken on the role of maximizing the availability of information of all types and forms to the entire citizenry. But they failed to realize the fact that millions of people were not able to use the information that libraries were so aggressively providing.

In 1970 ALA created the Office for Library Service to the Disadvantaged. Part of the office's mission was to increase and help maintain literacy skills among the disadvantaged. In 1980 the name of the office was changed to the Office for Library Outreach Services, although its mission regarding the provision of literacy services remained the same (Coleman 1986). One of the office's projects, begun in 1979, was a series of workshops "designed to train librarians in the techniques of establishing programs for tutoring in basic literacy skills for the functionally illiterate" (Coleman 1986, 211). Hundreds of librarians were trained, and they established literacy programs in their libraries around the country.

In 1981 ALA organized the Coalition for Literacy, which was formed from 11 independent groups working for literacy (see page 100). The coalition has raised public awareness about the literacy problem better than could the 11 groups working separately.

In many ways, libraries in general, and ALA in particular, have been in the vanguard of the literacy movement. By 1980 more than half of all U.S. public libraries were involved in some form of literacy activity (Smith 1981). Yet despite their efforts and the work of other groups, despite many individual successes, the overall illiteracy problem continues to grow.

In recent years, the federal government has supported literacy efforts through the library system with a variety of programs. Title II-B of the Higher Education Act established the Library Research and Demonstration Program. Since 1967 this program has provided grants to libraries and library organizations, about 5 percent of the total (more than $1.4 million) for literacy projects, mainly on Adult Basic Education or ABE (Mathews, Chute, and Cameron 1986).

Another source of federal funding for library literacy programs is the Library Services Program, established under the Library Services and Construction Act. This program has funded library projects since 1970 and has emphasized literacy efforts as a major priority since 1984. In that year, $4.2 million was spent funding 97 literacy projects, including tutoring in bookmobiles sent into prisons and teaching English to new immigrants (Mathews, Chute, and Cameron 1986).

Although not aimed primarily at libraries, the Federal Adult Education Act has focused on the illiteracy problem. Money funded through this act can be channeled to public libraries through state adult education departments or local adult education agencies. Funds may also be used to support literacy councils (see discussion that follows).

Other federal efforts have not so much provided funding as they have drawn attention to the problem. A report in 1984 by the Library of Congress recommended a national goal "to abolish illiteracy in the United States by 1989" (Fields 1984a, 11). Unfortunately, in the five years between the establishment of that goal and its proclaimed deadline, the problem grew worse. In reacting to the crisis of widespread illiteracy, President Reagan chose the bicentennial year of the American Constitution as the Year of the Reader. Said the President, "Every American should be able to read this national testament with full understanding. That goal alone should mobilize us to make ours a fully literate nation" (Nelson 1987, 27). More recently, 1990 was designated as International Literacy Year.

William J. Bennett, then Secretary of Education, indicated that "both the dropout problem and illiteracy ... are two national problems that do not lend themselves to a Washington solution" (Mathews, Chute, and Cameron 1986, 236). In other words, the federal government believes that the states must take the lead in tackling illiteracy. The federal government has provided financial assistance to help the states, in part through Library Services and Construction Act (LSCA) funds supporting the formation of literacy councils. The kind of state literacy activities supported by this federal Library Services Program include information and referral services, manuals and newsletters, literacy conferences, literacy hotlines and directories of service providers, and the use of military bases to provide rent-free buildings for literacy activities (Mathews, Chute, and Cameron 1986).

Some state governments have become involved in funding literacy programs as well. For instance, in 1985, the state of Illinois provided nearly half a million dollars to fund 17 literacy programs within the state. These programs involved local libraries cooperating with other groups to provide literacy services and to purchase reading materials (Illinois funds library literacy programs 1985).

Some cities have become involved in literacy efforts in a major way. For instance, New York City committed $35 million to the cause of adult literacy. Some of this money was used in 1985 by the Brooklyn Public Library to open five adult learning centers. These centers offer individual literacy tutoring, computer-assisted learning, and a reference collection for literacy professionals. The program employs 10 full-time and 16 part-time staff members in what has been described as the largest and most comprehensive literacy effort ever by a single library (Malus 1987).

In 1987 Kurt L. Schmoke became mayor of Baltimore, Maryland. His mayoral campaign stressed the need for literacy, and he affirmed at his inauguration his intent to make Baltimore "the city that reads." He sought to improve both the quality of the public schools and the availability of adult learning programs. He established the Baltimore City Literacy Corporation—the first of its kind—and sought cooperation and funding from other groups, such as the United Way and private corporations. Some of the specific projects in various stages of development include a literacy hotline and six adult learning centers based in the city's neighborhoods. These centers will provide testing and literacy services (Prete 1989). It is too early to assess the effectiveness of this very ambitious municipal program. Should it prove as successful as hoped, it may provide the blueprint for other cities around the nation.

Many businesses, including some of the nation's largest corporations, run literacy programs for their employees. It is unlikely, however, that a public library would become involved with an intrabusiness literacy program other than to provide literacy materials for tutoring and resource information for program coordination. Other private literacy programs target the public at large. Many libraries have worked with private groups trying to improve literacy in general. These cooperative efforts have proven beneficial.

Many publishers have become involved in literacy efforts because they realize that the future of their businesses depends upon having a population that reads. For example, the Business Council for Effective Literacy was founded by the chairman of McGraw-Hill, Harold McGraw, Jr., who donated $1 million of his personal funds. One of the council's first projects was support of the ALA's Coalition for Literacy (Fields 1984b). Like publishers, booksellers have a vested interest in promoting literacy. B. Dalton Bookseller, through its National Literacy Initiative, provided $12,000 in matching funds to the Dallas Public Library to help pay for the library's volunteer literacy tutoring program (Dallas Public receives literacy grant from Dalton 1984).

Project Literacy U.S. (PLUS) is one of the largest private groups to enter the fray. Founded in 1986, PLUS has 365 task forces scattered around the United States and Canada. The group sponsors a major media campaign of TV ads extolling the virtues of education (Dismuke 1989).

The U.S. portion of Laubach Literacy International (LLI) consists of 600 community groups with a total of about 30,000 volunteers around the country. Literacy Volunteers of America (LVA), founded in 1962, has over 230 groups scattered around the United States and Canada, with a total of about 12,000 volunteers.

Some professional organizations, such as the National Education Association, are helping to fight illiteracy. This organization, composed mainly of teachers and administrators in education, is cosponsoring PLUS (Dismuke 1989).

Finally, many churches have sponsored literacy programs. Some programs target church members. Often, programs extend to the surrounding community or to specific groups in the community, such as immigrants, which the church has identified as needing special help.

The following private and volunteer groups have played important roles in U.S. literacy efforts: Laubach Literacy Action (LLA)—the U.S. programs of Laubach Literacy International (LLI), Push Literacy Action Now (PLAN), Project Literacy, U.S. (Youth PLUS), Project READ, and Reading Is Fundamental (RIF). Much more could be said about the guiding philosophies, methods, and successes of these groups. That information is given in chapter 8 and appendix A.

Some Lessons Learned from the History of Literacy

Looking back over the panorama of literacy efforts throughout history and around the globe, some common threads appear. Certain approaches and styles seem to increase the likelihood of success, while others seem destined to produce little more than frustration. A brief discussion of the most important of these lessons follows.

Imposition. Just because a state is powerful does not mean that its leaders can impose literacy improvement on their people. In tyrannical situations, people tend to resist such imposition. In other words, if literacy is pushed too hard in the wrong way, the extra attention and effort can actually make things worse rather than better.

Motivation. Literacy programs seem most successful when they appeal to the dominant motives among the people being encouraged to seek increased literacy. Illiterate people may care little to spend the time and effort required to learn reading and writing if the purpose is to achieve some abstract national goal or please some political figure or party. If literacy conveys no direct benefit to themselves, at least as far as they can see, they may avoid help or even work against the program. On the other hand, when people can achieve one or more important personal goals through literacy, they are more willing to devote themselves to the effort. Such goals may be religious, political, social, economic, or personal. Therefore, the first task of those interested in spreading literacy is to show illiterate people how literacy relates to their own goals.

Focus. There are two logical ways to approach literacy: to teach reading and writing to youth going through school and to reduce illiteracy among adults who have avoided school or passed through it with deficient skills. Both approaches are important in controlling illiteracy. One should not be pushed to the detriment of the other. Historically, the main emphasis has been on achieving initial literacy in the schools. That succeeded when schooling was virtually universal and of sufficient quality to ensure adequate literacy. However, because both of those conditions have been called into question, current literacy programs cannot afford to ignore school literacy programs even as they encourage adult literacy training.

Level of Organization. Spreading literacy skills depends upon a one-to-one relationship between a tutor and a trainee. That is the most fundamental level of organization for teaching literacy. At the same time, without central organization at the national level, there is not sufficient public attention on the problem to stimulate volunteers and other support for literacy programs. To bridge the gap between the individual level and the national level, an organizational network at the state, regional, and local levels is needed. At the state and regional level, financial resources are allocated and lists of relevant organizations are maintained. At the local level illiterates within the community are identified and matched with tutors. In short, efforts are required simultaneously at all levels of organization for literacy efforts to achieve success. If active organization is lacking at any one level, the program will not proceed far, despite the dedicated efforts at the other levels.

Funding. It takes substantial sums of money to develop an extensive, multilevel organization to deal with the literacy problem. On the other hand, simply throwing money at a problem does not solve it. When there is no leadership and vision, major infusions of cash will accomplish little in terms of literacy. Too many well-funded programs fail to continue when the grant runs out, or they look good in theory but do not actually work, or they build a small bureaucracy but never have a direct effect on nonreaders. When there is motivation and commitment, a sense of people cooperating to achieve a vitally important goal, much can be accomplished with little extra money. For example, the library can donate facilities at no extra cost, volunteers work for free, the media can provide free publicity, and so on. This is not to say that money is unimportant, but only to encourage libraries and communities to begin literacy projects without waiting for grants. Of course, the best situation is a program that has both adequate human and financial capital.

Realistic Expectations. No literacy program has been completely successful. People who enter a program expecting complete success may become disillusioned and want to quit at the first sign of partial failure. However, it makes no more sense to stop supporting a literacy program because some trainees drop out than to stop supporting hospitals because some patients die. Partial success is better than none. Therefore, people embarking on a literacy program should be cautioned to have realistic expectations and to prepare for some setbacks.

More Help Required. Despite the lofty goals, the well conceived programs, the infusions of funds, the dedicated volunteers, only a small portion of the people needing help are getting it. Nationwide, four million or so illiterates are receiving help, which is about 5 percent or less of those who need it (Chall, Heron, and Hilferty 1987). If this were a test in school, a score of 5 percent would be considered an incredibly dismal failure. What is at stake here is far more important than a test: The very future of this culture and this nation is at risk. Much, much more effort is required to attack the seriously persistent problem of illiteracy.

THEORIES RELEVANT TO LITERACY—MASLOW, PIAGET, AND BLOOM

Maslow's Theory of Motivation

The late psychologist Abraham Maslow developed a theory that helps to explain how various types of motivation dominate in different personalities. Maslow posits that people do not merely have diverse needs but that these needs constitute a distinct hierarchy. As a person satisfies the lower needs, he or she is able to move up the hierarchy to more advanced needs.

The major levels of Maslow's need hierarchy, in order beginning with the lowest, most basic level, are described in the following paragraphs (Maslow 1959).

Physiological needs. Fundamental survival needs for food, drink, sleep, and so forth, must be met before a person can turn to higher needs. All infants begin life at this level of motivation. People of any age in desperately poor situations may be restricted to this level. The struggle for survival occupies all their energies, and they simply cannot see beyond it.

Safety needs. Provided that the first level is met, attention turns to safety needs. Motivations at this level are expressed in terms of building (or purchasing or renting) shelter, installing locks, supporting local police or military, or perhaps fleeing a dangerous situation. The person at this level saves money as a cushion against disaster, learns self-defense or to handle a firearm to protect against crime, or installs burglar alarms to ward off intruders.

Belongingness and love needs. The person who is able to satisfy basic survival and safety needs, at least to a certain extent, turns some attention to love, to belonging to a family and a community, to interacting in meaningful ways with friends and acquaintances, or to caring for pets. A person at this level needs to feel a part of a group or groups, to love and be loved.

Self-esteem needs. The person who has satisfied the lower needs and has established relatively stable and satisfying relationships can turn to seeking self-esteem. This may be done by participating in community organizations or civic work, or by excelling or earning attention in some field of endeavor—sports, career, finances, or the arts. The emphasis is on self-satisfaction rather than earning fame or fortune. In short, the person wants to feel not like a twig floating on an anonymous stream of existence but like an individual making a contribution to the world, doing something important.

Self-actualization needs. According to Maslow, few people reach this level. Self-actualization is related to self-esteem, but in this stage the person tries not only to make a mark but to reach full potential, to become a uniquely productive person. The focus at this level is on others rather than the self; the person seeks the greater good rather than personal satisfaction and esteem. Maslow credited only truly exceptional people, such as Abraham Lincoln, Albert Einstein, and Mother Teresa with advancing into this level, although he recognized that almost everyone may aspire to it.

According to Maslow, no one is situated securely at one motivational level. One may achieve a higher level then slide back to a previous level because of external interference. This necessarily interferes with attempts to reach yet higher stages. For example, many top scientists in Europe during the late 1930s, brilliant people who were scaling the heights of self-actualization, found their safety and survival threatened by war and persecution. Many abandoned their research immediately until they could relocate to safer countries, where they began anew. In the literacy context, the self-esteem a student may gain by regularly attending a tutoring program may crumble due to loss of a job.

Maslow (1954) focused much of his attention on people who had reached a prominent stage of self-actualization. After studying a number of such people, he concluded that they generally had 15 characteristics in common. Those of greatest relevance to the topic of literacy include:

- Self-actualizers have a deep social interest in all of mankind.

- Self-actualizers are highly creative, producing original insights and discoveries.

- Self-actualizers can rise above their own cultures due to their keen insights into the cultures' flaws as well as strengths.

It is difficult to imagine the illiterate person coming close to reaching the higher levels of need satisfaction and matching the traits of self-actualizers as described by Maslow. In other words, the illiterate person who chooses to remain in that state voluntarily cuts off an important avenue for personality development. In a society based on literacy, being able to read and write is required in order to build self-esteem through concern about issues threatening mankind, creation of original contributions in a particular field, or analysis of the foibles of the culture on which the society is based. In short, the illiterate person in an advanced culture may suffer stunted personality growth.

Piaget's Theory of Cognitive Levels

Piaget outlined four levels of cognitive development (1952). These levels are described in the following paragraphs, along with identifying characteristics and some comments on how each level affects literacy training.

The Sensori-Motor Level. This is the level normal in the first two years of life. At this stage the child learns to relate sensory information to muscular (motor) control. For example, the infant normally learns to roll over, sit up, crawl, reach out to grab things, stand, and walk. As muscular control matures, the infant is able to control, to some extent, what information reaches the senses. Similarly, the infant learns that things seen or heard can be approached or avoided by the correct motor movements. In short, the child learns to integrate sensory input with motor output in meaningful ways to achieve goals. A child at this level cannot achieve literacy, of course, but may appreciate being read picture books or simple stories. Only the most profoundly retarded adults remain at this level, and achieving literacy is impossible for them.

Level of Preoperational Thought. By operational Piaget means essentially logical. Thus, people at this level are prelogical, i.e., full of magical thinking. For instance, children at this stage often believe dreams are real, that monsters are hiding under their beds, that if you reassemble the pieces of a turtle run over by a car that you can fix it, that a big, shiny penny is more valuable than a tiny, worn dime, and so on. On the average, children operate at this level from the ages of approximately two to seven years. However, gifted children may develop logical thought prior to age seven. On the other hand, many adults with substandard mental capability may remain at the prelogical level. Just as few children can read well prior to age seven, many adults at this level have great difficulty learning to read and write. They are capable of elementary literacy, of learning to read traffic signs or write their own names, but a tutor expecting them to achieve advanced literacy is bound to meet disappointment.

Level of Concrete Operations. People at this level have the ability to think logically, but thought processes are rooted in the concrete, i.e., in personal, tangible experience. This person remains incapable of truly abstract thought. For instance, the person may have no trouble adding and subtracting real objects (coins or pieces of candy) but may grow quite confused in a discussion of algebra and solving equations for unknown variables. Coins fall within daily experience, but unknown variables do not. Similarly, a person at this stage may have no difficulty reading a map of a familiar region, e.g., a local neighborhood, but could become quite lost using a map of an unknown area. On the average, children remain in this stage from about age 7 to age 11 or 12. However, gifted children may certainly leave this stage earlier, although many adults never leave it.

Adults with mildly affected mental capabilities generally fall into this category. These are the people who did not advance very far in school, who may have grown discouraged, quit trying, or dropped out. Yet with the proper tutoring, they can achieve a reasonable level of literacy, approaching perhaps a normal skill level of sixth or seventh grade. With help they will be able to reach the level of reading want ads and filling out job applications. They can certainly perform meaningful blue-collar jobs. They will not, however, with any amount of tutoring, turn into budding college professors interested in discussing the fine points of eighteenth-century French philosophy, and they should not be expected to do so.

Level of Formal Operations. Formal operations refers to formal or abstract logical thought, i.e., the level of mature thought. The person at this level can deal with abstract and theoretical notions that go beyond direct experience, for example, comprehending science fiction stories about civilizations that do not exist or discussing philosophical notions about the meaning of life or the nature of society. It usually takes from about age 11 to age 16 to enter fully into this stage, and the adult who remains mentally active may progress in it throughout life. In other words, continued cognitive growth is possible throughout adulthood, too. The person may acquire more and more knowledge and wisdom but will remain in this stage, because it is the highest level of cognitive functioning. Relatively few adult illiterates have reached this stage, but those who have reached it have virtually unlimited literacy potential if they remain with a good literacy program long enough.

Application of Piaget's Theory to Literacy Training

To reach the patron at his or her level, the literacy trainer must first discover at what level the patron functions. One way to do this is to think in terms of Piaget's levels of cognitive ability and decide which one applies to the patron. This will not say everything important about the patron, and it will not disclose unique characteristics, but it does provide a convenient starting point. An approach to literacy training that may work perfectly for a person in the formal operations level, for instance, would fail miserably with a person at the preoperational thought level.

An adult at the sensori-motor level would be severely retarded and probably would not be encountered in a library literacy program. An adult at this level probably would be in an institution or under full-time custodial care. To discern the other three levels, the key diagnostic criteria are

- Does the person have primarily magical, illogical thinking? Such thinking indicates a person is at the preoperational level.

- Does the person deal logically with things within the realm of personal experience but lack comprehension of the abstract? This indicates the concrete operations level.

- Is the person capable of complex, abstract, logical thought? This indicates the formal operations level.

Most adult illiterates probably fall into the middle two categories. But remember—the purpose of classifying a person's cognitive level is not simply to stamp a label on the person and be done with it. Instead, the purpose is to guide the literacy teacher in selecting materials and in determining the best way to approach the student. The teacher should use information about cognitive function to help the illiterate in the most appropriate way.

If an illiterate is initially classified incorrectly, and later reveals a higher stage of cognitive function, or if the student progresses to a higher level, that's great! The concept of cognitive levels should not be used to limit or hold back a person in any way, but should provide a convenient starting point for improving literacy skills.

Bloom's Theory of Education

The educational psychologist Benjamin Bloom theorized that educational objectives can be best described as constituting a hierarchy with six levels (Bloom 1956). This is known as a taxonomy, or systematic classification. Reaching each of the various levels is markedly affected by literacy skills.

The following paragraphs briefly describe each of the six levels in Bloom's taxonomy, with some examples of each. As in the case of Maslow's hierarchy, a person must succeed at each lower level before reaching the next one.

Level One: Basic Knowledge. At the most fundamental level of education, the student learns simple facts, such as names, dates, and places, as well as terms and principles. The student may be able to memorize the correct answer for a test but not really understand what has been memorized. For example, a student may know Columbus discovered America in 1492 but may not have the slightest inkling who Columbus was, the significance of his discovery, or what the date means in terms of relative dates in world history. The student may simply parrot back what has been heard, relying on rote memory.

Level Two: Comprehension. At this level, the student understands the facts and principles that were memorized at Level 1. The student displays this understanding by using terms that differ from those memorized or by addressing an issue from a different reference point or perspective. The student can express the same thought in different words, for example, "Columbus discovered America about 500 years ago."

Level Three: Application. At this stage the student can take what is learned from a book or lecture and correctly apply it to real-life situations. Comprehension is demonstrated in action rather than words alone. For example, a student might build a model of Columbus's ship, dress up like Columbus, or act in a school play about the discovery of America.

Level Four: Analysis. Analysis is an abstract form of comprehension in which the student begins to break up an event or concept into its components and recognize the structure that holds them together. For example, a student might be asked to write an essay or engage in a debate concerning the discovery of America. The debate could deal with such questions as, Why did European nations sponsor exploration of the New World? What were some of the good and bad consequences of Columbus's discovery of America? Discussing these issues requires seeing the event in context and analyzing the relationship of each part to the whole.

Level Five: Objective Synthesis. Objective synthesis means developing original and creative perspectives on familiar material, i.e., learning to think for oneself and to generate new theories, insights, and ideas. An essay on the topic, "What would the world be like now if Europeans had remained in Europe for another 450 years and America had remained undiscovered until 50 years ago?" might exhibit an objective synthesis. Such an essay would not necessarily display objective synthesis, because many students, even quite literate ones, would flounder, producing an inadequate answer with little creativity. A good answer would show imaginativeness and original insights indicative of objective synthesis.

Level Six: Objective Evaluation. This highest level can be reached only by those who have mastered the five lower levels. In addition to possessing basic knowledge, comprehension, application, analysis, and objective synthesis abilities, the student can develop appropriate standards of judgment by which to evaluate those ideas. This level of thought is reminiscent of Maslow's self-actualization level and clearly is not achieved by many people. A scholar, for example, might not only develop a new theory about the psychology of Columbus but have the further insight to compare the theory to others and to evaluate its strengths and weaknesses objectively.

The illiterate person could certainly make some progress on basic knowledge (level one) and comprehension (level two) by interacting purely on a verbal level. But without the benefit of being able to write down what was heard or to read more about it, the ability to advance even within the two basic educational levels would be severely limited. The illiterate could make some progress in application—level three—demonstrating knowledge by producing something handmade, but it would be difficult to make any progress in the three higher levels.

Deficient literacy skills have a negative impact on all levels of educational objectives and make it impossible to fulfill the highest levels. As Richard A. Lanham said, "Until students have achieved conceptual literacy, they are not adequately equipped to gratify the need to discover their identity and seek order and intelligibility in the world around them" (Shrodes 1974, 11). Just as better education is needed to achieve higher literacy, higher literacy improves education. Better education of today's students produces better teachers, and other professionals, for the next generation of pupils.

Readability Assessment

When developing a reading program for literacy improvement, acknowledging readability levels is important. It would be senseless to throw college level material, for example, at a beginning reader. It would be insulting to provide third-grade reading material to an adult with eighth-grade literacy skills. Many publishers provide their own estimates of the reading level of the materials they produce. These may or may not be very accurate, however, for they sometimes depend on nothing more than the author's intention and subjective evaluation.

The best way to determine or verify a reading level is to conduct a brief but formal readability assessment. There are a number of ways to do this. Two of the simplest and most popular are the Fry Readability Graph and the Gunning Fog Index.

The Fry Readability Graph

Edward B. Fry (1968, 1969) developed a readability assessment technique that depends upon checking out in depth any three short passages from the text in question. These are the steps:

1. Three 100-word samples (not counting proper nouns) should be chosen randomly from somewhere near the beginning, in the middle, and near the end of the text.

2. Within each 100-word section, count the number of sentences and also the number of syllables (not counting those in proper nouns). To simplify the sentence count, begin the 100 words at the start of a sentence, then estimate the fraction of the final sentence (to the nearest tenth) which fits within the 100 words.

3. Compute the average sentence length and the average number of syllables across the three passages. For instance, if the sentence counts were 6.2, 6.5, and 5.6, then the average is 6.1.

4. To determine the approximate grade level, use Fry's Graph in figure 2.1, plotting average sentence length against the average number of syllables.

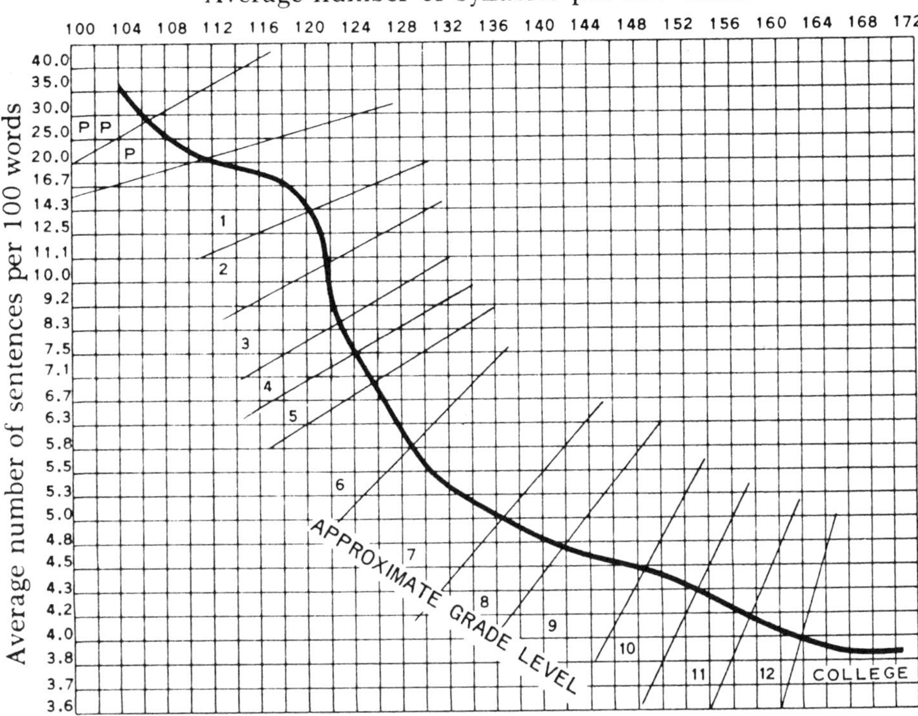

Fig. 2.1. Fry's Readability Graph (from G. H. Maginnis, "The Readability Graph and Informal Reading Inventories," *The Reading Teacher* 22 (March 1969): 516-518, 559.

The Gunning Fog Index

Robert Gunning (1968) developed a readability assessment technique which does not depend upon a graph. The reading level is computed directly. The name "Fog Index" refers to his contention that difficult writing basically *fogs* the meaning. His scale is meant not only to assess reading as it stands, but to encourage writers to simplify their writing to aid their readers' comprehension.

To compute the index:

1. Choose three samples (near the beginning, middle, and end of a text) of approximately 100-words each, keeping only complete sentences (not fractions as in Fry's formula).

2. In each, count the number of complete sentences.

3. For each sample divide the total number of words by the number of sentences to obtain the average sentence length.

4. In each sample, count the number of hard words with three or more syllables (however, do not include long proper nouns, long but simple

compound words like "woodcutter," or long verbs in which the third syllable just reflects a tense change, such as "created").

5. Add the average sentence length to the number of difficult words. Multiplying this sum by 0.4 provides the actual grade level directly. For example, if the average sentence length is 12.2 and the number of hard words is 6, then 18.2 x 0.4 = 7.28, indicating seventh grade reading level.

6. Take the average of the three sample grade levels to compute the overall grade level.

The advantage of this technique is that no chart need be consulted. Indexes ranging from 1 to 12 correspond to reading levels of grades one through twelve, while indexes from 13 to 16 correspond to reading levels of the four years of college.

REFERENCES

American Library Association. Commission on the Library and Adult Education. 1926. *Libraries and adult education: Report of a study made by the ALA*. Chicago: American Library Association.

Arnove, R. G., and Graff, H. J. 1987. National literacy campaigns: Historical and comparative lessons. *Phi Delta Kappan* 69 (November): 202-206.

Bethell, T. 1983. But can Juanito really read? *National Review* 35 (30 September): 1196-1199.

Bloom, B. 1956. *Taxonomy of educational objectives, handbook 1: Cognitive domain*. New York: McKay.

Brandt, A. 1980. Do we care if Johnny can read? *American Heritage* 31 (August-September): 4-13.

Chall, J. S.; Heron, E.; and Hilferty, A. 1987. Adult literacy: New and enduring problems. *Phi Delta Kappan* 69 (November): 190-196.

Coleman, J. E. 1986. ALA's role in adult and literacy education. *Library Trends* 35 (Fall): 207-217.

Dallas Public receives literacy grant from Dalton. 1984. *Wilson Library Bulletin* 59 (December): 252.

Dismuke, D. 1989. NEA joins national literacy drive. *NEA Today* 7 (May-June): 3.

Fields, H. 1984a. Library of Congress report: Abolish illiteracy in five years. *Publishers Weekly* 226 (14 December): 11-12.

———. 1984b. McGraw funds literacy council. *Publishers Weekly* 225 (3 February): 291.

Fry, E. B. 1968. A readability formula that saves time. *Journal of Reading* 11 (April): 513-516, 575-577.

______. 1969. A readability graph for librarians, Part 1. *School Libraries* 19 (Fall): 13-16.

Gunning, R. 1968. *The technique of clear writing.* Rev. ed. New York: McGraw-Hill.

Illinois funds library literacy programs. 1985. *Wilson Library Bulletin* 59 (June): 651.

Johnson, Alvin. 1938. *The public library: A people's university.* New York: American Association for Adult Education.

Learned, William S. 1924. The American public library and the diffusion of knowledge. New York: Harcourt Brace.

Malus, S. 1987. The logical place to attain literacy. *Library Journal* 112 (July): 38-40.

Maslow, A. H. 1954. *Motivation and personality.* New York: Harper & Row.

______. 1959. Psychological data and value theory. In *New knowledge in human values,* edited by A. H. Maslow. New York: Harper & Row.

Mathews, A. J.; Chute, A.; and Cameron, C. A. 1986. Meeting the literacy challenge: A federal perspective. *Library Trends* 35 (Fall): 219-241.

Nelson, D. 1987. Reagan proclaims year of the reader. *Wilson Library Bulletin* 61 (February): 29.

Piaget, J. 1952. *The origins of intelligence in children.* New York: International Universities Press.

Prete, B. 1989. Baltimore, the city that reads. *Publishers Weekly* 235 (4 August): 71-72.

Shrodes, C. 1974. Anachronistic pedagogy, humanistic goals. A review of *Style: An anti-textbook* by Richard A. Lanham. *The Chronicle of Higher Education* 9 (13 May): 11-12.

Smith, E. G. 1981. *Libraries in literacy volume 1.* Washington, D.C.: U.S. Department of Education.

Unesco and the struggle against illiteracy. 1984. *Unesco Courier* 37 (February): 33.

War on illiteracy wins applause for Ethiopia. 1981. *Jet* 59 (8 January): 14.

Williams, P. 1988. *The American public library and the problem of purpose.* New York: Greenwood Press.

3

REMOVING THE ROADBLOCKS
Solving and Preventing Problems

One of the most satisfying feelings an administrator can have is in removing roadblocks which have thwarted the organization's ability to respond to a particular need. Organizations that thrive are ones which are able to solve existing problems and prevent others from happening. Applying these principles to a contemporary and pervasive problem like illiteracy—and witnessing the positive results—can be one of the most rewarding experiences an individual or organization can have.

The library, like any organization that embarks on a new direction or proposes nontraditional service, can expect challenges. Some of these challenges are intangible—they may involve philosophical matters or librarians' perceptions of literacy. Most organizations must contend with one or more issues related to personnel. Other problems are tangible—logistics and, of course, funding dilemmas.

This chapter presents capsule descriptions of representative literacy-related problems or questions that may confront librarians, followed by discussion or possible solutions. Although not every library will encounter difficulty in each of the areas discussed, it is useful to scan the list to identify the obstacles that must be overcome. After dealing with the appropriate situations, the library is ready to choose the direction and scope of its literacy efforts.

PERCEPTIONS AND OPINIONS

Throughout the history of library service, few positions or goals have been universally embraced. Literacy is no exception. Librarians and libraries of all types have been slow to respond to the national crisis of illiteracy. Unlike pioneers, such as Helen H. Lyman, a large number are not convinced that an emergency exists in the area of illiteracy. Much of the time and effort that could have been devoted to literacy has been expended discussing the need for and merits of literacy programs. But Lyman, who has spent five decades working with adult education, continues to assert and praise the library's role in literacy efforts. "Over the last decade librarians have been providing and cooperating in literacy programs," she explains, even though their efforts have at times been unnoticed or even ignored (Davis and Fitzgerald 1989, 47). "I know that across the country many libraries and librarians are involved in highly successful literacy programs" states Lyman. "They present models of services and resource collections" (Davis and Fitzgerald 1989, 47).

Below are some of the intangible issues that may arise among the library's professionals and other employees.

Are libraries responsible for eliminating illiteracy?

What about government, society, schools, and service agencies? Aren't they responsible for eliminating illiteracy?

Yes. Government, society, schools, and service agencies have major roles in reducing illiteracy. But the problem has become so pervasive that every available resource must be utilized. Libraries and librarians represent key resources that can greatly assist in the overall efforts. But no, it is not the sole responsibility of libraries to eliminate illiteracy. Libraries are an important part of the literacy team, and they must work with other member agencies.

Should illiteracy be handled by educators?

Is this education's problem? Can we consider it "their" problem that does not directly concern "us"? How can we do more than educators have done?

The education establishment must play a major role to reduce illiteracy. But it cannot single-handedly correct illiteracy—particularly in out-of-school adults who lack basic skills.

While some librarians and educators work closely together, there are many communities in which the two have maintained a certain distance. This has allowed each profession to exist separately even as both worked (occasionally together) on the broader goal of enlightening the populace. Librarians have assumed that as long as they maintain the storehouses of information, there will always be citizens who will require their services. The machinery of education, at all levels, seems so well established that occasional breakdowns do not cause significant alarm within the library community. As librarians struggle to keep up with the information explosion, the campus, the curricula, the budget, and the faculty may not represent significant concerns. In fact, librarians may be so absorbed that the only "academic" issue they can seriously address is interlibrary loan.

Both librarians and educators are concerned with information and materials; most members of each profession would probably prefer more communication and cooperation.

Will the federal government step in?

Will literacy soon be institutionalized (assigned to an institution)? Can libraries and other agencies wait and see where literacy's ultimate home will be? Will a new agency be created to deal with it?

A glance at the proliferation of programs in the former U.S. Department of Health, Education, and Welfare (HEW) clearly proves the problem that is big enough, loud enough, and squeaks long enough usually gets the grease.

Individuals holding this precept wonder whether they should establish programs to fight illiteracy or wait until the federal government gets involved. They expect to see a federal Literacy Department or perhaps an undersecretary who will head the national literacy effort. In this scenario, state literacy offices would probably follow suit, creating offices through which funding would be channeled.

But bureaucracy is typically an inhospitable environment for people with social consciousness. What will happen to volunteers if and when the federal government or a national institution takes the reins of the literacy movement?

Recently, the U.S. Congress has taken significant steps to address illiteracy with the Sawyer and Simon bills, and the new Equity and Excellence in Education Act. But do not wait for literacy to be assigned to a government department or other institution before beginning a library literacy program. No one knows what the outcome of these bills will be or if they will be effective in reducing illiteracy. Meanwhile, libraries can begin the battle against illiteracy on a local level.

Is the literacy hysteria a new fad?

What are the odds that in a few years almost everyone will realize libraries cannot help much with illiteracy after all? What happens to these new library patrons if the literacy emphasis becomes passé?

The library profession, like most professions, has a history of jumping on bandwagons. When a movement is signaled at a conference or in an important publication, concern washes over the country and many libraries respond. In their enthusiasm, some libraries spend a great deal of time, effort, and money to retool, only to look around a few years later and discover they are among the very few still involved in that effort. This is not necessarily bad; important innovations can be made by capitalizing on fads. One simply must be careful when jumping on the bandwagon and not be crushed by the wheels.

One must wonder whether, with the next presidential election or a new first lady, the new federal budget, a different state government, or fresh ALA leaders, the emphasis on illiteracy might shift to something else. That is not likely. Almost all experts agree that the illiteracy problem has reached such enormous proportions and has such widespread deleterious effects that it will continue to be a major concern of our entire society for some time. Libraries that are already participating in the improvement of literacy will find themselves in a very favorable position when government, business, education, and society formulate a successful alliance to propagate the new information age.

Why can't illiteracy wait?

Why should libraries jump into literacy now? When is the deadline and what is the rush? If our predecessors would not or could not become involved, why are we suddenly in the spotlight?

With financial woes and advancing technology steamrolling libraries, many librarians believe literacy should be ranked third—or lower—in a list of priorities. They believe literacy can be handled in a couple of years, when both the technology and the budget are under control.

But illiteracy cannot wait: the problem grows worse each year. The longer we wait, the more difficult it will be to reverse the cycle and the effects of illiteracy.

Is it enough for libraries to support reading?

Is a general endorsement of reading enough? What is the library's role in the literacy effort? Should libraries be concerned with reading instruction?

Library professionals have always espoused reading, usually in the general contexts of education, fulfillment, and enlightenment. Over decades, institutions have invested untold sums in collections to support the arts, humanities, and sciences—the higher pursuits of the informed mind.

The library community has devoted relatively little thought to the needs of those who cannot read and write at all. It was generally assumed there were illiterate people "somewhere," but the unspoken assumption was that the numbers were small. Now it appears those assumptions were false. Illiterates are not "somewhere"; they are here. Their numbers are growing, and their lack of coping skills affects our entire society.

What is the library's proper role?

What can the library do? Can another agency do it better? How will the library's literacy activity be implemented? Is there any certainty it will help?

Chapter 4 discusses several specific areas in which libraries can help improve literacy. After receiving input from appropriate agencies, the library should define for itself its roles, purposes, and responsibilities to adult education. These determinations should not come from external sources, but from the library professionals themselves. After laying the groundwork in this way, the library should establish a literacy program, set up a timetable, and become involved in the local literacy network.

How does the library cooperate with other agencies?

How do we identify the network agencies and locate the contact people? In what functions can we cooperate with others? How can continuity be retained if there is a change in the coordinator at either end?

The library must discover what the principal agencies are, what they are already doing, and where libraries can fit in (see chapter 7). If the literacy network already exists, it should be easy to locate. If the community does not have a literacy network, the library should help form one. In many cases, the network exists, but it may lie fallow or may be loosely organized.

Illiteracy is such a vast area of need that "libraries must not repeat work already being done by other groups and individuals" (Lyman 1977, xi). Use the library's resources wisely by performing functions that complement or further efforts made by the literacy network agencies. Determine which agency has the knowledge and experience and ask for their assistance.

The library should have at least one member participating fully in the literacy network. But in most cases, the library administrator and the literacy coordinator should avoid assuming primary leadership of the network in order to devote their energies to specific projects. Leading the network is a job in itself; the leader probably will not have the time or energy to handle a specific project as well.

Continuity can be a problem for large activities in which many of the participants are volunteers. Frequent changes in the contact people at particular agencies or departments make keeping a current roster difficult. But libraries specialize in handling and updating information, and keeping a current list of literacy network members is not much different than maintaining the files of cabinet members, federal and state politicians, or municipal department heads!

What are the proper definitions and terminology?

What is the concise and authoritative definition of illiteracy? How many kinds of illiteracy are there? Which aspects should we tackle?

Many experts disagree about everything from definitions and numbers to causes and solutions. But the lack of consensus should not impede library progress and projects. The fact is, definitions and numbers are not the most important factors. Chapter 1 gives an overview of basic types of illiteracy and statistics on the numbers and general demographics of illiteracy. This basic information is enough to help you set goals and direction, determine activities, and get started!

PERSONNEL MATTERS

Starting a new project of any type involves change, hard work, and risk. The library literacy activity must be assigned to one or more principal figures. In addition, the organization needs to train support employees and should inform other workers to a certain extent. In some libraries, a literacy project may face staff resistance for various reasons, and some of these perspectives may be difficult to counter. The previous section supplies answers to some of the questions employees may ask. Following are additional questions or problem areas a library might encounter, with suggested courses of action or response.

Who leads the library's literacy project?

Who has the "right stuff" to handle literacy efforts? Who has the savvy or time to interact with other agencies and individuals? Who is available and who chooses them?

One person should take primary responsibility for the library's literacy effort and coordinate with the local network (see chapter 7 for more on interfacing). If someone on board is willing and able to handle this responsibility, turn him or her loose. The person with responsibility for the project should have the authority to carry it out—with administrative support, of course.

If no one on the staff has the time or skills necessary, consider hiring a tutor or a trainer. Someone with several years of experience in literacy tutoring will have a great deal of insight into the needs of the clientele. Libraries with a tight salary budget should try to recruit a skilled volunteer.

It is by no means essential that the literacy coordinator be a qualified librarian. If you select a nonlibrarian, provide some orientation in the workings of the library system. If you choose a volunteer coordinator, establish mutual understandings about his or her commitment to see the project through as well as the library's level of commitment and support.

How do other staff members get involved?

What do the other staff members need to know? To what extent should they be trained? Does an employee's rank or position determine the amount and type of information needed?

Adult new readers and nonreaders have needs which are quite different from those of mainstream library clientele. It is important to keep the staff informed of the direction and extent of the library's involvement in a literacy program. Some refer to this education process as "sensitizing staff" to literacy (Johnson and Soule 1987, 9). Your program needs the support and assistance of the staff, and they need to know what is being done so they can interpret it to the inquiring public. Generally, the higher the level, the more the employee should know about the library literacy program and its interaction with other community efforts. At the lower levels, everyone should know these points: whether the library has a literacy program, who coordinates it, and where the coordinator can be reached.

How do employees obtain information and training?

What kind of training is required for a librarian to be of specific use to the literacy effort? Do you have to be a reading expert, an instruction professional, or a certified tutor to work with literacy programs? Who is the replacement when staff turnover occurs, and how does he or she get trained?

Generally, librarians do not need specific literacy training to be effective, but they certainly do need awareness of the illiteracy problem and familiarity with the community's involvement. Of course, the more they know, the better they will be able to understand the unique needs of clients and program providers. Employees who have completed tutor training are particularly valuable to the library's overall literacy program.

The ALA and its sections offered several good literacy programs in recent years (Coleman 1986, 212), and these are likely to continue. For the 1990 ALA conference in Chicago, literacy assumed a marque position at the opening general session. In part 2 of a theme begun at the Midwinter Meeting President's Program, Patricia Berger explored whether ALA should adopt an association-wide literacy strategy.

Other opportunities, however, are relatively unknown, such as the single literacy poster session at the 1989 ALA conference in Dallas. But there is increasing momentum on state and regional levels for more workshops on literacy. If your library has an adequate travel budget, it is an excellent idea for several of the staff, or at least the literacy coordinator, to attend such programs as early as possible in the project timetable.

If travel is not practical or affordable, there is another way the library staff can quickly gain familiarity with the illiteracy problem. Gather several recent articles on a variety of adult illiteracy topics and assign one to each branch supervisor, department head, or other key staffer. Set up a morning meeting in which each person gives a five-minute report on the assigned article. Then conduct a roundtable discussion and brainstorming session. Not only will each librarian gain a close-up view of at least one aspect of illiteracy, but the whole group will receive balanced exposure to the main components of the problem. Several good ideas that can be used in the project may also develop. Make sure, however, that good ideas do not commit the presenter to implement those suggestions—that can quickly shut down the creative process.

Since staff turnover does occur, it is a good idea to have at least two staff people with fairly detailed knowledge of the library's literacy operation. One person is the project coordinator, of course. The other may be the library director, the public services coordinator, or perhaps the supervisor of the building in which the literacy project is housed. This key participant can provide valuable training and assistance to the new literacy coordinator.

What do you do if staff resist literacy involvement?

What causes librarians to resist? Can those factors be changed? Can a fledgling literacy program survive staff resistance?

When change occurs in a library, it may meet with resistance. That does not necessarily mean the staff opposes the literacy program, however. Resistance may reflect the belief that their departments' spending will be hurt by the allocation for a new program. Or it may be a matter of the materials or supplies that were appropriated from their departments for use in the literacy program. It could even be jealousy over the attention the literacy coordinator may receive in the early phases of the program. A good administrator or coordinator should be tuned in to the possible underlying reasons for staff resistance and should try to neutralize sources of friction. If the resistance stems from a simple misunderstanding about supplies or funding, for example, the resistance may subside when the matter is explained or corrected.

While it is important to realize that all librarians are not going to enlist in the illiteracy battle, literacy activities should move ahead. The library's involvement in literacy is too important to wait upon the elusive consensus.

What about those who believe libraries should not be involved?

Does everybody have to fall in step with the First Lady, the educators and sociologists who write the books, and the librarians who write the articles?

A number of people believe libraries and librarians should not play a role in the adult literacy effort. Among their reasons are these: (1) we are not in the business of teaching reading; (2) we should not waste money on adult reading material that is heavily diluted and aimed at the lowest common denominator; (3) book budgets should be used solely for reference material, authoritative nonfiction, quality fiction, and sturdy children's books; (4) the reading public is the voting public, and they are the ones libraries should serve; and (5) illiteracy in the aged is society's responsibility and illiteracy in the young is education's responsibility.

These views are generally considered a bit musty by today's standards. For staff members who honestly believe literacy programs are beyond the scope of library service, explain what you are doing and request their cooperation to the extent that it involves their areas, but do not expect them to change their minds. It is not essential for everyone to agree.

What about libraries that cannot handle literacy involvement?

What about differences in libraries' sizes and budgets? Will some communities have needs the library cannot handle?

Of the individuals who believe that librarians have a responsibility to share in the literacy effort, a sizable number are convinced that their libraries cannot handle the task. Among their convictions are the following: (1) we cannot redesign the whole public service program; (2) there is too little time to handle what we already do; (3) we do not have the training, and it is better to do nothing than do something poorly; (4) we are already bursting at the seams and there is no extra work space or collection room; (5) our existing budgets are continually threatened, and there is no new funding on the horizon; and (6) if we start a literacy project and it flops, it will be embarassing and will generate bad press.

Unlike people who are steadfastly against involvement in literacy programs, these people believe the library should be involved, but they fear the obstacles and ramifications. Among their ranks may be quite a few strong librarians you can depend upon for assistance. You may have to choose your project coordinator from this group—and that can be good. Many librarians of this ilk have tempered their naive idealism with strong doses of practicality and logic. Your project needs clear-thinking people who can recognize limitations and identify red herrings. The library must provide assistance to these employees and assure them that they will not be cut adrift once the project is underway.

LOGISTICAL PROBLEMS

Many librarians who are interested in literacy—even those who have settled all the philosophical matters—have allowed tangible problems to keep their libraries from becoming integrally involved. Several obstacles, some of which may seem impossible to overcome, can interfere with a library's ability to assist literacy efforts. These problems are discussed in the following paragraphs. Although each library probably will not encounter every matter discussed, it will certainly have to contend with some of them. To insure against unpleasant surprises later in the program, use this section as a checklist. Examine each problem, decide whether it applies to your situation, and work on the ones which need solving.

Will literacy be too complicated for the library?

Which reports are involved? How many? How can we keep all the proper records? What kind of system will we use to keep track of things?

The library should keep only as many reports and records as are required by the funding agency (if using outside monies). Otherwise, just take a few sample statistics (e.g., number of callers, number of items circulated, number of new patrons registered), and write brief narrative summaries for each calendar quarter. Personal information about clients (adult nonreaders and new readers) should be minimal and strictly confidential.

The following bit of levity illustrates how complicated things can become in a library.

> Question: How many librarians does it take to change a light bulb?
>
> Answer: It takes only one librarian, but it takes six months because of verification, ordering, encumbering, waiting for library rate delivery, receiving, cataloging, classifying, bibliographic record, ownership stamp, spine label, theft label, jacket, pocket and card, filing cards, and shelving.

The wide range of a librarian's duties is no joking matter. Many aspects of library work are very exacting and should be so. Still, there are times librarians should streamline the processes, bypass the rigidity of the system, and expedite a solution.

What about the library's routine problems?

> *If we turn our attention and energy toward the literacy effort, who and what will keep the organization going? What about the processing backlog, the unfinished reports, the overdue weeding project?*

Of course, the library cannot abrogate its responsibility to service, operations, and ongoing programs. Without a strong organizational structure, the library may be unable to implement something new or to extend service to additional areas or groups.

The old maxim, "if it ain't broke, don't fix it," is certainly valid. It is tempting to try to gather, clean, sort, and alphabetize everything before starting a new project. But that reaction can be counterproductive; the nonliteracy work might never be finished. It can delay the literacy project indefinitely and provide a handy excuse: "We have to get *this* straightened out first."

Libraries must have priorities: It is routine to have some things on a back burner, and some ongoing activities may never end. Those things need not prevent a library from participating in the literacy effort. Chapter 4 describes some literacy activities that almost every library can perform.

Where do we find the time and space?

> *How many hours or days are needed each week? How can we juggle staff responsibilities to make time for the program? Will the coordinator be forced to deal with the literacy program between patrons and calls?*

Constraints on time and space are sometimes responsible for killing literacy initiatives. There are no magic numbers for the hours needed or the square footage necessary.

Literacy activities will likely expand to occupy the designated staff, no matter how large in number. The best solution, if the organization has the resources, is to create a half-time or full-time position for a literacy coordinator and designate a couple of hours of clerical support each day. That may be all of the scheduled hours the literacy program needs. But many libraries will be unable to add a new staff position solely to coordinate the literacy program. In these cases, responsibility for the program will fall to a current employee who has responsibilities that must be shifted, in part or in their entirety, to someone else. Clerical support may come from the director's secretary, if there is one, or from another department with skilled office workers (e.g., technical services clerks). In some settings, the director will coordinate the literacy program and assign most of the specific activities to employees in various departments.

Unless the library is housed in a new facility with vacant offices, there is probably no available space for the literacy program. Many literacy programs may be fortunate to have a desk, chair, and telephone as a starting point. While it is certainly preferable, it is not essential for one space to house all of a library's literacy activities. As long as one person keeps tabs on all literacy activities, the individual functions can reside with the employee performing them. Of course, when planning to construct new headquarters or a branch library, space for a literacy office should be included.

Cope with the schedule and facilities that you have; do what you can with what you have. Do not wait for a new staff position or a new wing before committing the library to literacy involvement.

Which people are afflicted by illiteracy?

Who are these people? How many reside in our jurisdiction and how do we identify them? What do they need that we can provide? Do they really want our help?

There are many statistical studies; additional studies by the library are probably a waste of time. There is, and will continue to be, considerable variety in the figures and what they mean. Beyond such broad coverage as the U.S. Census and related research, state reports, education analyses, and economic studies give solid information, from different perspectives, on various aspects of the problem.

In many areas members of the literacy network probably have already completed local statistical research. If that is not the case, a discussion or request at the network meeting might generate an offer by some agency to perform the study. The library probably is not the logical agency to conduct such research—the library's role should be to collect the studies and make them available to others. Usually, the most that a library should undertake in this area is an informal needs survey or other relatively small sampling of users and nonusers.

However, the library's literacy team should not operate without some information on the target group. It is a mistake to assume what the needs of the disadvantaged are—those who suffer from discrimination, poverty, or lack of education—because their needs differ from the needs of the middle class.

How can libraries meet the needs of nonreaders?

How can libraries start helping people who cannot read when all these years our efforts have been directed toward readers and their children? How will we get nonreaders into the library? Failing that, how can we extend library resources to illiterates?

For nearly 50 years, the library community has been aware that a disturbingly small percentage of people read and an even smaller number use libraries regularly. A notable 1975 Gallup poll revealed, among other chilling statistics, that 35 percent of American adults had *never* used a library to obtain information (Eberhart 1976, 207).

For many years, library professionals thought of nonreaders as people who *could* read but who did not practice that skill regularly. When the subject of literacy arose, it was often overwhelmed by the disagreement among librarians over whether nonreaders could be encouraged to read more and whether the general public even wanted a library. While these colleagues realized that many adults were not reading and did not use libraries, it was not apparent that illiteracy handicapped millions.

The point here is that even if the library's *reach* to literate adults was vastly successful and already served *all* of its literate adults, it still would *not* be effective in reaching nonliterates. These clients must be approached through different means, with different messages. In other words, just plugging in some extra literacy materials will not reach nonreaders. Because, in fact, the library is probably used regularly by only about 20 percent of the adults who *do* read! (Eberhardt 1976, 207)

The library should try to reach nonreaders by working through the literacy network's member organizations, the community's social service agencies, or the city/county human resources departments.

DOLLARS AND SENSE

The appropriate role for each library will depend a great deal on community needs, the degree of organization in place, and many other factors. No single dollar amount is appropriate for all libraries; some literacy efforts have little or no direct extra costs, while other programs may require substantial investments. Few libraries in the country have unclaimed resources in hand, but the price tags need not keep them out of the literacy effort. More and more sources of funding are becoming available as literacy gains national momentum.

The following sections discuss some of the funding concerns that the library may need to consider.

Will funding fix everything?

Is federal financial stinginess the reason for increasing illiteracy? Will a massive injection of funding correct the whole illiteracy problem?

Grants are not the complete answer to the illiteracy problem. Too often, funding becomes merely a placebo or a quick fix to a small part of the greater problem, which continues to exist long after the money runs out. Some literacy programs that look good on paper simply do not work because they are not properly formulated. Other projects may function in a technical sense but are not effective – they do not reach a significant number of nonreaders.

It is a mistake to assume money will *cure* illiteracy any more than decades of designated federal funding were able to fix education.

Where will the money come from?

Can it be squeezed out of the regular budget? When will other funding be available, and from what source? How will the funds be handled in the library's budget? What kinds of reports and applications will be required?

Most librarians want a clear idea of who is responsible for literacy funding: federal, state, local government, or the private sector. They also need to know what requirements or obligations may accompany the funding.

Many libraries will not be able to act without the requisite extra funding in hand. A library without enough revenue to compensate a full staff and to purchase the books and magazines needed for the regular patrons will have a difficult time justifying any new expenditures for literacy. It can be difficult, or impossible, to cut an existing activity to start something new.

Lacking any extra financial resources, try to obtain grants through sources like the LSCA Title VI Library Literacy Program, which began in 1986 offering grants up to $25,000 to approved projects. Many libraries have compiled information on foundations and funding entities; often, this includes guidelines and forms. A particularly helpful source is the Foundation Center's annual publication *Grants for Libraries and Information Services*, which lists more than 900 grants of $5,000 or more from more than 250 foundations. This source includes statistical analyses, grant listings, indexes to the grants by recipient, location and subject, and foundation addresses and limitations. The volumes list total grants of some $85 million each year; as many as 18 foundations have each granted over $1 million to libraries annually. There have been a small number of listings for literacy grants, so literacy applications have to compete with many other categories of programs.

Some states, such as California, Kentucky, and Illinois, have designated funds for library-based literacy programs. In some areas, state adult-education agencies can help programs secure funding. Several cities and urban areas, such as East Harlem, Brooklyn, and Baltimore, have secured monies for literacy projects. Libraries should find out whether they can apply directly to the state or city comptroller for funding or if they must send applications through an agency like the state library.

Book-based companies, such as B. Dalton Bookseller, Waldenbooks, and Baker & Taylor, have spent considerable sums on projects, some of which have featured libraries. Some businesses (e.g., Southland Corporation's 7-Eleven Stores in the Washington, D.C. area) emphasize libraries as part of their literacy promotional efforts. Some provide grants to nonprofit organizations like LVA (e.g., New York Life Foundation's recent grants) and may be willing to extend consideration to libraries that develop a sound program. Companies such as the Ford Motor Company, which have invested in literacy training for employees, may be interested in a cooperative arrangement with libraries which could play a strong supporting role in their program. Other possible sources of funding include regional or local foundations, philanthropic entities, social organizations, or service clubs.

As noted in chapter 4, some of the library's contributions to literacy may cost very little.

How do you apply for grants?

> *How much paperwork is involved? Will we spend all of our time on reports and follow-ups? What are the chances of being accepted? What do the grant people look for?*

There probably have been more workshops and seminars on grant-writing than on literacy, and there are differences of perspective among the grantsmanship experts. The clearest advice, however, is to

- Keep the program simple. Focus on a few objectives and do them well.
- Show clearly the relationship of proposed expenditures to the objectives of the project.
- Indicate which activities will meet each objective.
- Identify the agencies you will cooperate with and what form that interaction will take.
- Seek input from local agencies and literacy providers to be sure the proposed project does not duplicate existing efforts and to be certain the proposed program will actually fill a need.
- Compose a statement of purpose, a program summary, and an outline of the objectives and activities. Send these with the grant application, even if they are not requested.
- Show how, by whom, and on what criteria the project will be evaluated.

What kinds of things do most grant agencies prefer to fund?

Are most grant agencies so finicky that few applications will pass*? How can we configure an acceptable program that involves the activities appropriate for our library?*

Most grant agencies prefer to fund start-up or build-up projects; many will not finance ongoing expenditures or operating costs. They look askance at expenditures that appear to feather the nest. Most legitimate grant entities want funding to go for projects that (1) put as much of the money as possible into the target area for the named clientele; (2) work cooperatively within a network or community; (3) have a clear concept of what to do and how to do it; (4) demonstrate that the project will produce measurable benefits; and (5) are handled by honest, capable, and qualified people.

Most entities publish their criteria, and many even explain on what basis they evaluate the applications. Many, such as LSCA Title VI, have only one application window each year, and often there are waiting periods of several months to find out whether the application has been approved. The library should study the grant entity and its guidelines thoroughly before submitting an application for funding. If you do not qualify, do not apply.

What are the funding possibilities on the local level?

Is all the funding locked up with foundations and government? Are there sources of grants that do not require all the paperwork?

If foundation funds or government grants do not match program needs, the library should try local businesses and individuals. Be sure to make it easy for them to participate. Just as it is difficult for a library to embrace an activity as large and daunting as literacy, it is difficult for others to participate in a general program that might require more of them than they can offer.

Most donors find it easier to respond when project needs are broken down into manageable pieces. Instead of requesting general support, make a list of needs that is simple and specific: books, tables, personal computers, shelves, or money for particular items. Retailers who would not give money might be willing to donate new or used items that are on a shopping list. Individuals who cannot or will not tutor may have other valuable skills, such as transportation, child care, or carpentry. Citizens who cannot finance an entire project may be able to give amounts of $50 or $100, which can buy a large number of books for adult new readers.

How do you spend the money wisely?

At what level should the money be spent? On what kinds of things can it be spent? What kind of money management is required?

Grant money and other literacy funding should be spent primarily to obtain literacy materials, training, or promotion. The program should fund activities that specifically help teach illiterate people to read or the functionally illiterate to cope. Do everything possible to bypass bureaucracy, both in the library and in the other network agencies, and eliminate as much of the overhead and administrative costs as possible.

Funding alone does not make an effective literacy program. Even well funded projects can become a quagmire of errant organizational machinery, or they can disintegrate into fragments of redundant efforts, misguided aims, and disconnected thinking. When seeking grants and funding becomes the primary interest of an organization, there may be a tendency for that body to take on the mantle of self-perpetuation rather than service to others.

The library's literacy project must be properly conceived and appropriately executed—being funded is not enough. It is important to consider what happens to the program, and to the people it served, when the money runs out. Will the library be able to pick up operation of the essential aspects or will the entire effort grind to a halt?

DISPATCHING THE PROBLEMS

After identifying problems and giving your best effort to solving them, it is time to go ahead with the literacy project. Some problem areas may never be solved to your satisfaction, and other solutions may take time, so you must not expect a perfectly clean slate before you begin. The library's literacy project should be able to survive most problems of implementation. Allow for serendipity: Some things will work themselves out and some problems may never develop. No prayers are unanswered, states a noted clergyman, but you may not receive the answer you requested—sometimes it's "yes," sometimes it's "no," and often it's "wait" (Lowery 1986, 43). It can also be said that there are no unsolved problems, however, the solutions presented may not always be expected or appreciated: "yes," "no," or "wait."

The solutions to most of the problems associated with implementing a literacy program are relatively unique to each library and must be solved in light of its situation. The advice or general approaches suggested here are intended as starting points for the literacy team at each library.

REFERENCES

Coleman, Jean E. 1986. ALA's role in adult and literacy education. *Library Trends* 35 (Fall): 207-217.

Davis, Nancy H., and Fitzgerald, Pam. 1989. Literacy clearinghouse. *Library Journal* 114 (December): 47.

Eberhart, W. Lyle. 1976. A closer look: Gallup survey of American adults assesses the role of libraries in America. *American Libraries* 7 (April): 206-209.

Foundation Center. 1987. *Grants for libraries and information services.* New York: The Foundation Center.

______. 1988. *Grants for libraries and information services.* New York: The Foundation Center.

______. 1989. *Grants for libraries and information services.* New York: The Foundation Center.

______. 1990. *Grants for libraries and information services.* New York: The Foundation Center.

Johnson, Debra W., and Soule, Jennifer A. 1987. *Libraries and literacy: A planning manual.* Chicago: American Library Association.

Lowery, Fred. 1986. *Starting here starting now.* Bossier City, LA: Love Publishing.

Lyman, Helen H. 1977. *Literacy and the nation's libraries.* Chicago: American Library Association.

Monroe, Margaret E. 1986. The evolution of literacy programs in the context of library adult education. *Library Trends* 35 (Fall): 197-205.

4

LITERACY INVOLVEMENT

How Libraries Can Help

Libraries should react promptly to the illiteracy crisis. In response to *A Nation at Risk* (National Commission on Excellence in Education 1983), the library profession called for "forming an alliance among teachers, education administrators, parents and other citizens, and the nation's libraries" (Center for Libraries and Education Improvement 1984, 2). Although many experts agree on some of the roles libraries should play in literacy, there is not a clear consensus on when, how, or how much should be done.

What *is* clear is that effective literacy involvement will require some adjustments on the part of the library. Although referring primarily to public libraries, the following description might be apt for other types of libraries: "It sometimes appears that libraries never change, or are the last to change, or *cannot* change from a rigid, institutional, establishment role" (Lyman 1976, 6).

This chapter examines why the library should be involved in literacy, what is the library's unique role, several areas of activity at different levels of commitment, types of libraries and their responsibilities, and information on library literacy programs already underway.

MOTIVATION FOR INVOLVEMENT

Even after handling or preventing all the problems associated with implementing a literacy program, some librarians still will be reluctant to get involved in adult literacy programs. Some think the stress on literacy is a passing fad, others will not become personally involved even if the emphasis is permanent, and many still believe the library's work is solely with people who already read. Influential leaders in our profession believe otherwise: The library "must have a full partnership in the Learning Society that will *have* to be brought to life if we are to be competent, knowledgeable citizens in the Information Age" (Center for Libraries and Education Improvement 1984, 4).

ALA and National Priority

When the Coalition for Literacy was formed in 1981, the leadership of ALA "took a giant leap into its commitment to literacy education" (Coleman 1986, 213) by bringing together 11 organizations that had a history of involvement in working to promote a more literate population.

Many years before the scheduled July 1991 conference, participants in the White House Conference on Library and Information Services Taskforce (WHCLIST) focused on adult literacy as one of the key initiatives in the second WHCLIS (WHCLIST pledges to aid adult literacy initiative 1983, 636). By the tenth annual WHCLIST meeting, literacy had become one of three primary conference themes for the 1991 conference (DeCandido and Rogers 1990, 14).

In her inaugural banquet address, Patricia Berger, ALA 1989-90 president, announced her focus by declaring, "First, we must win the battle against all the illiteracies—functional, informational, and numerical" (Gerhardt et al. 1989, 39). Berger also announced her intention to showcase literacy programs in libraries during her presidential year. At the January 1990, midwinter meeting, she presented the first part of a major study regarding ALA's association-wide literacy strategy; the second part was scheduled for the annual conference in June 1990.

Why the Library?

Many national authorities on libraries and literacy education have written widely on the matter of why libraries should be involved. Adult literacy "is an important and logical area of involvement for all types of libraries" (Johnson 1986b, 5). One of the 13 main recommendations of the *Alliance for Excellence* is that libraries "become active in adult literacy education programs at local, state, and national levels" (Center for Libraries and Education Improvement 1984, 31). The widely distributed booklet *Opening Doors for Adult New Readers* notes, "As a member of your community, the new reader is as significant as any other user group and his or her needs are often greater than those of others" (Bayley 1984, 2).

Lyman, whom many consider the dean of library literacy, reminds us, "Every library in the country—no matter what its size, function, purpose, and resources—has a place in the national literacy effort. The responsibility that libraries and librarians have for developing and interpreting collections of communication media places them in the forefront of the nation's effort" (Lyman 1977, 2).

There should be no doubt that libraries have a significant role and a definite responsibility in adult literacy. It is up to librarians to accept the challenge and implement a sound program.

UNIQUE ROLE OF THE LIBRARY

Ever since Melvil Dewey placed his first decimal, librarians have been concerned with information in its broader context. They collect it, arrange it, maintain or update it, and make it accessible; they purchase it, borrow and copy it, and loan it to others. With technological flair, librarians input information, output it, index it, and even network it. Clearly, the library already supplies a well-rounded information service that no other agency could provide. Unfortunately, many of these libraries' smooth-running information machines do not include important literacy data that almost every community needs in order to become part of a Learning Society.

What Is Unique about the Library's Role?

Libraries are considered to have "a major educational responsibility as well as unique services and resources to contribute to the development and maintenance of lifelong literacy skills and knowledge" (Lyman 1977, xiv). No other institution "has a schedule quite so attractive, or an atmosphere quite so nonthreatening, for adults" (Center for Libraries and Education Improvement 1984, 27).

Specialty of the House

Librarians specialize in lists and indexes. Some find validation in such routine, but exacting tasks. Librarians list books, bibliographies, serials, guides, indexes, annotations, and they even list lists; they index books, newspapers, magazines, journals, quotations, maps, realia, trivia, and almost anything else patrons might request. Librarians should be listing and indexing the services and programs of literacy providers, too.

These programs, services, contacts, addresses, schedules, and phone numbers can be assembled by the library in many ways. One very efficient method is a computer software spreadsheet program (e.g., Lotus 1-2-3), which allows the user to sort the information by many different fields of information. Many word-processing programs can handle directories or rosters, which could be adapted to the literacy effort. Finally, there is the old standby—the file box of 3-by-5 cards—which is still easy to use.

Almost every library has a vertical file. It is a simple matter to make several extra folders for literacy programs and resource information and then conduct a literature search for articles on the subjects (e.g., funding, promotion, or workplace programs) that would interest local literacy providers. If copyright considerations allow, articles can be photocopied and filed in the folders. The very least that should be done is to compile lists of articles on pertinent topics and file the lists in the folders. It is a good idea to send these lists to the literacy network members and other program providers. Finally, the availability of the new literacy information resource center should be publicized.

To go a step further, the library could assemble a vertical file of useful information on coping for literacy students. An excellent list of typical subjects appears in the "Literacy Clearinghouse" column of the May 15, 1990, issue of *Library Journal* (Davis and Fitzgerald 1990, 25). The editors refer to the material under these topics as "street smart" and cite two other valuable sources for similar information (see Lyman 1977 and Bayley 1984).

Mechanism in Place

Libraries have the mechanism in place to provide significant assistance to illiteracy victims and literacy volunteers. Libraries currently possess several important things that literacy program providers need desperately—professional material, program information, and grant and funding data. The history of literacy programs is filled with examples of information and programs falling through the cracks, of people reaching out for help and hitting walls, of citizens wanting to volunteer but not knowing how, where, or to whom. For example, people responding to a national literacy ad campaign might call one number and receive a different local number, which, if no active mechanism is in place, may lead to a dead end.

Making Alterations

Libraries need little adaptation to make available to adult nonreaders and new readers places for tutoring, referral to tutors, and materials written at appropriate levels, including information and entertainment. Some of the library's major ongoing activities, which are desperately needed by program providers, tutors, and students, may be unknown to them and should be promoted appropriately. Some endeavors, such as assimilating information, need not be changed except to include literacy-related information among the many other subjects already represented. Other resources, such as collections, need be altered only to the extent of locating and purchasing additional materials on appropriate reading levels for the new adult readers.

Facilitation and Neutrality

Librarians, by nature of their work, often play a facilitating role. Patrons of all ages receive help in locating and understanding almost everything in the library's collection (with the exception of legal and medical information, which, due to possible liability issues, should not be interpreted for patrons). It is a simple matter to extend those facilitating functions to literacy providers and illiterate citizens.

Libraries, especially public libraries, offer a sense of neutrality and the assurance of acceptance and service. Unlike many institutions and government offices, which can seem ruthlessly unhelpful at times, libraries emphasize service. The perception of the library as a place of service can help overcome some of the unique problems facing literacy pupils and tutors.

Frame of Reference

Libraries cannot do everything for everybody. That is clearly impossible and would dilute the library's effectiveness in performing the services that are integral to its program. Librarians should be innovative but should not stray far beyond reasonable bounds of library and information service and its support systems.

Functions like assisting, facilitating, and cooperating are important roles for libraries. Obviously, most libraries should not act as day-care centers, transportation providers, soup kitchens, medical aid stations, or shelters for the homeless. Librarians should assist people needing these facilities and services; they should provide information and referral to the agencies that are equipped to handle those activities. But the library must retain its own identity.

WHAT THE LIBRARY CAN DO IN THE LITERACY EFFORT

Thus far, this chapter has discussed the motivation and rationale for library involvement in the literacy effort and some of the unique features of the library as an institution. The remaining portion of the chapter examines some of the specific roles and activities that libraries could include in literacy programs. Materials, perhaps the most obvious component, is covered separately in chapter 5.

Many library authorities agree that one of the foremost roles for the library in regard to literacy is cooperation and collaboration. Among the other primary functions are education, community awareness, services, and materials. It is not necessary to limit these roles as long as all of them are logical and appropriate to the library's frame of reference.

Cooperation and Collaboration

In *Alliance for Excellence*, librarians are remonstrated to "leave behind their relative isolation and develop more effective interactions with the communities of which they are a part" (Center for Libraries and Education Improvement 1984, 26). Some colleagues, dispirited because of inadequate budgets and staffing, have fallen into isolation. Others are transcending those limitations and discovering mutual support among cooperating agencies. The report further suggests that "libraries, newly energized, freshly chartered, can become centers of the Learning Society" (p. 5). Some writers describe this as a virtual transformation. "Librarians have before them the invigorating activity of joint venture and the unparalleled opportunity to collaborate" (Lyman 1977, 2).

In their valuable manual, Johnson and Soule (1987) offer a continuum of possible cooperative efforts: contact and meet other literacy service providers and publicize their services, cosponsor tutor training sessions and coordinate community awareness and recruitment campaigns, advocate literacy with legislators and the public, and publish booklets or newsletters on illiteracy problems and literacy services. They recommend forming a coalition or council, expanding its membership, formalizing its structure, and soliciting funds from outside sources for future activities (Johnson and Soule 1987, 8).

Others with whom libraries should cooperate are "other libraries and other educational agencies in the community, region, or state ... teachers, researchers, reading specialists, citizens, volunteers from many fields, other librarians, and interested families, friends, and neighbors of the new literates ... members and staff of churches, high schools, colleges, universities, international houses, armed services" (Lyman 1977, 2).

True collaboration is hindered by differences in such areas as funding sources, responsibility, and administrative structure. Chapter 7 provides additional insight and assistance for libraries embarking on cooperative ventures.

Service: What the Library Does Best

Other than books, service is the best understood and most expected "product" of library and information service offerings. It is, quite simply, what librarians do. To compare, let us look at the world of retail where service was something you used to receive when you went to a store to find what you needed. Now it refers to a department you visit when the item you purchased goes awry. In many public and governmental environments, offices and bureaucrats do not offer service in any of the term's positive connotations. What they provide is a mandated function—rife with waiting lines, forms, rules, inconvenient schedules, and brusque demeanors.

The library offers assistance, without judgment or cost, to all who request it. All that needs to be done in order to extend this service to adult nonreaders and new readers, is to make appropriate materials available, understand the clients' special needs—and, of course, find ways to reach out to or attract clients.

Included in the Johnson and Soule continuum are these possible literacy services

- gather information on adult education opportunities for referral of questions, expand information on each literacy agency, collect literacy information for resource file for advocacy or display, and follow-up on referrals to agencies;

- provide space for tutoring and adult education classes, provide tours and orientation to adult education students, conduct literacy workshops for staff, and make presentations to community groups on literacy and the need for services;

- solicit funds for library literacy services, publicize the literacy collection, produce bibliographies of materials, and conduct tutor recruitment and training and student placement (Johnson and Soule 1987, 8).

The Johnson and Soule continuum differs from this listing in that it groups these services by complexity.

Other service activities could include the following: serve as resource centers for materials both for clients and professional personnel, assist in recruitment of participants, encourage potential learners or readers, produce information bulletins, make periodic assessments, evaluate services, keep relevant records, and exchange nonconfidential information about learners (Lyman 1977, 7-9). Lyman's summary is an inclusive charge: "Libraries should place their skills and knowledge, their science of evaluation, organization, and interpretation of reading and audiovisual media at the service of the teachers and administrators of literacy or relevant adult education programs" (Lyman 1977, 9).

Community Awareness

Lack of public awareness is the chief reason that the nation has failed to progress in eradicating illiteracy, even though bell ringers have echoed the call to action for nearly twenty years. The best literacy programs, in libraries or in other agencies, cannot thrive without the awareness and support of the community or without participation by the clients targeted by the program. As long as citizens are not aware of the magnitude of the problem or believe it does not affect them, they will not be roused to action. "To reverse this situation, marketing strategies for all types of libraries have to be developed" (Center for Libraries and Education Improvement 1984, 35). Advocacy is part of the awareness effort; it involves "providing information on national and state legislation regarding literacy services, addresses of legislators, and displays ... a public hearing or community meeting to discuss the literacy problem and identify services" (Johnson and Soule 1987, 9). Many of the services and cooperative efforts previously discussed are appropriate to help the public become more aware of the illiteracy crisis.

Many activities already performed by libraries can improve the public's awareness: public service announcements, posters, flyers, bookmarks, book talks, adult programming, exhibits, and tours. Without too much organizational stretch a library can mount a modest publicity campaign for literacy, featuring any or all of the following: local celebrities (media, politics, and society) posing with their favorite book, a profile of "Tutor of the Week" or "Student of the Week" (or month) in newspaper and on TV, or a spotlight on a particular book title in the adult new readers' material. Other promotional information is discussed in chapter 6.

Taking the Initiative

While many agencies wait for literacy to be adopted by an institution or department, some would impose that mantle upon community libraries. While it is probably not appropriate for libraries to become the official institution of literacy (with regard to funding, legislation, and so forth), it is true that libraries and literacy are intimately related. Because of that close relationship, libraries cannot afford to lag behind in literacy efforts. In fact, some experts assert that libraries should assume the initiative. "Without question, librarians ... must now take the initiative. They must reach more vigorously for their fair share of public attention and support; they must shake off invisibility and neutrality; they must be far more dynamic than is their custom. They must become stronger leaders" (Center for Libraries and Education Improvement 1984, 25). Although that heady directive implies that librarians fit a somewhat negative stereotype, the intent is to encourage the profession to assume leadership. "With all reasonable speed," the report continues, "librarians must retool their public presence, learn ways of active partnership, and ready themselves to lead their cohorts. On national, state, and local platforms, they must now stand up and be counted" (32).

Leading in Education?

Although some experts continue to believe libraries should not undertake primary educational roles, other notables believe differently. The library, "like the school, has permanence in every community; it is the major information resource and should be linked directly with all educational services to ensure continuity of educational opportunity and support" (Lyman 1977, 27). Pursuing that goal, libraries could assume a more active role, such as that of a learning center, providing educational programs and activities, such as Adult Basic Education (ABE) classes. This is an area that should be examined against the library's frame of reference to determine how far the library should advance into the camp of its educational allies.

Family Literacy Activity

A new area of literacy involvement that should interest libraries is family literacy activity. Libraries already have a great deal of experience and investment in developing the reading interests of young children. Most of these youngsters, except those arriving with day-care centers, are in the company of at least one parent. To be sure, the majority of parents who bring their children to preschool library programs are readers themselves. Nevertheless, the mechanism is in place to add programs aimed at both the child and the nonreading parent, if these clients can be identified, convinced to attend, and if necessary, assisted with transportation.

The Barbara Bush Foundation for Family Literacy recently published *First Teachers: A Family Literacy Handbook for Parents, Policy-makers, and Literacy Providers* (Barbara Bush Foundation for Family Literacy 1989). Among the programs featured are: Kenan Trust Family Literacy Project, Parent and Child Education (PACE) Program, Parent Readers Program, Mothers' Reading Program, Arkansas Home Instruction Program for Preschool Youngsters (HIPPY), and Parents as Partners in Reading.

Some federal legislation is taking a stronger stand on literacy as a requirement for welfare benefits (e.g., the Family Support Act of 1988). It is possible that the instruction phases of such programs may be contracted out to local entities since insufficient classes are in place. Creative libraries may be able to launch some of the instruction programs funded by such legislation. At the very least, libraries should participate substantively in the support of these programs.

Other Activities: Something Old, Something New

Several common library activities can be helpful to the literacy effort: information and referral, meeting rooms, high-interest/low-vocabulary (hi/lo) reading materials, adult programs, and information on job banks, transportation, day care, and other topics.

Libraries can handle the materials they have differently: reclassify selected hi/lo titles from juvenile to adult new reader collections, consolidate vertical file material on selected agencies, and place new adult reading materials in high-profile areas other than the library (i.e., satellite sites).

Other ideas to investigate include the following:

- Assemble deposit collections of hi/lo materials and rotate them among library branches or other public buildings.

- Establish a mini co-op, with librarians from school, public, academic, and special libraries getting together, at least quarterly, to provide collective library input to the literacy network.

- Establish an information clearinghouse in which books, articles, manuals, flyers, brochures—anything related to literacy efforts—are collected and publicized for use by tutors, trainers, or interested citizens.

- Offer special assistance with library card registration or other forms of citizen validation (for example, driver's license or social security card) for literacy pupils; promote this service in communities where the average educational attainment is lower than normal for your geographic region.

- Establish a support group for pupils and tutors; schedule and host meetings in the library on a regular basis.

- Obtain federal, state, or local funding to buy adult new reader materials for neighboring libraries that cannot afford them.

- Publish a regular newsletter for tutors and students to share information about programs and to print input from pupils. The newsletter must be written at a level that can be used by students and tutors during tutoring sessions.

- Conduct a family literacy program that brings parents who are new readers and their preschool children together.

- Advise churches, community centers, adult day-care centers, and nursing homes that the library has special hi/lo materials and arrange to make the items easily accessible.

- Identify the nonreading clients; recognize their needs, abilities, fears, and limitations. Give them understandable information about the library's services.

- Adopt a new mindset that the library belongs in the literacy business. Accept the challenge of serving the adult nonreader or new reader in addition to the library's existing clientele.

TYPES OF LIBRARIES AND THEIR RESPONSIBILITIES

Many of the roles and activities already discussed apply to all types of libraries. Libraries have a great deal in common, in terms of materials and services, and the major differences relate primarily to the ages or special interests of their specific clients. One characteristic common to all libraries is this: Nonreaders perceive libraries differently than do readers. Obstacles arise "when the users or nonusers and the librarians are unable to relate to each other, are even hostile and fearful; when concentration is on administrative efficiency, centralized organization, automation, systems development, and expressed information needs" (Lyman 1976, 4). Lyman is not referring specifically to the adult illiterate but to groups of unserved people, which certainly include nonreaders, and her remarks are still valid after 15 years. After accepting the fact that the library may be forbidding to the nonreader, one should explore ways to make it more inviting.

Nonreader Perceptions of Libraries

It is somewhat oversimplified, but nonetheless true, that adult nonreaders can find little comfort in school, academic, or special libraries. Each of these has a rather specific clientele, a particular type of collection, and a location that may not welcome the general public. It is important to realize that libraries may represent significant barriers to citizens who lack basic reading skills.

Public Libraries

Public libraries are more accessible to ordinary citizens than other types of libraries, but they represent significant barriers to nonreading adults. People with low self-esteem who are self-conscious about their inability to read may feel out of place in a facility, even a public library building, that seems clearly aimed at educated users. If nonreaders enter the building, it is probably for directional assistance (e.g., to the water fountain or rest room); they are not likely to remain and browse the collection. Most are not aware of what type materials the library offers, they are certain they cannot locate it, and they are fearful they will not understand it. They are not likely to request help if the staff seems unapproachable, if there are other people nearby, or if there is a chance they will be found to be illiterate.

Most of the literacy efforts discussed in this book are within reasonable reach of a public library that is serious about literacy efforts. Some experts believe the public library is the only type of library that can hope to reach adult nonreaders because of location, access, and perceptions. *Alliance for Excellence* recommends that public libraries provide service to parents of preschoolers, help to increase independent learning, supplement school libraries' efforts, enable adults "to enhance the quality of their life through learning pursuits," and assist others "who must be given special help because they have weak academic backgrounds or related problems" (Center for Libraries and Education Improvement 1984, 28-29).

Public libraries could make efforts to serve as a catalyst, taking a coordinating and leadership role; direct and sponsor group instruction and conduct tutorial programs; furnish materials in the languages of all client groups; follow-up on reading programs and provide follow-up reading materials; and use bookmobiles, book vans, and books-by-mail to distribute adult education materials (Lyman 1977, 61-62).

School Library Media Centers

The school library media center/learning center is uniquely designed to support classroom activity, teach library skills, provide supplemental learning, reinforce teachers' programs, and offer casual reading material for students. Few school libraries have the budget, staffing, security, or policy permission to remain open very long after classes are over. Even if it were open, nonreading adults probably would not be drawn to the library in a school complex that failed to help them while they were enrolled or that bypassed them entirely.

Of the 13 major recommendations in *Alliance for Excellence*, 9 deal with school library media centers, relating to such matters as services, standards, policies, collections, staffing and cooperation. "With their captive audiences, school library media centers have the best, most consistent opportunity to turn the introduction to independent learning into a lasting acquaintance" (Center for Libraries and Education Improvement 1984, 30). The report encourages school librarians to "work with teachers to introduce children to basic learning skills, build their enthusiasm for learning by themselves, guide them in homework, motivate their uses of libraries for studying and for extracurricular activities, and encourage the lifetime habit of reading for pleasure and information" (29).

Because of its direct relationship to the education system, the school library media center also has opportunities to reinforce basic literacy instruction, if the center: supports curriculum and instructional goals, consults on individualized reading guidance programs, offers reading laboratories, provides library group activities, instructs students in library skills, helps teachers appraise student skills, conducts workshops and discussions to help parents support children's learning, and collaborates with the public library on reading programs (Lyman 1977, 59-60).

Academic Libraries

Typically, academic libraries are even more uninviting than school libraries to adults without reading skills. While most academic libraries observe schedules that could support the needs of out-of-school adults, the campus itself probably seems forbidding to the nonreader. The library's collection features vast sections of materials written at levels accessible, for the most part, to professors; the classification scheme often is so complex that even students can become disoriented. This facility is custom-fitted for the institution of higher learning it serves.

But the college and university library "has an essential role by extension of its traditional functions and responsibilities into the area of literacy" (Lyman 1977, 62). The following activities are appropriate for academic libraries: develop literacy material collections for teacher education and training; develop research data collections and promote and disseminate that information; support the academic curricula; provide instruction in the use of dictionaries, encyclopedias, and reference aids; provide advice and counsel to students on the use of media materials; assist students who are tutoring individuals in ABE, General Education Development (GED), College-Level Examination Program (CLEP), English as a Second Language (ESL), and Teachers of English to Speakers of Other Languages (TESOL) programs; collaborate with the literacy programs in school, public, and prison libraries; develop instructional materials on what the library can do for the professional student and faculty; provide a resource center for teachers in programs of ESL and for speakers of other languages; provide bilingual and bicultural materials; develop reading and writing laboratories (Lyman 1977, 62-63).

Alliance for Excellence recommends that academic libraries staff the library with strong advisers to lead students toward advanced learning skills, provide subject-oriented bibliographic instruction, and offer remedial help in basic information skills (Center for Libraries and Education Improvement 1984, 31).

Since the campus already has educational and instructional professionals, classrooms, and laboratories, the academic library should be an excellent setting for workshops, tours, or training sessions. Such activities could help make illiteracy problems and literacy solutions more understandable to tutors, trainers, donors, volunteers, coordinators, politicians, clergy, community leaders, and other librarians.

Special Libraries

Obviously, special libraries are the most inaccessible to nonreaders. These collections are specifically assembled to meet the particular needs of the companies or agencies that house and fund them. Most deal extensively with relatively narrow topics that are of interest to the company personnel and their activities. Rarely does a special library have material of general interest, except for newspapers, magazines, and very basic reference tools. Most nonreaders would not be aware of the existence of special libraries and probably could not gain access to them unless the nonreaders happened to be employed by a company that operates a special library.

Although some special libraries are part of a governmental complex, most belong to a corporation, company, business, or other private enterprise. Consequently, many of these special libraries may not be affected by the momentum of national initiatives that affects school, public, and academic institutions. However, with increasing attention on the alarming statistics about workplace illiteracy, special libraries may soon feel more pressure to become involved in literacy efforts. Thirty-six percent of the Fortune 500 service and industrial companies offer employees remedial courses in reading, writing, and reasoning. And more than three-fourths of the people entering the nation's work force between now and the year 2000 will have limited reading and writing skills, which will be suited to fewer than half of the jobs being created (Barbara Bush Foundation for Family Literacy 1989, 1). Surely, the impetus soon will be evident for special libraries to assist directly in the efforts of their parent companies to reduce illiteracy.

State Library Agencies

The state library agency's role is typically one of leadership, assistance, coordination, and interaction with state and federal government. Its possible literacy activities include efforts to create awareness and understanding of literacy among legislators, decision-makers, and trustees; coordinate literacy activities of local and federal staff; provide funds for the outreach efforts of regional and county library systems; emphasize nonusers, adult beginning readers, and the disadvantaged; help librarians and trustees plan literacy programs; provide training for trustees, librarians, and paraprofessionals on how to sustain a literacy program; help fund and coordinate workshops, institutes, and courses on literacy with library schools; develop English and bilingual and bicultural collections of literacy materials for long-term loan or rotating collections; develop media collections to help promote community awareness; assist small- and medium-sized independent libraries in rural and isolated areas; inform librarians, trustees, and legislators on a continuing basis of significant literacy developments; initiate and support demonstration and experimental literacy projects; and assist librarians in writing proposals for demonstration literacy projects (Lyman 1977, 63).

INFORMATION ON LIBRARY LITERACY PROGRAMS

Library literacy programs are becoming more plentiful and considerably more varied. Some focus on obtaining special adult literacy materials, while others embrace automation technology to equip computer-assisted teaching labs. The wide variety of literacy activities can include the types listed by LSCA Title VI: innovative approaches, programs for targeted populations, urban and rural programs, librarian training, tutor recruitment and training, building coalitions, employment-oriented projects, computer-assisted approaches, public awareness campaigns, collection development, and general literacy services.

One library may spend a few hundred dollars on materials, while another may purchase expensive audiovisual or computer equipment to help with tutoring classes. There is no standard profile against which to examine these programs. Rather than discussing individual library literacy programs, this section examines sources that treat these programs more fully. A detailed case study of an actual public library literacy program is presented in chapter 9.

LSCA Title VI Library Literacy Programs

An excellent source for examining the literacy programs of individual libraries is a publication of the U.S. Department of Education. Covering LSCA Title VI Library Literacy Grant programs that have been funded since 1986, the annual reports give considerable information about individual projects. The first report, entitled *Library Programs: Library Literacy Program Abstracts of Funded Projects, 1986*, features the 239 projects funded that year. Abstracts are arranged by the type of project and an appendix lists the projects by state (Office of Educational Research and Improvement 1987).

There were 245 projects funded for 1987 and 224 selected for 1988. The 1988 report contains analyses of the funded projects rather than abstracts. The report lists each project, its level of funding, and a code to the type of activities it conducted. More than one-third of the 1988 grantees also received grants in either 1987 or 1986; many received grants in both of the previous years. In the first three years of this program, fewer than half of the applications received were approved. For 1989 there were 214 programs funded with an average of $22,103 each; for 1990, 237 programs averaged $22,637 each.

Other Sources Describing Library Literacy Programs

An excellent source of information on family literacy programs, from the Barbara Bush Foundation for Family Literacy, is entitled *First Teachers*. It features detailed descriptions of 10 programs, including the Kenan Trust Family Literacy Project, which is active in a dozen states and has received national media attention. Each description contains information on the program's background, funding, components, setting, and evaluation. The most unusual component is the advice to policy-makers and practitioners, which follows each program description. Near the end of the handbook is a program summary chart, which allows convenient comparison of the different aspects of the featured programs.

The Fall 1986 issue of *Library Trends* is a theme issue devoted to adult education, literacy, and libraries. Editor Darlene Weingand assembled 12 articles covering the full range of topics related to libraries and literacy. Karen Gaughan's article, "Literacy Projects in Libraries" (1986), discusses many programs, including an LVA cooperative program in Connecticut and the California Literacy Campaign. Two other articles in that issue have a direct bearing on library literacy programs: Debra Johnson's "Evaluation of Library Literacy Projects" (1986a) and Margaret Monroe's "The Evolution of Literacy Programs in the Context of Library Adult Education" (1986).

Gary Strong's article, "Public Libraries and Literacy: A New Role to Play" (1984), features the California Literacy Campaign and mentions several specific projects. In an appendix to *Literacy and the Nation's Libraries*, Lyman details six library literacy projects (1977, 161-181). Johnson and Soule present three sample programs, each of which focus on a different activity: collection development, instruction, and support services (1987, 10-11). The *ALA Yearbook of Library and Information Services* has featured an article on library literacy projects annually since 1976. The bibliography to *Literacy and the Library* lists scores of articles on individual library literacy programs.

REFERENCES

Barbara Bush Foundation for Family Literacy. 1989. *First teachers: A family literacy handbook for parents, policy-makers, and literacy providers.* Washington, D.C.: Barbara Bush Foundation for Family Literacy.

Bayley, Linda. 1984. *Opening doors for adult new readers.* Syracuse, N.Y.: New Readers Press.

Center for Libraries and Education Improvement. 1984. *Alliance for excellence.* Washington, D.C.: U.S. Department of Education.

Coleman, Jean E. 1986. ALA's role in adult and literacy education. *Library Trends* 35 (Fall): 207-217.

Davis, Nancy H., and Fitzgerald, Pam. 1990. Literacy clearinghouse. *Library Journal* 115 (15 May): 25.

DeCandido, Graceanne A., and Rogers, Michael. 1990. *Library Journal* 115 (15 March): 14-15.

Gaughan, Karen K. 1986. Literacy projects in libraries. *Library Trends* 35 (Fall): 277-291.

Gerhardt, Lillian N., et al. 1989. Presidential focus. In Deja vu in Dallas: ALA's 108th annual conference. *School Library Journal* 35 (August): 33-39.

Johnson, Debra W. 1986a. Evaluation of library literacy projects. *Library Trends* 35 (Fall): 311-326.

______. 1986b. Libraries and adult literacy education. *RQ* 26 (Fall): 5-7.

Johnson, Debra W., and Soule, Jennifer A. 1987. *Libraries and literacy: A planning manual.* Chicago: American Library Association.

Lyman, Helen H. 1976. *Reading and the adult new reader.* Chicago: American Library Association.

______. 1977. *Literacy and the nation's libraries.* Chicago: American Library Association.

Monroe, Margaret E. 1986. The evolution of literacy programs in the context of library adult education. *Library Trends* 35 (Fall): 197-205.

National Commission on Excellence in Education. 1983. *A nation at risk: The imperative for educational reform.* Washington, D.C.: U.S. Department of Education.

Office of Educational Research and Improvement. 1987. *Library programs: Library literacy program abstracts of funded projects, 1986.* Washington, D.C.: U.S. Department of Education.

______. 1989. *Library programs: LSCA VI library literacy program analysis of funded projects, 1988.* Washington, D.C.: U.S. Department of Education.

Strong, Gary E. 1984. Public libraries and literacy: A new role to play. *Wilson Library Bulletin* 59 (November): 179-182.

Weingand, Darlene E. 1986. Introduction. *Library Trends* 35 (Fall): 183-186.

WHCLIST pledges to aid adult literacy initiative. 1983. *American Libraries* 14 (November): 636, 638.

5

MATERIALS FOR ADULT NEW READERS

This chapter deals exclusively with materials for new adult readers: which ones to choose, where to find them, and how to handle them. Almost every library has the resources to acquire some specialty materials for adult nonreaders and new readers. In addition, "the role of providing print materials may be the most comfortable for libraries, because it is something libraries are used to doing" (Johnson and Soule 1987, 7).

Many literacy materials are priced like paperbacks, and most are quite a bit less expensive than hardcover library books. Any library should be able to afford a modest collection, even without additional funding. Even if a library ignored all of the other literacy responsibilities and opportunities, such as cooperation, services, and promotion, the commitment to materials must be honored. This is the library's minimum level of involvement in the community's literacy efforts.

DIFFERENCE IN PHILOSOPHY

Before examining which library literacy materials to choose, where to get them, and how to handle them, this chapter briefly discusses what is different about these materials and which philosphical matters should be settled in order to maximize their use.

What Is Different about These Materials?

Adult literacy materials are quite different from any other collection in the library. They vary by type, format, level, and subject matter; they require special selection, handling, and promotion. Typically, adult subjects are written on adult levels while topics of interest to children are aimed at their reading level. In literacy material, however, subjects crucial to adults' daily survival are presented at reading levels from grades 1 to 6.

Collections best meet literacy needs when they include "a variety of media formats from multiple sources, a range of skill levels, and useful and meaningful content and appeal to potential users" (Bayley 1984, iii). These materials may be used independently by new readers or in tandem by tutors and pupils; in some cases they are obtained as supplements to computer-assisted tutorial programs or lab activities, such as IBM's Program-Assisted Learning System (PALS).

What Should Libraries Do Differently?

A balanced adult literacy collection differs in many ways from the library's other material regarding the target clientele, reading level, subject, format, and type. Because of those differences, some adjustments must be made in the library's handling, control, organization, promotion, and training. Acquisition or selection policies may need to be revised or expanded to include these atypical materials. For example, some public libraries' selection policies include a specific statement that they will not purchase textbooks. If so, the policy could be reworded to allow the buying of literacy textbooks and workbooks.

How extensive will the literacy collection be? Which subject areas will be covered? Can the library purchase workbooks, which are designed to be written in? Who on the staff will be responsible for selection and handling? No single set of answers will fit each library that chooses to develop a literacy collection. But all of these issues must be addressed, and library officials should establish policies to cover the extenuating circumstances of these unique clients and their specialized needs.

Loosening the Grip

The main philosophical adjustment necessary for a library embarking on a literacy program is to loosen its institutional grip. Before an adult literacy collection can be used to its potential, it may be necessary for the library to rethink its policies and relax on such matters as inventory control, registration requirements, and overdue fines. A first step, however, should be to examine applicable legal issues. It would be a mistake to change a policy only to find later that the new policy is legally questionable. If the library relaxes its stance on certain policies for adult new readers, what criteria will be used to classify the patrons to determine who receives exemptions from the regular guidelines? What will be the reaction from other patrons?

Decisions should be made regarding the relative importance of inventory control versus potential use by the target clientele. Should there be a longer or shorter loan period? How vigorously will the library pursue items that are not returned? Will there be a fee for lost items? Can the library afford to write off an item by rationalizing that it is being used by someone who needs it? Is that practice legal?

Rules, Forms, Fines, and Fees

Because completing application forms is a daunting task for the functionally illiterate, the library may consider relaxing its registration process for these patrons. A short form could be developed or specific assistance could be made easily available for those who need it. Will these special patrons be restricted in how many items or what kinds of material may be borrowed, or how long it may be borrowed? Should the electronic patron record be coded, or should their borrower's cards be labeled in some way to reflect these privileges?

The library should examine its structure of fines in light of the degree of economic disadvantage frequently associated with population groups having high illiteracy rates. Since many of the materials are in workbook formats, they probably will be returned with marks or answers written in. Will there be a penalty for defacing the book? Here is another choice between upholding traditional library rules versus finding ways to extend service to people who otherwise may not be helped. Should these materials have lower fines or no fines? Is that legal?

These questions are posed because every library should make conscious decisions about each one. The organization should enter a literacy program or build a literacy collection with full awareness and should not allow the project to evolve by default. While each library must make decisions based on its own situation, a general attitude is suggested: relax as many requirements as you can; simplify procedures and forms; build in the flexibility to meet clients' needs on their level; expect and accept a higher loss rate; compose riders to applicable policies that state how the policy will be adjusted for illiterates and the reasons for such adjustments.

Determining Patrons' Needs

Most of the library's regular patrons—from toddlers to geriatrics, from students to professors, from kindergarteners through senior high schoolers—have relatively predictable needs. Libraries have served these groups for generations and have built collections by responding to positive and negative feedback from patrons and employees. But with adult illiterates, a group largely ignored in most libraries over the years, there is no long record of service to examine. Most librarians do not know from experience what is useful to this new clientele.

Some experts recommend conducting surveys, which consume a great deal of thought, planning, and effort. Such activities also delay the beginning of the library's literacy project. If a library is compelled to do a survey, the study should be limited to an informal needs survey with a simple one-page list of topics and formats. This checklist should be distributed to a sampling of regular patrons, new readers, tutors, coordinators, or instructors.

What Do Adult New Readers Want?

There are many variables to consider in developing a literacy collection: low reading levels and high interest content are not enough by themselves. Uncertain or general purposes will not provide sufficient motivation for adults to learn to read or to use such material. The adult new reader must be able to recognize that the material has a specific, everyday purpose that is relevant to him or her; the material must be practical and pertinent to daily survival. Material for pleasure reading should be on subjects or issues of importance to adults (Lyman 1977, 54).

WHICH MATERIALS TO CHOOSE

There are various ways to group the types of materials that should be included in the library's adult literacy collection. What one writer calls informational material may be described by another as life skills or coping skills. One author refers to study materials when discussing basic skills or reading skills in another's context. Some topics (e.g., use of computers) could be considered informational, instructional, or coping. It is not important to nail down the precise sorting method for these subject areas. These materials are essential to the developing reader, and the important idea is to get balanced coverage of the subjects.

Types and Subjects

Librarians may prefer to think of the following distinctions for literacy materials: (1) instructional, which teaches and reinforces the processes of reading, comprehension, writing, and basic arithmetic; (2) coping skills, which includes material on life skills, daily survival, and coping situations; and (3) enrichment, which includes reading for pleasure, leisure, or recreation.

Instructional Materials

As used here, instructional material refers to items that help teach basic literacy skills, including reading, writing, spelling, and mathematics. Some professionals also include U.S. history, science, and social studies. Laubach Literacy International (LLI) and LVA have developed two distinct teaching methods that have a wide variety of instructional materials and workbooks available on several reading levels.

For some individuals, the only incentive to read may be to pass an important test, such as GED, driver's license, or citizenship tests. Instructional material geared for these tests is not really on the same level with basic literacy skills instruction. Most libraries have study guides for common tests in the regular collection and may or may not want to duplicate them in the adult literacy collection.

Coping Skills Material

For the purposes of this book, coping skills material includes information on subjects that are also referred to as life skills or survival skills—the "skills and knowledge needed to interact effectively in one's environment" (Lyman 1976, 137). The following list includes some of the topics that are considered important to adults with substandard literacy.

Consumer Needs

Financial: budgeting, planning, family finance, money management, banking services, credit, taxes, economics, insurance.

Housing: utilities, home maintenance, renting, housecleaning, household appliances, furnishings, relocation.

Shopping: food and grocery, comparison shopping, clothing, refunds, Better Business Bureau.

Miscellaneous: transportation, auto repair, conservation, gardening, farming, home crafts, pollution.

Health Needs

Personal: family care, birth control, pregnancy, childbirth, nursing, child care, personal care, nutrition and diet, grooming, aging, preventive health care, sickness, venereal disease, sickle cell anemia, drug abuse, alcohol abuse.

Agencies: hospitals, emergencies, disasters, health service, mental health, pest control, animal control.

Employment Needs

Finding work: want ads, job vacancies, application forms, interviews.

Working: job training, tax withholding, employment rights, job benefits, group insurance, unemployment compensation, workmen's compensation, retirement.

Legal Needs

General: citizen's rights and responsibilities, voter registration, political process, elections, privacy act, human rights, advocacy.

Specific: legal aid, choosing lawyers, legal documents, arrests, bail, trials, divorce, child support.

Community Resources

Social Security, employment office, welfare programs, health department, recreation entities, various public assistance agencies.

Other Information

Marriage, family, children, community, religion, leisure, recreation, etiquette, education, personal development, self, relating to others.

Enrichment Materials

Some libraries may place less emphasis on this type of material, particularly if funding or space are limited, in order to concentrate on instructional and coping skills materials. But new readers have a definite need for enrichment material to obtain balance in their new medium of information. In the library's general or young adult collections, there may be several titles appropriate for literacy pupils. Be careful to select items with subject appeal to adults, and do not include those with covers or illustrations that look childish.

Adult new readers who are reading for pleasure may turn to comics, the new graphic novels, regular hi/lo materials, or easy reading fiction (realistic stories, romance, or science fiction). Abbreviated and heavily illustrated biographies of sports figures, music stars, or other prominent personalities are particularly popular and usually easy to obtain. Libraries can also "publish" stories—particularly humorous ones—to supplement the collection (see appendix B).

Balancing the Collection

What topics should be covered in the adult new readers collection? Literally hundreds of topics and subtopics have been identified by various studies; a complete list would not be practical nor particularly helpful. Regardless of how one groups the subjects or names the skills, it should be clear that adults who are illiterate or functionally illiterate are not able to cope as easily with everyday situations that the reading population may take for granted. Adults who are new readers need material on key subjects in a format they can use and at a level they can understand.

For each beginning literacy collection, the library's literacy coordinator should:

- Select a dozen titles on various levels, in both Laubach and LVA methods, for instructional materials.
- Pick a half-dozen topics in each of the six coping skills categories; purchase at least three different titles on various reading levels in each chosen topic.
- Choose a dozen titles in enrichment material.

This shopping list provides a starter collection of about 150 titles to unveil right away. Later the gaps can be filled in by assessing the results of the abbreviated needs survey sheet. Consult authoritative sources, such as the Project: LEARN bibliography (Pursell 1989) to choose additional recommended titles and series.

Format, Content, and Level

Librarians are accustomed to dealing with material of every conceivable size and shape, from oversized art books to Beatrix Potter's Peter Rabbit series, from unabridged dictionaries to paperback romances. They are accustomed to ordering titles on every imaginable level, from picture books with no text to the most scholarly, authoritative treatises available. Adult literacy material also comes in a variety of sizes, shapes, and reading levels.

Format: Size and Shape

A large amount of literacy material is 8½ by 11 inches with paper covers and stapled spines; many of these are about 75 to 125 pages long. Another popular size is 5 by 7 inches, with about 50 to 80 pages; many are even smaller. The covers are typically illustrated with photos or artwork that is clearly aimed at adults.

Many covers depict adults in situations such as interviewing for a job or shopping at a market, which gives the literacy student a clear idea of the book's content.

Some titles have teachers' guides, which accompany the pupil text and may share the same cover art. Some materials are designed like color comics, while others appear in a tabloid newspaper format. There are also video and audio cassettes that can be used as primary or supplementary material. More and more companies are developing computer software for use with PCs or in computerized reading laboratories.

There is hardly a limit to the size, shape, binding, or format of this material. As publishers become more deeply committed to decreasing illiteracy, they produce a greater number and a wider variety of material for literacy tutors and students. That proliferation significantly affects the selection and handling processes in the library.

Content: What Is Inside?

Much instructional material is in workbook form, with questions, exercises, and answer blanks. Many are heavily illustrated with drawings or photos that depict what the text explains. Some contain simple graphs or charts to help pupil comprehension. Depending upon the reading level, there may be short word lists at the beginning of each section or at the end of the book.

In coping skills material, there may be an illustration of an item next to the word or words describing it. In some of the material, scenes are shown in cartoon fashion, with speech "balloons" for dialogue. The size of the lettering and the use of boldface type varies with reading level. The following describes generally how illustrations, exercises, and lessons are used in instructional and coping materials.

> *Illustrative Matter.* Photos should be simple, well composed, and specifically related to the text they accompany. Subjects (individuals in the photo) should have reasonably contemporary clothing and hairstyles.
>
> Artwork should be clear and obvious, but not childish, and it should directly reinforce the adjoining text. When evaluating artwork, notice whether the characters appear contemporary and seek balance in the racial/ethnic representation.
>
> Some illustrations use exaggerated facial expressions to show contrasting situations like "good and bad" or "right and wrong" (Pasley and Williams 1988, 1). Some use preposterous situations (e.g., a VW Beetle approaches a city intersection and encounters an army tank coming from the right) to help reinforce the point that drivers should yield to the vehicle on the right (Richey 1980, 7).
>
> *Exercises.* Some of the exercises a literary student encounters in instructional and coping skills material may include filling in blanks, writing short lists, answering "yes" and "no" questions, writing check marks in boxes, circling the numbers of correct responses, copying (writing) phrases and short sentences, underlining words within a sentence in response to a question, and drawing lines to match exact items or related terms.

Lessons. Lessons should include a clear statement of the lesson objectives, directions that are brief and easy to understand, a glossary of the words used in the lesson, and pronunciation keys for unfamiliar words. A particularly effective presentation is one which uses repetition and variety to help the student understand. One example of an excellent coping skills lesson focuses on "want ads." It has a brief (one sentence) description of a type of want ad with artwork which depicts the activity being advertised and a sample of the actual ad (Jew and Tandy 1977, 8-9).

Enrichment material is mainly text, with some illustration, but no need for blanks and exercises. Many contain short glossaries, however, and both the word selection and sentence length are carefully fitted to specific reading levels. Some of these titles resemble traditional hi/lo material, except that the plots are aimed at an older audience and contain comparatively fewer pages.

Reading Levels: Low, Medium, or High?

Experts frequently disagree on how to assign grade levels to reading material and what those grade levels really mean. It is a bit like having maps of a given county: there are road maps, topographic maps, and maps showing property ownership. All three types of maps depict the same territory, but each describes it in a different way and for different purposes.

Many educators classify an individual with basic illiteracy as having a grade level from 0 to 4.9, while functional literacy refers to grade levels between 5.0 and 8.9. Some publishers group titles along different lines, for example, Adult Basic Education (2.0 to 7.0) and GED (8.0 to 12.0). Many literacy programs take students to the point where they can begin ABE classes. Other programs are geared to help students through level 6.0, where they are graduated to pre-GED or GED classes and literature.

The library should purchase materials in a wide range of reading levels, particularly on subjects that are most useful to the struggling reader. If the literacy budget is very limited, it would be wise to concentrate the collection on the lower reading levels while still covering the full range of levels. The range of reading levels for most small and medium literacy collections probably should have a ceiling of 6.0 to 7.0.

Often, there is no indication of the reading level on a book itself, but publishers' catalogs usually indicate the range for each series or title. Some materials have an indicative numeral in the title or subtitle (e.g., *Skill Book 2* or *More Stories 3*). Despite such clues, in some cases the reading level may not be clear to the librarian, coordinator, selector, or cataloger. Someone in the education community, an independent reading specialist, or an experienced tutor can be consulted for assistance in this area. The local literacy network will almost certainly have a member who is able to help.

The physical appearance of the pages will indicate whether the text is aimed at a very low or very high level. However, differences between third- and fourth-grade levels, for example, may not be easy to determine. Libraries wishing to conduct their own analysis may consult Fry's Readability Graph or the Gunning Fog Index (see chapter 2).

Other Evaluation Criteria

In addition to types, subjects, format, content, and reading level, other criteria should be used in selecting adult literacy collection materials. These include a limited number of pages, short chapters, short paragraphs, ample white space on pages, and sizable, but not juvenile, print; a small number of characters, unstereotyped people, uncomplicated plots, minimum description, and adult characters, situations, action, and conversation; and finally, clear explanations, emphasis on use or application, and repetition of significant information (Pursell 1989, vi-vii). Lyman devotes an entire chapter (1976, 157-218) to evaluation of reading materials and includes samples, charts, and reproduction of Fry's Readability Graph, and an explanation of the Gunning Fog Index.

WHERE TO FIND LITERACY MATERIALS

Some librarians have not started a literacy collection because they were not sure what to purchase or where to get it. Fortunately, several sources can help. As recently as the late 1970s, librarians writing about literacy noted the relative scarcity of high-quality material on appropriate subjects written at the proper levels for the beginning adult reader. Much has changed since then. Publishers have now recognized their stake in the illiteracy crisis and are turning out a wide range of material.

Bibliographies

Several bibliographies of materials for adult new readers are included in this book's bibliography. Particularly helpful among them is *Books for Adult New Readers* (Pursell 1989), which was developed by Project: LEARN. Originally compiled and annotated by Roberta L. O'Brien, the fourth revised edition was edited by Frances J. Pursell. Arranged by fiction, biography, and nonfiction (in broad Dewey categories), it contains entries for about 650 titles and recommendations for a core collection of about 100 titles. It features a section on publishers and contains indexes by title and subject. An extremely valuable section lists and describes various series. The titles included in the bibliography are cited with a number for quick reference to individual annotations. Other helpful sections contain suggested readings for the librarian, materials for the tutor, books already in most libraries' collections, general readings on literacy, and computer learning. If the library can afford only one bibliography of literacy materials, this is the one to purchase.

Publishers of Literacy Material

Libraries just beginning a literacy collection, or those with limited budgets, should concentrate on publishers that specialize in literacy, such as LLI's New Readers Press or LVA. This eliminates much guesswork, because the materials are specifically developed for literacy programs. But it is important to realize that many LVA tutors will not use Laubach materials and vice versa. Each program has a different approach to the teaching of reading: the Laubach method is very structured, with emphasis on phonics; LVA stresses flexibility, with customized lessons and materials tailored to student interest and needs. Both LVA and Laubach have long histories and are certain to thrive, so a library needs materials that are useful to each group.

It is important to realize that publishers focus on different aspects of adult literacy. Some produce entire series with a very specific application, such as ESL programs, while others publish titles effective for a variety of uses. For instructional material in basic literacy skills, good examples include: the Laubach Way to Reading series, LVA's Read On! II series, and Lakeshore's Working with Numbers series. Although much of the instructional material is written near the 4.0 level, there are some creative series on the prereading levels, such as the Longman Photo Dictionary workbooks and ARCO's Reading Power series. For students who have already attained basic literacy, the library should purchase a wide variety of coping skills material that assists with daily life. Examples of these are Follett's Coping Skills series and Success Skills series, and Lakeshore's Math for Everyday Living. Some publishers adapt their regular hi/lo list and sell it as adult literacy material in the enrichment vein. A few publishers provide a mixture of instructional, coping skills, and enrichment materials.

Several literacy books and bibliographies include lists of publishers (e.g., Johnson and Soule 1987 and Pursell 1989). Most libraries already have some of these publishers' catalogs in the director's office or the acquisitions department. Some catalogs show reduced-scale sample pages from the text of the literacy material so the librarian can determine its approximate reading level. Other catalogs have charts showing each series and title and where they fit on the reading level scale.

Other Sources

Other sources of information on literacy materials include various community agencies, organizations such as Laubach Literacy Action (LLA), which is the U.S. program of LLI, and LVA, and input from tutors and students. Many community agencies will be represented on the local literacy network, which provides an easy point of contact for the exchange of information on types of material most helpful to adult new readers. If a list of materials has not already been developed, the library's delegate could poll the network members or distribute a self-addressed, stamped envelope with a request for 10 favorite titles from each member. Organizations like LVA and LLA have publications that are distributed by the parent organizations as well as lists produced by the local affiliates; these should be easy to obtain from local chapters.

Do not overlook the tutors and the students themselves as sources of information on what type of reading material will be valuable in your literacy collection. Tutors may be able to recommend certain titles they have been using for years. Some students may not have particular titles in mind, but they can certainly relate which subjects most interest them.

HOW TO HANDLE THE LITERACY COLLECTION

In order to get the most use from the library's adult literacy collection, pay special attention to the way in which the materials are classified, cataloged, placed, arranged, and promoted. Because adult new readers have specific needs and the material comes in a variety of sizes, shapes, and formats, handling these materials correctly requires special care and planning.

Selection and Ordering

The library's literacy collection selector should examine several catalogs, study a few of the bibliographies that recommend specific titles, and visit a neighboring library that has a literacy collection. The selector should then purchase some books and get the collection rolling. Having several librarians review the list is a waste of time, as is any mechanism that requires someone to approve the selections, since they probably know very little about specialty literacy material. Later, after the literacy collection is established, is the time to evaluate what is being used and what has been requested by tutors or students. That information can be used when replenishing the collection in subsequent budget years.

Classification and Cataloging

Rather than alter the existing catalog scheme to accommodate literacy materials, many libraries will be tempted to use the standard classification numbers and descriptive cataloging. But such handling may render the materials largely inaccessible to a struggling reader who cannot understand that system.

Most libraries of any appreciable size use Dewey numbers carried out to as many as four decimals. In a library with LC classification, the problem is even worse, with its bizarre (to the nonlibrarian) alphanumeric-decimal combination. Such classification systems are confusing even to the reading population: the call numbers are more difficult to locate and harder to remember.

Descriptive cataloging, under the influence of MARC records and AACR2, has evolved into a rigid system of information that is helpful to libraries sharing resources but is confusing and unnecessary to ordinary patrons. Most readers simply do not care how many centimeters tall a book is or how many leaves of plate it has; most do not care about those inverted subject headings that must be so precise in their awkward phrasing. These devices have been adopted for the convenience of librarians and in most cases offer nothing of direct benefit for patrons.

Keep It Simple

Both classification and cataloging should be greatly simplified for literacy materials. If the library's rigid scheme is confusing and unnecessary for many of its regular clients, imagine what it represents for the struggling reader. The library should be willing to sacrifice technical rigidity if the fundamental issue of access is at stake. A successful literacy collection does not have to adhere to the same classification scheme as other nonfiction; it does not need four decimal places to provide the necessary organization. This collection does not require the precise subject headings that hold all the other titles in their grip.

Many experts recommend not cataloging the literacy collection at all. Bayley proposes subject categories such as money management, travel, transportation, community information, law and government, study skills, history and culture, self-improvement, arts and crafts, and others (1984, 12-13). It is certainly possible to make a case for having no numbers at all—just an arrangement under a few dozen categories, such as jobs, home, safety, and health. Another option is to use those topical categories in conjunction with a simplified Dewey number (for example, 641 Nutrition), so both the librarian and the client can be satisfied.

Librarians who prefer to use a standard classification scheme may be willing to keep Dewey to its second summary (e.g., 150, 240, 780, and so forth). The library would be well advised, in any case, to allow Dewey numbers no more specific than the third summary (e.g., 031, 248, 647) by eliminating the decimal and anything that follows.

Rethink the reasons the material is classified and cataloged. Consider the clients and evaluate their special needs as opposed to the library's predilection for order and uniformity. Be creative with classification—you could even use symbols instead of numbers or words!

Placement and Arrangement

Experts disagree on whether to interfile new reader materials with the general collection. Adherents to collection integration maintain that new readers may be stigmatized by being referred to a special collection or may be reluctant to be seen in that area if they are trying to hide their inability to read. Other authorities suggest keeping literacy materials separate. "Reluctant readers are not likely to pore over the shelves looking for something they want" (Bayley 1984, 14-15).

If a library places literacy items in a separate collection, it should pick a good location and have adequate signage. Bayley (1984) recommends highly visible browsing stations that are colorfully marked and generally appealing. She suggests using signs that say Find Out Here or Information You Need rather than more typical collection designations. Some libraries have responded by separating the literacy material and naming the collection Adult Education, Adult Basic Education, Adult New Reader, or other somewhat neutral descriptions.

If a library decides to interfile the materials, it may be possible to apply color-coded dots or tape to the materials in order to identify them quickly.

Staff Familiarization

It is very important for the library staff to understand the purpose of this new collection, in addition to becoming familiar with its various formats and reading levels. The staff may attend a training session in which the literacy coordinator or a community tutor briefly presents an example of each reading level and a sampling of typical subject areas and prominent series available. This training should include emphasis on the manner in which library employees handle requests for this material and the type of assistance that may be required by these patrons. After securing copyright permission if necessary, photocopy sample pages from several representative titles; then distribute the copies to branches and departments so employees can learn more about the literacy collection materials.

Publicity and Promotion

After the library staff has been informed of the collection's purpose, content, location, arrangement, and labeling, the literacy materials should be publicized and promoted. Merely owning a collection of literacy materials will not ensure its use by the target clients. Because most of these individuals are not already using libraries, special efforts will be necessary to make them aware of the collection.

With the cooperation of the media, produce public service announcements (PSAs) to announce these materials to the nonreader or new reader. To keep the public aware of the literacy collection, ask the local radio and TV stations to air the PSAs periodically throughout the year. If the media does not respond to an ordinary press release announcing the new collection, perhaps you should have a ribbon-cutting or dedication ceremony.

To help inform the public about the collection, the library can produce inexpensive announcements, flyers, brochures, and book lists for distribution to churches, schools, colleges, other libraries, social service agencies, community centers, tutors, and other literacy program providers. Be sure to include the community and political leaders on your list. Remember, a wordy brochure or book list may not be accessible to a struggling reader, but should be sent to anyone who has regular contact with illiterate citizens. When designing promotional material for struggling readers or nonreaders, use symbols and concepts rather than text wherever possible.

Other Ideas

There are several activities libraries may undertake with regard to literacy materials. These could include efforts to evaluate current holdings; collect available materials into a separate collection; identify other collections in the area; expand the collection to include audio cassettes for ESL and video cassettes on topics such as unemployment or GED; place deposit collections at adult education providers' sites; expand collection to include micro-assisted instructional software (Johnson and Soule 1987, 8).

It is hoped tutors and students will learn to use the library's literacy collection and rely upon it in the areas of instruction, coping skills, and entertainment. One way to help them identify it as their collection is to collect stories and other pieces that are written by students in tutoring classes. Pick a dozen or so and publish them in a chapbook, spiral-bound booklet, or even a three-ring binder. Checking out a small collection of stories produced in class can give a genuine thrill to a student who has struggled to attain basic literacy.

Providing books and materials in support of community literacy efforts is clearly an appropriate, significant activity for libraries. These materials require an enlightened philosophy, they have unique selection criteria, they come from specialized sources, and they need atypical treatment. Most important, they will be helpful to the literacy effort only if the providers, coordinators, tutors, and students are aware of their availability.

REFERENCES

Bayley, Linda. 1984. *Opening doors for adult new readers.* Syracuse, N.Y.: New Readers Press.

Jew, Wing, and Tandy, Carol. 1977. *Using the want ads.* Hayward, Calif.: Janus Book Publishers.

Johnson, Debra W., and Soule, Jennifer A. 1987. *Libraries and literacy: A planning manual.* Chicago: American Library Association.

Lyman, Helen H. 1976. *Reading and the adult new reader.* Chicago: American Library Association.

______. 1977. *Literacy and the nation's libraries.* Chicago: American Library Association.

Pasley, Sally G., and Williams, Dee K. 1988. *Forms and applications.* Englewood Cliffs, N.J.: Cambridge Adult Education (Prentice-Hall).

Pursell, Frances J., ed. 1989. *Books for adult new readers: A bibliography developed by Project: LEARN.* Syracuse, N.Y.: New Readers Press.

Richey, Jim. 1980. *Driver's license language: A survival vocabulary.* Hayward, Calif.: Janus Book Publishers.

PART 2
Implementing Literacy Programs

6

REACHING OUT TO THE ILLITERATE

Without encouragement, only a few illiterates will approach a library—or any other institution—seeking help with their problem. For this reason, the library should concern itself with seeking out and communicating to the illiterates in its community on a group level, letting them know what is available and encouraging them to seek help. When illiterates do come forward for assistance in overcoming illiteracy, the librarian or tutor who is literate but perhaps a novice at illiteracy training needs to be careful to reach out to the student in a suitable way on an individual level. This chapter deals first with the proper handling of patrons who approach the library for help with literacy and then with reaching out to illiterates in the community.

HOW TO REACH PEOPLE AT THEIR LEVEL

No one would disagree in principle with the abstract statement to help people you must realize where they are and contact them there. Obviously, it would be useless to give oral instructions to someone who is deaf or to speak French to a person who knows only English. In these two examples, it is dramatically clear that method and need would be terribly mismatched. Usually, however, the discrepancy is more subtle, although perhaps equally serious in consequences.

Although all may accept the tenet that the teacher should reach the student at the student's level, almost all teachers frequently violate it. Here the word *teacher* includes all persons engaged in the act of teaching—supervisors, parents, older siblings, friends, librarians, and countless others—as well as those with recognized career roles in the education field.

Most people behave as if everyone shares the same basic background knowledge and mindset. People tend to accept their own beliefs, knowledge, or mental level as the norm and subconsciously react to anything that varies from that personal standard as if it were abnormal. This is not a planned or deliberate reaction, but rather an unwitting tendency. The person who knows math very well, for instance, may have little patience with the student who does not understand the simple background to a problem which the tutor takes for granted. Naturally, each person sees the world through a uniquely personal frame of reference, and it may be difficult to fully appreciate what someone from a different background thinks, feels, and understands.

Most people have no idea how to assess what level of mental functioning another person has reached. The teacher may overestimate or underestimate the student or may unconsciously assume that the student has achieved the same approximate level as the teacher. This is not a matter of graded levels of reading material; it is relatively easy to assess a student's reading level with standardized tests. The level of mental functioning refers to the level at which the illiterate can comprehend and utilize the information the tutor offers and the way that information is communicated.

Realizing That People Differ

The following exercises demonstrate not everyone feels, thinks, values, and understands the same things in the same ways.

- How many hours of sleep each night do you normally need? Imagine someone who needs only half that much, feels that quantity is normal, and believes that any other amount is abnormal. He or she says to you, "You are just lazy to sleep so much. If you'd just quit being a baby you could get by on less. Why don't you try to be more like me? Think of all you could do with the extra hours each night." How would you respond?

- Assume you know little about auto mechanics. You ask a friend, who is an expert, for help on a specific problem. Without a pause, he or she tells you a half-dozen steps to follow, mentioning about 20 mechanical terms you have never heard before. Your friend rattles off the paragraph once, expecting you to comprehend it fully. In other words, the mechanic responds as if both of you share the same professional qualifications, experience, and background. When you say, "Wait a minute, I couldn't follow all that. Could you explain that bit by bit?" your friend looks at you as if you are stupid.

- You are driving in a strange town and pause to ask a passerby for instructions on how to find the local library. You get these directions. "Well, you know the Westco station down by the mayor's house, you just turn left there and zip up to the bridge by the Ice Cream Barn, then turn right and there you are." This person assumed that you, a stranger, knew the town as well as a resident does. Rather than communicating to you as someone new to the territory, the resident communicated in terms of his or her own familiarity with the town.

- A library patron asks if the library has *Using WordPerfect* by Beacham and Beacham. You suggest looking it up in the card catalog. The patron says, "What's a card catalog?" How do you respond? What do you say, not only in words, but in your tone of voice? What does your facial expression or body language convey?

Such exercises may seem silly or irrelevant. But it is important, when talking to a student who has little education or literacy skill, to identify feelings of superiority or, perhaps, discomfort, and to eliminate subtle signals of "looking down on" or feeling awkward with the student. The teacher must also take care to avoid the tendency to say things pitched at the teacher's level. Instead, the teacher should try to discern the student's level of understanding and discuss matters accordingly.

Understanding a few simple concepts about levels of cognitive functioning can greatly enhance human interaction skills.

Understanding Levels of Cognitive Functioning

It is important to realize that people, even those similar in such characteristics as size or physical maturity, operate at different levels of cognitive or mental functioning. This is not a matter of age or experience or amount of education. People at disparate levels of cognitive functioning do not merely have different amounts of facts stockpiled in their memory banks. They actually think and perceive the world in often radically dissimilar ways.

The late Jean Piaget, an eminent Swiss psychologist, dedicated his life to exploring the cognitive or mental differences among people. Most of his work concerned the developmental progress of children growing normally through the levels of cognitive function, stepping higher and higher as their minds matured. But despite growth in bodily size, not all individuals reach the higher mental levels. Some people get stuck at the lower stages of development. Severely retarded persons may remain fixed at the lowest level. Even physically mature adults may operate at a fairly low cognitive level.

Piaget's work provides a number of identifying characteristics for each level. Using these characteristics to categorize a person will help the teacher respond to each person in an appropriate, individualized way. (See chapter 2 for discussion on Piaget's theories.)

Dealing with the Illiterate's Concerns and Fears

Reaching illiterates at their level requires more than estimating cognitive levels. It is also important to understand and sensitively address the anxieties and concerns with which they may approach the literacy program. One reason for the lack of success in literacy programs is the high drop-out rate among the adults attending them. Drop-out rates are as high as 50 percent on the average (Bernardon 1989). To lower the rates, the literacy program must identify and ameliorate the causes. Success in meeting these concerns will not only improve retention among those already in literacy programs but will help lure some illiterates who so far have not revealed themselves.

There are several major concerns or fears that the library literacy program should seek to dispel.

False Pride

For a variety of reasons, adult illiterates may feel too proud to accept help. It may threaten their egos or senses of identity to admit they have a problem. Or, if they can admit the problem, they may feel they cannot accept charity to solve it. The literacy trainer should try to deal with this false pride. Students should be encouraged to take pride in achievement and in self-improvement, not in avoiding growth. In regard to charity, it should be pointed out that as taxpayers, the students are actually helping to fund the program in the first place. As citizens, they have earned the right to attend. Dealing with concerns that involve the ego requires great empathy, tact, and sometimes, subtlety.

Fear of Exposure

Steven Peck of the Jones Memorial Library in Covington, Virginia, put it best: "In reality individuals are motivated by fear, especially in small-town America. The stigma of not knowing how to read or write is great in a close-knit community, and it might seem unbearable to make a public disclosure of the need for help" (Peck 1988, 56). This fear cannot be entirely overcome. But at the very least, the library should make it clear that literacy trainers will maintain strict confidentiality. They will not release names of illiterates in the program to employers or others. They will not provide progress reports to anyone other than the trainee. The illiterate will have the same confidentiality as a client seeing a lawyer or a patient seeing a doctor. An illiterate who knows there is no need to fear exposure by the library may be more willing to reveal his or her need for the literacy program.

Fear of Program Equipment

Modern literacy programs often involve desktop computers, videotape players, books on audio tape, microfilm projectors, and other high-tech equipment. Many illiterates, particularly those who attended school before some of this equipment was invented or widely used, have no experience with such equipment. Consequently, they feel intimidated by it and may evade the program to avoid putting themselves into the embarrassing and anxious situation of sitting before a high-tech monster they cannot control. To relieve this fear, the library must reassure patrons that all equipment will be set up for them initially and that they will be given training and all the help needed to operate systems on their own.

Fear of Personal Treatment in the Program

Many illiterates harbor bitter memories of school, of being looked down upon or branded as a failure. Some would rather continue as illiterates than voluntarily subject themselves to any program even vaguely resembling their schooling. To help relieve this fear, the literacy center for adults should look like an adult place. For instance, even simple books for beginning adult readers should look like adult materials, not childish ones (Mathews, Chute, and Cameron 1986). School implies an authoritarian teacher setting goals for and controlling children. If they expect this type of setting, trainees may fear paternalistic treatment by tutors, whom the trainees may feel look down on them. For these reasons, adult literacy training should resemble a partnership, with the trainee establishing goals and the tutor providing support. Only by controlling the nature of the relationship can the trainee become motivated enough to persist in and learn from the training (Gintis 1984).

All people tend to shy away from something new and about which the outcome is uncertain. Many people give up their dreams to become athletes, writers, or actors because they fear possible failure more than they treasure possible success. The library literacy program can allay some of this fear by stressing that there are no tests for grades, as in school. There is no passing or failing in the literacy program—trainees get out of it exactly what they are willing to work for. Fear of failure also may be relieved by stories of success, testimonials from previous trainees who are delighted with the new life opened to them by literacy training. Such testimonials may be anonymous or signed. Written ones may adorn advertisements for the program and bulletin boards in the literacy training room. At open meetings held to discuss the program with potential trainees, one or more successful graduates may be willing to come forward and speak about their successes, encouraging others to overcome the fear of failure.

Reaching a person at his or her level means becoming aware of what that level is and then dealing with the concerns and motives as they are expressed—not as some armchair theoretician may predict them. For instance, looking at a heavy-set, successful, blue-collar worker who is inquiring about the literacy program, you might guess that his hesitancy reflects a fear of exposure. But such a guess may be completely wrong—perhaps the person feels intimidated by talking to someone who is educated. The trainer should not project personal thoughts about possible fears onto the trainee or waste time guessing what the latter's fears are. Rather, the trainer should create an environment in which the trainee can express concerns. Once these concerns have surfaced, the trainer should seek clarification, if needed, and then deal with the concerns in a sensitive, compassionate, and reassuring way.

To reach illiterates on their level may require more than understanding cognitive levels and reservations about participation in the program. It may also help to know more about the learning process itself.

Understanding How a Person Learns

Every person learns, but exactly how learning takes place remains largely a mystery. Educational psychologists and others have discovered much about certain key factors that affect the learning process, but many puzzling questions about how learning actually occurs remain unanswered (Thompson 1976). Important factors seem to be motivation, technique, and feedback.

The Importance of Motivation

A person unmotivated to learn will not learn, or at least will not learn the intended lesson. To learn how to read and write, the illiterate must be motivated to do so. Society has built-in incentives for achieving literacy, and the literacy program should continually point them out. As Guerra put it, "Strong incentives are needed to provide adults with the motivation to undertake and persist in the considerable effort required to achieve literacy. Such incentives may take a variety of forms: cultural, religious, economic or political" (Guerra 1984, 7). It is not enough to list these factors by rote. "Literacy is good for several things, all of which have to be demonstrated personally; they are not compelling if simply talked about" (Smith 1989, 357).

Cultural incentives for literacy include wider opportunities to participate in society. Religious incentives consist of being able to read the Bible or other religious literature. Economic incentives include better opportunities for finding a job, keeping a job, and moving up to better jobs. Political incentives include the opportunity to learn more about competing candidates, register to vote, and independently cast a ballot. Family incentives include the parents' wish that their children do better in school than the parents did.

In addition to pointing out incentives, the library can enhance motivation by providing literacy materials of intrinsic interest to the trainee. These materials can be tailored to the trainee's community as well as personal interests. For example, adult trainees from a Hispanic community may prefer reading materials about Hispanic history rather than Black studies; the converse is likely true for Blacks. Furthermore, the trainee's individual preferences, vocation, and hobbies should be taken into account. A farmer, for instance, may care little for reading materials about embroidery and quiltmaking. The garage mechanic, on the other hand, may care nothing for books about farming. Reading becomes more exciting when the material read is strongly related to the new reader's principal interests (Fader 1966). Thus, each library should continually assess the major reading interests within its community and stock materials accordingly.

The Importance of Technique

People learn best in different ways. One person, for instance, likes to be led by the hand until familiar with the material; another prefers greater independence from the start. One works best alone, perhaps using computerized instruction; another feels motivated only when part of a group. One likes to move forward at a rapid pace; another likes to savor the luxury of advancing slowly but surely. Tutors should be able to use enough different techniques so that the trainee's preferences can help shape the nature of the training sessions.

Whatever technique is used, one thing to be cautious about is the negative impact of anxiety on learning (Salter, Meunier, and Triplett 1976; Ward and Salter 1974). If the trainee appears nervous and tense, forging ahead with the training will be ineffective, for the anxiety will interfere with, and perhaps even prevent, any learning. The anxiety should be dealt with first. After the trainee feels more comfortable with the program, he or she will be far more receptive to learning from it.

The Importance of Feedback and Reward

People learn best when they receive feedback, i.e., information about how well they are doing. Imagine trying to learn how to shoot basketball alone and blindfolded. Improvement would be virtually impossible. Similarly, in literacy training, the trainee's improvement and motivation to continue in the program can be boosted with some words of encouragement during and after each session. This communication should include the two major forms of evaluation. First, there should be some simple feedback, factually stating what has been accomplished, for example, "You read that passage aloud with only one error." Then there should be some reward, some words of praise, for example, "You've improved so much since last month. I'm really proud of you!"

A great deal of research demonstrates how effective simple feedback and reward can be in enhancing learning and making the process more enjoyable (Bruner 1966; Emmer 1987-88; Watson 1963). The literacy training program can become a mutually reinforcing experience for both tutors and trainees. The tutor's attention, help, and praise reward the trainee. The trainee's progress, joy at learning, and gratitude reward the tutor.

REACHING OUT TO ILLITERATES IN THE COMMUNITY

Not every illiterate who needs help will come forward and request it. What can be done to reach out to those who will not?

Communicating Program Availability to the Public

Illiterates who do not know about training programs certainly cannot become involved in them. Because their reading skills are limited, it is not enough to do simple things, such as placing articles or advertisements in the local newspaper. More creativity is required to promote a literacy program.

Public Service Announcements

Television and radio stations donate a certain percentage of advertising time to help nonprofit groups that are of service to the community. When they become aware of the great illiteracy problems in their regions, most media executives will be glad to place frequent, short announcements about the availability of literacy training programs in the area. The Advertising Council estimated that in 1986 print and electronic media had contributed about $20 million in free advertisements to the Coalition for Literacy (Coleman 1986). It certainly cannot hurt to ask local electronic media executives for their support. If you know what kinds of radio or TV programs tend to draw the most illiterates, you might suggest that the public service announcements be used during those shows.

Posters and Brochures

Written materials advertising literacy programs must be composed in the simplest language possible. They should include visuals to attract attention and express the meaning of the text (e.g., a cartoon of an adult with a smile on his face while reading). A phone number to call for more information should be included.

Mathews, Chute, and Cameron (1986), at one time employed by the Library Programs section of the U.S. Department of Education, suggest that posters and brochures might be distributed

- in restaurants, bars, and laundromats;
- in doctors', dentists', and optometrists' offices;
- in welfare, employment, unemployment insurance, and food stamp offices; and
- on buses, subways, and elevated trains.

In one case, brochures were used in fast-food restaurants as tray liners! The more creative the means of distribution, the greater the impact. Using multiple outlets not only helps to reach a greater number of people but it virtually guarantees that many individuals will see the advertisements in several places. When this happens, the whole concept makes a greater impression, and the overall image of the program is given a greater sense of importance and legitimacy.

Using Successful Trainees as Personal Contacts

Illiterates often come from poor and disadvantaged neighborhoods that house many other illiterates. Who better to spread the word among illiterate acquaintances and relatives than a former illiterate who has achieved success in the program? This kind of personal contact conveys far more than simple communication of the information – people trust someone they know to tell them what the program is really like, and they can see the benefits for themselves in the success of their friend.

Canvassing Neighborhoods

If enough money and people are available, it is possible to go house to house, knocking on doors and informing those who answer about the availability of the program. Census data could be used to target the neighborhoods most likely to house illiterates. This approach is too complicated and expensive for routine use, although it may be helpful in comprehensive research studies about literacy programs.

Overcoming Obstacles to Helping the Illiterate

Even if illiterates know about the literacy program and are motivated to pursue it, many obstacles may stand in the way. Some of these barriers may lie beyond the reach of the library and are not discussed here. Others can sometimes be overcome with insight and compassion on the part of the program's sponsors. Discussed here are a few problem areas in which the library might possess the resources to make a difference.

Child Care

Many illiterates are young adults with children. The parents may strongly desire to attend the literacy program but be unable to do so because they have no one to watch the children. This problem is one of the major causes of high dropout rates in adult literacy programs (Mathews, Chute, and Cameron 1986). The solution, if the library can afford it, is to provide some form of day care or a children's library program that coincides with the time of the tutoring session. A less effective, although more affordable option for the library with a tight budget, is for the library to provide a list of babysitters or low-cost day care centers that will accept children for short periods.

Transportation to the Literacy Program

Illiterates who are also poor may not own or have access to a car. They may also lack access to public transportation or the money to pay for it. The solution, if finances permit, is for the library either to take the program into the neighborhoods with a van or bookmobile or to provide some form of transportation to the library for trainees. If providing buses is too expensive, perhaps an arrangement could be worked out with the local transportation authority to provide special rates for service to the library. Perhaps the city government would be willing to sponsor a program of free bus passes for the underprivileged to attend literacy training—passes that would be validated by the library or other training site to ensure only authorized use.

Reputation of the Program

The illiterate may have heard bad things about the library literacy program and avoid it for that reason. For example, a friend in the program may have felt "burned" by one of the tutors. Sometimes trainees come to respect and depend on a given tutor, who then quits abruptly, leaving the trainees feeling rejected. To avoid this situation, Peck suggests, "Tutors must make a serious commitment to attend all training sessions and to volunteer services for a minimum of one year" (Peck 1988, 56). An approach that may help when a tutor quits is to play down its impact on the trainees, making clear they were not at fault and facilitating their shift to another tutor.

Similarly, some tutors are simply unqualified to teach and do a poor job of it. One evaluation of a literacy program found that many of the tutors themselves had substandard literacy skills (Mathews, Chute, and Cameron 1986). To overcome these kinds of problems, the program must be carefully established, with tutor volunteers being screened and properly instructed in teaching techniques. It is better to have a few good tutors than many bad ones who ruin the reputation and effectiveness of the entire program.

CONCLUSION

The library, of course, cannot be held responsible for every obstacle that might prevent an illiterate from attending the program. But every time it can identify and remove a hindrance, it can lead yet more illiterates to a new life of reading and writing. The next chapter describes how libraries can work with other organizations to establish and sustain literacy programs.

REFERENCES

Bernardon, N. L. 1989. Let's erase illiteracy from the workplace. *Personnel* 66 (January): 29-32.

Bruner, J. 1966. *Toward a theory of instruction.* Cambridge, Mass.: Harvard University Press.

Coleman, J. E. 1986. ALA's role in adult and literacy education. *Library Trends* 35 (Fall): 207-217.

Emmer, E. T. 1987-88. Praise and the instructional process. *Journal of Classroom Interaction* 23: 32-39.

Fader, D. N., and Shaevitz, M. H. 1966. *Hooked on books.* New York: Berkeley Publishing.

Gintis, H. 1984. The political economy of literacy training. *Unesco Courier* 37 (February): 15-16.

Guerra, M. 1984. The cultural roots of literacy. *Unesco Courier* 37 (February): 6-8.

Mathews, A. J.; Chute, A.; and Cameron, C. A. 1986. Meeting the literacy challenge: A federal perspective. *Library Trends* 35 (Fall): 219-241.

Peck, S. D. 1988. Teaching literacy training. *Library Journal* 56 (15 April): 113.

Salter, C. A.; Meunier, J. L.; and Triplett, N. M. 1976. Multiple measurement of anxiety and its effects on complex verbal learning. *Psychological Reports* 38: 691-694.

Smith, F. 1989. Overselling literacy. *Phi Delta Kappan* 70 (January): 353-359.

Thompson, R. F. 1976. The search for the engram. *American Psychologist* 31 (3) (March): 209-227.

Ward, C., and Salter, C. A. 1974. The effects of trait and state anxiety on verbal learning. *Psychology* 11 (3): 56-62.

Watson, G. 1963. What do we know about learning? *NEA Journal* 52 (March): 20-22.

WORKING WITH OTHER ORGANIZATIONS TO MEET THE LITERACY CHALLENGE

Regarding the illiteracy crisis, the one thing all librarians probably would agree on is that the library cannot solve the problem by itself. Whatever literacy efforts it does engage in, the library severely restricts its own effectiveness if it tries to work in isolation. A vast and strong network is required to hold back the tide of illiteracy. A library program acting in isolation is like a twig trying to stop the tide. This chapter provides some general guidelines on how the library should interact with other organizations involved in the literacy campaign. It also gives general information on several key groups, including their goals, level of organization, approach, and membership size. Appendix A provides more information on these organizations, including addresses and phone numbers.

GUIDELINES FOR WORKING WITH OTHER LITERACY ORGANIZATIONS

Each library has its own structure and standard operating procedures. Each library staffer has a distinct personality and preferred way of doing things. The same holds true for other organizations and their staffers. Problems sometimes arise when these differing systems conflict and when the respective staff do not recognize the differences in structure and style.

Things to Keep in Mind

The staff in other groups combatting literacy probably are open to the concept of cooperative effort, but will resent intrusiveness and outside attempts to direct them. Many potential problems can be avoided by putting yourself in the other individual's shoes.

Other Groups Are Hyper-Busy, Too

Every library staffer knows how it feels to be burdened with too many responsibilities and yet be faced with one more. Here is a representative scenario: the holiday staffing schedule was late yesterday, the revised budget is due today, the boss wants to see you in five minutes, there is a check-out clerk in your office wanting to talk, and the phone rings. It is a staffer from a local literacy group who wants to get together to discuss some cooperative plans. You are all for literacy, but.... You glance at your watch—late again.

This scenario focuses on the librarian's point of view when a call comes in. Reverse the roles to get a better perspective on how staffers in other organizations feel. A lukewarm response does not necessarily mean the contact person is not all for literacy; it may mean only that he or she is busy when the call comes in. Contact the other agency, but remain flexible if the response is less than enthusiastic.

Other Groups May Have Differing Goals

If a group is working for literacy, clearly one of its paramount goals is to increase the reading and writing skills of the citizenry. However, beneath that overall goal, the precise goals of the organization may differ quite a bit from yours. To use an obvious example, UNESCO (the United Nations Educational, Scientific, and Cultural Organization) is interested in literacy efforts around the world. In fact, one of its top priorities is to encourage greater literacy. But its goals are directed mainly at a high level of national and international concern, e.g., raising awareness of the problem and influencing national policies concerning it. UNESCO does not include in its organizational goals the establishment of individual literacy centers in the various towns of a given state. It would not respond in the affirmative to overtures from a library concerning such a joint effort—not that it would disagree with the notion, but because UNESCO's goals target a different level. On the other hand, if the library contacted a local volunteer literacy group interested primarily in establishing literacy centers in the same town, the group probably would be overwhelmingly interested in supporting the library's goal.

Other Groups May Have Differing Approaches

Groups not only differ in goals, but also in their approaches to meeting those goals. Two groups may have identical goals but be so widely divergent in approach that they would be unable to work closely together. For instance, a public library is interested in setting up a literacy center that is run entirely by volunteers. Imagine a group that shares the goal of establishing a center in the same town, but its approach is to solicit donations or raise tax revenues for a program based on paid permanent staff. The primary goal of improving literacy and the secondary goal of establishing a center in the town would be the same. But with such opposing views on how to reach the goal, the two groups might be able to cooperate only very little in terms of organizational structure.

The Other Group Does Not Want to Be Swallowed Up

Some groups are established and run by people fiercely loyal to their particular organization. They may see the value of true cooperation with other groups, perhaps even very different groups, but they do not want their organization to lose its identity in the process. The group represents a part of themselves, and they may fear the loss of their own independence in a joint venture. It is important, therefore, when contacting other groups, to stress the ideal of cooperative interaction, not an annexation or a hostile takeover that reduces the other group to a mere subsidiary of the library or the new umbrella coalition.

General Pointers on How to Make Contact

The Importance of First Impressions

Research in social psychology (Luchins 1957a, 1957b) reveals that first impressions are very important because they tend to endure, even if later information contradicts the initial data. It will take much work to overcome an initial bad impression; it may be impossible. Conversely, if you present a polished, professional image as an expert with something to contribute, you will make a good first impression. This will tend to last even if things do not work smoothly in the future. In other words, a good initial impression earns a bit of credit that you can draw upon if unexpected problems are encountered or if a few mistakes are made later.

To create a good first impression, project yourself as a thorough professional in all communications with other groups. Making a good impression when writing depends in part on all letters, memos, and other written communications being literate, concise, and to the point. When on the phone, smile and sound positive, as if you were talking to the other person face-to-face. In personal contacts, the importance of sensible dress, good grooming, a pleasant demeanor, and eye contact cannot be overemphasized.

Learn about the Other Group

The primary way to make a good first impression is to learn all you can about the other group before making the first few contacts. The title of the group or an off hand comment heard at a conference may give a false idea of the group's goals and procedures. This can lead to misunderstandings or uncomfortable situations when trying to develop cooperative efforts. To avoid these problems, look for information about the group in the library or request literature from the group. Talk to individuals who know more about the group. The state library association may know some literacy experts who can talk knowledgeably about literacy groups in various regions of the state. If someone on the library staff has had dealings with the group, find out what he or she knows, or let that person make the first approaches about the proposed cooperative effort.

Write First

Staff in other groups are likely to be hyper-busy, harassed with a deluge of tasks and details to monitor. If the first contact is by phone or in person, you might find yourself in the position of an unwanted intruder. Instead, write first, explaining who you are, what you want, and what you would like to talk about. Avoid making demands of any sort, but ask if someone from the group would be willing to discuss the idea of cooperation over the phone or in a meeting. When developing a coalition, by all means invite members of each group to a meeting with pre-established time, place, and agenda. If you simply want to meet with a member of the group, do not try to set an exact time in the first letter. Ask when is a good time and let the other person get back to you.

If you get no response after a week or two, follow-up with another letter restating the key question (whether they are interested in meeting to discuss cooperative efforts). Wait another week or 10 days after the second letter. Then, either take the lack of response as a negative answer or, if it is important that you contact the group, call. In this call, do not castigate him or her for failing to respond! Say something like this: "I'm sure you're busy, but I really need to know whether you'll be able to accept our invitation to the first meeting next Tuesday of the Mill River Literacy Coalition." Accept the decision graciously, and do not try to change a negative response.

Get to the Point and Be Specific

Whether communicating in writing, over the phone, or in person, do not waste time in idle chitchat. If you know each other, of course, it is appropriate to ask about the other person's family, program success, and so on. But with relative strangers, get to the point as soon as possible. This does not mean to act stiff, formal, or abrupt. It does mean to avoid tangents and get to the heart of the matter. For example, in a first letter, do not spend the first page describing your library literacy program and your goals for the future and only on the second page broach the topic of cooperative endeavors. Instead, summarize the whole point of the letter right up front—why you wrote it and what you want. Then expand a bit, if needed. For example,

> Dear Director:
>
> I am writing to see if your organization would be interested in joining the Mill River Literacy Coalition, which we are sponsoring. In particular, I hope you or others on your staff will be able to attend the first organizational meeting on Tuesday, June 10, at....

Only after you have stated the reason for the letter should you begin to describe your goals, method of approach, and so forth. Even then, be as brief and concise as possible. Always be specific about what it is you want.

Stress Your Willingness to Work

Make clear what you want, but do not make demands. For example, do not write someone for the first time to say, "We hope you will accept our nomination as chairperson of the committee" or "We would like to see your fine organization take the lead in this effort." Big demands up front scare many people away – it sounds as if you are trying to rope them into doing your work for you.

Instead, when you make subsequent contacts (letters and phone calls), stress first what the library is willing to do and be subtle and flexible about the work you hope the other group will do. Put your contact person in the position of seeing the need and volunteering, not in the position of someone trapped in the spotlight. For instance, do not say, "We would like you to provide all the volunteer tutors and their transportation for the coalition's new program." Instead, say, "We have set aside library space and literacy materials for the program. We have plenty of trainees eager to acquire more advanced literacy. All we need are a few good tutors...." This approach encourages others to join you in truly cooperative work.

Be Encouraging and Positive

In all meetings and other forms of communication, try to stress the positive. Doom and gloom over the terrible illiteracy crisis does not motivate people. Go beyond the problem to the hope of a solution. Stress how the cooperative effort can help improve the situation.

Stressing the positive is especially important if you want to persuade people who at first remain unconvinced. Research on the social psychology of persuasion (Janis 1967; Leventhal 1972) demonstrates that frightening people does not generally motivate them to change. For instance, showing frightful pictures of lung disease to college student smokers does not by itself motivate them to quit. Rather, this entirely negative approach encourages them to avoid the communicator and the communication that is so frightening – they just turn a blind eye to it. On the other hand, mentioning the negative and then proceeding rapidly to the positive – exactly what can be done to improve the situation – raises motivation considerably. To extend the previous example, after showing the pictures of lung disease, the communicator can describe a program to quit smoking and then show pictures of the clean, healthy lungs that result.

Similarly, when talking to another organization or a group of potential volunteers, start with how bad the illiteracy situation in your region is. Then move rapidly to the program you are starting, discussing how with their help it can improve things. Include a couple of true success stories about former illiterates who have found new lives through literacy.

Being encouraging and positive helps foster recruitment, increases retention of volunteers, and promotes continuation of the cooperative arrangement. To see how this works, compare the leaders described in the following paragraphs. Which leader would provide more motivation and be more pleasant to work with day after day, week after week?

Leader A – This person grows disturbed over every problem, large and small, that threatens to disrupt the literacy program. Whether the problem is a budget issue, tutor no-shows, or a bit of bad publicity, Leader A stews and frets over how the very survival of the literacy program is being threatened. Whenever you approach to ask for or impart information, Leader A appears harried and distracted and exudes a sense of depression and anxiety.

Leader B—This person does not shoot the messenger bearing ill tidings but greets all—whether friends or new acquaintances, whether bringing news of success or problems—with a smile, courtesy, and complete attentiveness. Leader B does not gloss over crises but confronts them head-on with the attitude that they are hurdles to be leapt over, not terminal barriers to the program. Leader B exudes confidence and warmth, a sense that success may not be in sight now, but is just around the corner.

Note that differing behavioral styles do not stem simply from differences in the objective problems and crises that crop up. Every new program has its share of struggles and successes. Both enthusiastic and disparaging leaders face emergencies and predicaments. The difference is not in the situation, it is in the leaders' reactions, which result in part from their lifelong development of personality and in part from their conscious or unconscious decisions, moment by moment, to act in a negative or a positive way.

Reward Cooperative Helpers

Everyone appreciates being appreciated. Paid staffers may come to work every day even if they do not receive acknowledgment and praise from their bosses. After all, they are getting paid for the work they do. But volunteers and agencies interacting on a purely cooperative basis do not have a paycheck to fall back on as their ultimate motivation. Instead, they do have their concern for helping solve the illiteracy crisis, but that may not be enough if they feel their efforts are going unappreciated.

Therefore, when trying to establish cooperative arrangements or trying to maintain those that exist, remember to reward people for helping you, for cooperating with you, for fulfilling their end of the bargain. At the very least, offer intangible rewards. It costs nothing to smile, to say "well done," to thank people for their help. Yet many leaders forget to do this or to do it often enough—then they wonder why others do not persist long in the cooperative organization.

In addition to intangible rewards, there should be some opportunity for tangible rewards. Certainly in a volunteer arrangement or interaction you would not offer bonus checks. But letters of appreciation, framed certificates of participation, plaques, and other physical forms of recognition and reward cost little, and they can mean a great deal to the recipients. Occasional sponsored dinners and picnics are often good ideas. The library may not be able to fund these out of its own budget, but a sponsor may be coaxed into providing an annual awards and recognition banquet. Such tokens of appreciation may keep a weary volunteer or cooperating agency from throwing in the towel.

Following Up

In addition to maintaining a positive atmosphere and encouraging and rewarding those who help you, make sure you fulfill your end of the bargain. This means not only doing the work you initially agreed to do as part of the overall plan, but also following through on requests that members of other organizations make. For instance, three months into the program, the head of another cooperating literacy group asks you to provide a report of all the contact hours, by month, that people from the group have contributed on your site. You agree, but in the daily press of competing responsibilities, it begins to slide down the priority list. The next thing you know, you are past the deadline and have failed to provide what you promised. One occurrence like this makes a bad impression; repeated occurrences may rupture the cooperative agreement altogether. Agree to do only those things you can realistically expect to complete. Once you have agreed, let nothing stand in the way of fulfilling the commitment.

KEY LITERACY GROUPS

Groups with a Local Focus

Some literacy groups in your area may be entirely local in focus and virtually unknown outside your region, except for listings in literacy networks. For example, a local community college, church, or civic organization may have initiated a literacy program without affiliating with a larger state, regional, or national group. To find out about such local groups, consult the business telephone directory under Literacy Services or a similar designator, check with the local chamber of commerce, or ask a statewide literacy organization for a list of local literacy providers in your region.

When starting a new library literacy program, it is important to link up with all of the existing literacy organizations in your immediate area. Otherwise, you may put yourself into the position of reinventing the wheel, or confronting and solving local problems the hard way after another group has achieved the same end. Following the guidelines for interaction discussed earlier in this chapter, contact all of the local organizations. Some may be eager to help and be very useful. Others may be unable to contribute anything more to the local literacy effort. You will not know which organizations can and will help until you contact them.

Be sure to contact the local newspaper. Like book publishers, newspaper publishers are concerned about their futures in a world of increasing illiteracy. Often, they commit time and money to do something about it. For example, the *Burlington County Times* in New Jersey distributed 180,000 bumper stickers to subscribers. Each sticker included a clever drawing of a dinosaur reading a copy of the *Burlington County Times* and the slogan "Read. Avoid Extinction" in bold print. Not only were the stickers provided free, but owners of cars displaying the bumper stickers were eligible for a daily prize of $30 and a drawing among those daily winners for a $10,000 grand prize. Thus, people were strongly motivated to display rather than discard their literacy bumper stickers ("Read. Avoid Extinction" 1989). Max Heath, writing in a trade journal for newspaper circulation departments, provided the following recommendations for a model newspaper literacy program.

1. Offer assistance to local volunteer literacy programs.
2. Supply free papers in the amounts and on the days needed to fulfill tutor needs.
3. Supply teaching aids to literacy programs to help encourage wise use of newspapers.
4. Urge employee involvement in literacy training as tutors.
5. If no program exists in your community, then be the catalyst.
6. Most importantly, donate free gift subscriptions to anyone successfully completing a local literacy course.
7. Encourage your publisher, community-service director, or in-house charitable committees to key on literacy programs in their giving (Heath 1989a, 1989b).

Any newspaper with a program approaching this magnitude would be an ideal cooperative partner. In addition to newspapers, every community, no matter how small, probably has several businesses or community organizations that have a vested interest in or concern with literacy. Many local chambers of commerce have educational chairpersons who can help libraries solicit support from businesses in their communities.

These small-scale local efforts will, by their very nature, vary from locality to locality. There are other, larger-scale, well-known organizations that also may be of great benefit in the local sphere. These organizations are listed in appendix A with their headquarters mailing addresses or phone numbers. The remainder of this chapter offers brief descriptions of these major organizations.

National and International Literacy Groups

These groups are listed in alphabetical order to avoid giving any sign of priority to one or the other. All of the groups are deeply involved in improving literacy on a broad scale. Which ones a library interacts with will be determined by program goals and the kind of literacy organization being built.

American Reading Council (ARC). This organization was founded in 1976 to distribute information about reading programs it considers successful. Its special focus is on programs aimed at both parents and children. It also assists groups wishing to establish new literacy programs.

Business Council for Effective Literacy (BCEL). Founded in 1983, this foundation aims to help mobilize the corporate world in combatting functional illiteracy, not only in the work force but throughout the country. It encourages corporate funding of governmental and local literacy programs and also provides businesses with in-house literacy training workshops. It provides a free newsletter on literacy, which may prove helpful.

Christian Literacy Associates. Founded in 1977, this group has over 2,300 members who help local congregations and church councils sponsor their own literacy training programs. These programs are designed not to serve just the congregation but to reach the disabled, refugees, and prisoners. The organization also prepares and distributes through churches a series of adult literacy training materials.

Coalition for Literacy. The ALA formed the Coalition for Literacy in 1981, bringing together 11 organizations committed to and experienced in the literacy effort. The member organizations are the American Association for Adult and Continuing Education (AAACE), the American Association of Advertising Agencies (AAAA), the American Library Association (ALA), B. Dalton Bookseller, Contact Center Inc., International Reading Association (IRA), Laubach Literacy International (LLI), Literacy Volunteers of America (LVA), the National Advisory Council on Adult Education (NACAE), the National Commission on Libraries and Information Science (NCLIS), and the National Council of State Directors of Adult Education (NCSDAE). The coalition is an excellent example of success in interacting with other literacy groups. By pooling their influence and resources, the members of the coalition sponsor a national Ad Council campaign.

Contact, Inc. Contact, Inc., or the Contact Literacy Center, is one of the members of the Coalition for Literacy. Founded in 1964, it functions at the national level to provide referrals to local resources. Its staff of 25 maintains a computer database of literacy programs. Contact also publishes a guide to literacy services nationwide.

International Reading Association (IRA). The IRA has about 60,000 members dedicated to improving the teaching of reading. Members are professionals who teach reading or supervise the teaching of reading. The IRA encourages research in the field of reading and reading problems and publishes several journals, including the *Journal of Reading* and *Reading Research Quarterly.*

Laubach Literacy International (LLI). Laubach Literacy International is a member of the Coalition for Literacy. This group has about 600 local chapters around the United States and in many foreign countries. Each chapter organizes and coordinates volunteer tutors for adult literacy training. The group has approximately 30,000 volunteers and its own publishing division, New Readers Press.

Literacy Volunteers of America (LVA). Formed in 1962, the LVA is a member of the Coalition for Literacy. Like LLI, it organizes and trains 12,000 volunteer tutors to help illiterates improve their reading and writing skills. The tutors are organized into over 230 chapters in the United States and Canada.

REFERENCES

Heath, M. 1989a. Newspaper in education for the small newspaper. *Circulation Idea Service* 4 (July): 27-30.

______. 1989b. Literacy programs: A must-do effort for all newspapers. *Circulation Idea Service* 4 (December): 26-27.

Janis, I. L. 1967. Effects of fear arousal on attitude change: Recent developments in theory and experimental research. In *Advances in experimental social psychology*, edited by L. Berkowitz, vol. 3. New York: Academic Press.

Leventhal, H. 1972. Fear—for your health. In *Readings in psychology today*, 2d ed., 627-631. Del Mar, Calif.: CRM Books.

Luchins, A. S. 1957a. Experimental attempts to minimize the impact of first impressions. In *The order of presentation in persuasion*, edited by C. I. Hovland, 62-75. New Haven, Conn.: Yale University Press.

______. 1957b. Primacy-recency in impression formation. In *The order of presentation in persuasion*, edited by C. I. Hovland, 33-61. New Haven, Conn.: Yale University Press.

"Read. Avoid Extinction." 1989. *Circulation Idea Service* 4 (November): 7-8.

8

EVALUATING ONGOING LITERACY PROGRAMS

New programs often begin with a burst of excitement and enthusiasm. Hope seems boundless. The program appears destined to solve all the problems it was created to handle. Sometimes people develop a feeling that now the machinery has been set in motion, it will run itself, and everyone can virtually sit back and relax. A staff group approaching a new literacy program with that attitude, however, will soon find that things do not work out so well. The publicity and outreach system may produce few new candidates. The training and supervising system for literacy volunteers produces a trickle, then a flood of defections from the volunteer ranks. Murphy's Law—if anything can go wrong, it will—sets in, and people in charge feel bewildered and unable to cope. The program continues to regress, until finally it withers and blows away in the next storm of budget cuts.

The best way to avoid this scenario is to begin a new program with the realization that no matter how well it has been designed, it is not perfect and will require ongoing evaluation and revision to fulfill its original goals.

This point bears repetition, for it is the most often overlooked facet of new programs. To survive in a changing and often capricious world, a new program must be subject to continuing evaluation and refinement. This chapter provides a general outline to guide such efforts. For more information, refer to books on this subject, some of which are listed in the references at the end of this chapter.

TRAITS THE EVALUATOR WILL NEED

The person or group with the most interest in the new literacy program, the people who have helped the most and invested the most of themselves in it, are probably not the best ones to evaluate it. Meaningful evaluation requires a set of personal traits often at odds with those characteristics most valuable among the creators and major supporters of a new program. The following paragraphs describe a few of the traits required for a systematic and thorough evaluation.

Objectivity

Fortune 500 companies, among countless others, realize the importance of having outside consultants survey the enterprise, assessing strengths and weaknesses. It is taken for granted that outside experts are more objective and can cast a cold eye on even the most cherished of notions held by those who are utterly caught up in ongoing events.

Of course, a library strapped for funds generally can not hire high-powered consultants like profit-oriented private companies can. It may, however, be able to coax a literacy expert from a neighboring program or from a higher-level of organization (e.g., ALA, state literacy office, state library agency, or literacy grant official) to take an objective look. This kind of outside evaluation may be free, but the library cannot count on obtaining it whenever it is needed.

In the final analysis, most libraries will have to depend on their overworked staffs to provide some form of evaluation. When selecting a person or group of people to evaluate the program, it is important to choose those not too heavily involved in the program (e.g., a staffer from a branch library could survey the program at the main library). In some cases, those who resisted the program to begin with and played no part in it may be the best evaluators, as long as they can remain relatively objective and do not carry axes to grind. Prejudices either for or against the program will mar the quality of the evaluation. The objective person can see through both extremes of bias—not getting caught up in the rose-colored views of devotees to the program and not getting stuck in the rut of stubborn, close-minded criticism. The truth about strengths and weaknesses, about needed directions for change, can rarely be found in either of these opposing camps.

Goal Orientation

In addition to objectivity, the successful program evaluator must possess a very strong goal orientation. The process of evaluation cannot depend on aesthetics, on deciding what looks innovative, original, exciting, or dynamic. These kinds of buzzwords fill countless evaluations but, while they may provide emotional kudos to the developers and managers of new programs, they convey little information of help in refining programs. When taxpayers' money is being spent, when staffers and volunteers are putting in long hours, when library space and budget is being sacrificed from other areas to support literacy, the overriding question is: Does it work? Whether the program is nice, admired, praised in library journal articles, or provides a warm feeling of involvement in an important social issue is, in the long run, irrelevant. The evaluator must first, last, and always focus on the goals of the program: Does it work? Is it meeting or at least approaching its goals? Ego gratification, admiration, and praise will quickly fade—may even turn into hostility—if the program does not work.

To use an analogy, think of the program developer or manager as the driver of a bus. The staffers, volunteers, and illiterates seeking help are like passengers. They go along for the ride because they all want to reach Disney World. The driver takes them on an interesting route through scenic country. For a time people enjoy the ride; they appreciate each other's company. They may even admire the driver's dedication, insight, and industry. But after a long time, if they find themselves still sitting on the bus, no closer to reaching the amusement park, their positive feelings will fade. They may grow angry, demand an explanation, or insist on leaving the bus. They did not come along just for the ride; they joined in the hope of reaching Disney World. At this point, the driver feels exhausted and wants to take a cab home. However, if the driver had focused on the destination rather than on the pleasures of the ride itself, he or she would have realized the need to continually assess the bus's progress against the road map and corrected the course accordingly. Eventually, the persistent riders would have reached their goal.

Just so, the main thing to determine in an evaluation of a literacy program is not whether people like it (although it is hoped they will like it, too), but whether they are learning to read. If not, then something is wrong and should be changed.

Insight

Regardless of the methodology by which the program evaluator gathers and interprets data, a key trait for the successful evaluator is a high degree of insight. Sometimes the necessary information is obvious, yet an evaluator can make no sense out of it, can come to no appropriate conclusions and recommendations. Good insight is more than intelligence, more than simple objectivity—although without both of these, insight is virtually impossible. To achieve insight, the evaluator must become deeply immersed in the material, able to think it over again and again. The evaluator must care about the program and want the evaluation to help. Then, sooner or later, ideas will come bubbling up from the cauldron of busy thought. At this point wisdom and judgment are required to determine which ideas are potential gems of insight.

For example, say that the literacy program is unable to retain its volunteer instructors. The evaluator conducts phone interviews with some of the instructors who quit and interviews some of the remaining instructors as well as some of the students. A number of different comments are received, many of them contradictory, many biased by a fear of being honest or by bitterness against the program or by a desperate longing for the program to succeed. It takes great insight to sort through the material, sifting down to the roots of the problem, and deciding what to do about them.

Realism

Good insight stems from a realistic attitude, with sensible expectations of what a literacy program should be able to accomplish. Perfection is the ultimate benchmark, but it makes a poor short-term or intermediate goal—particularly if the success is defined as having achieved it and not achieving it implies failure. A program that is less than ideal provides no grounds for disbanding it or for extensively revamping it in the vague hope that change will somehow shake things up and improve everything. Realism keeps the program evaluator from trusting in excessively demanding goals and from making impractical budget recommendations. It goes without saying that any program could include in its evaluation a plea for more funds. But the realistic evaluator will balance that tendency with concerns about how much more money is likely to be approved. What priorities should be served first? Failing an increase in budget, what internal rearrangement could be made?

Willingness to Serve

Busy professionals always find themselves with more tasks than they have time to handle. The job of program evaluation is one task that should not be dumped on an unwilling victim. Without some personal concern and involvement in improving the literacy program, the overworked staffer is likely to do only a perfunctory job. The evaluation may look good on paper or sound good in an oral presentation, but if it lacks the spirit of commitment and dedication, it may fall far from the mark. Changes based on the evaluation may produce little improvement. Without a partially willing volunteer, then, the evaluation is useless.

On the other hand, willingness to serve means little unless the person has a fair measure of the necessary other traits. A willing person without insight and realism, for example, may produce an exciting, glowing report with recommendations impossible to implement.

To recap, the most promising candidate to conduct or lead a literacy program evaluation will have a healthy portion of these traits: objectivity, goal orientation, insight, realism, and willingness to serve. No staffer excels in all of these areas, perhaps, but among the candidates available for the job, the one who best matches this profile should be chosen.

CONDUCTING THE EVALUATION

Depending upon the size of the literacy program, one person or a small team of staffers is enough to conduct the program evaluation. Assuming these people have been carefully chosen, the next step is to make sure that they conduct the evaluation in a rigorous yet nonthreatening way. Following are some suggestions on how to perform this delicate balancing act.

Relieving Evaluation Anxieties

Nobody likes being evaluated. Students do not like being graded. Teachers do not like being rated by students. Staff members do not like performance reviews by their superiors. And literacy program workers do not like being evaluated, either. The core anxiety behind this fear can never be totally assuaged, but much can be done to reduce it and to prevent it from hampering the evaluation.

Take the Job Seriously

One of the best things the evaluator can do is approach the program members with the attitude that he or she is committed to the task, interested in the literacy program, and dedicated to making the evaluation useful to all concerned. Such an approach will relieve the program members of anxiety and encourage them to invest all possible effort or insight into refining their own programs.

Be Honest

Honesty on the part of the evaluator is very important. According to the old saw, "Some of the most frightening words in the English language are, 'I'm from the government and I'm here to help.' " To reassure literacy workers being evaluated, be straightforward and matter-of-fact. For example, say, "I'm here to conduct the annual review and analysis of the Mill Grove Library literacy program. This won't take more than 30 to 40 minutes of any one person's time, but I'll need everyone to fill out some questionnaires and I'll want to interview a few key people. I may even spend some time observing some of your procedures or tutoring sessions. My findings may be used to refine certain aspects of the program, so it's important that everyone help me get the most accurate view possible." As mentioned, some will experience an innate fear of evaluation, but this no-nonsense approach makes it clear that they can count on the evaluation to be fair.

This introduction could be used with each individual consulted or could be given at the beginning of the evaluation period to the assembled staff of the program. Either way, almost certainly some people will have questions. They may ask such things as when the report will be complete, whether they can see a rough draft, whether they will be quoted or identified by name, whether their budget is going to be cut, whether the program is going to be cut, and so on. In general, such questions should be answered in a calm, nonthreatening, cooperative way. If you do not know the answer to a question, admit it and add that you will answer it later (unless it is the kind of question you simply cannot answer).

Be Non-judgmental

When interviewing people, when observing them at work, or when answering questions, it is vital that the evaluator not take sides in a dispute, get embroiled in controversy, or express openly any criticism toward any part of the program. The evaluator must remain open to receiving information, data, and sense impressions. Later, in private or in a closed session, all data can be processed with insight and a critical eye. If the evaluator slips into the trap of taking sides too soon or too openly, some uncomfortable situations may occur. For example,

- An assistant literacy staffer asks, "Is this a good idea for a recruitment poster? If you don't like it, I can change it." Here the evaluator is being cast into the role of a supervisor or manager.
- Two staffers ask, "We've been arguing for months about which is the best system of literacy materials. What do you think?" Here the evaluator is being treated as an expert in a specialized area.
- A literacy instructor is nervous about the evaluator's presence and almost goes to pieces during a training session. Here the evaluator is seen in a punitive light.

To avoid these kinds of situations, simply refuse to take sides or express an opinion until your report is ready.

EVALUATING THE PROGRAM'S GOALS AND OBJECTIVES

The starting point for the evaluation itself is the literacy program's goals and objectives. Determining the program's goals is the first step in evaluation. It may not be as easy as it sounds to determine the real goals of the program. In new or informal programs, goals may not be written down. In older, better established programs, people who knew the goals in the beginning may not have transmitted them clearly to newcomers. In other words, people may have varied, even contradictory, concepts of what the program's goals are. If so, they may be proceeding based on their own concepts rather than the actual program goals. Thus, they may operate in ways that interfere with, rather than mutually support, each other. To determine program goals, find out whether there is a written statement of goals. If so, get a copy. In private interviews, find out whether staffers' goals are in line with the officially sanctioned goals. If not, find out why. Find out what trainees perceive as the program's goals and what are their personal goals. Compare the goals—do they mesh, or is there substantial conflict? If there is, find out why.

Are Goals Realistic?

After identifying the goals, ask whether or not they are realistic, attainable ends or vague expressions of noble intent. For example, the goal statement, "The purpose of this program is to lead Mill Grove County into a golden age of literary enlightenment," sounds good in literature designed to solicit financial contributions. It may be a good goal to mull over when trying to motivate volunteer tutors. But as an expression of realistic program goals, it misses the mark.

A realistic goal for one person may be too low for another yet too high for a third. In other words, the same literacy goals cannot apply to each individual. Neither can the same goals apply to all programs. A goal regarding, for example, the size of the literacy budget, the number of books purchased, or the number of clients served must clearly vary from program to program to remain realistic.

Are Goals Expressed in Measurable Terms?

Even if goals are clearly stated and realistic, they may be expressed in ways that make it impossible to assess progress toward the goal or even to know when one has reached it. The goal of leading a certain county into a "golden age of literary enlightenment" has this problem. This phrase certainly denotes something very positive and laudable, but how can a "golden age of literary enlightenment" be measured? To use an analogy, when you get into a car, your goal may be expressed as "to reach 117 Bilhingham Road, San Francisco." With that goal, you know at any moment where you stand in regard to accomplishing the goal, and you certainly know when you have succeeded. But if the goal when you got into the car was expressed as "to reach a higher stage of consciousness," you would have real problems with objective assessment of progress toward that goal.

In literacy programs it is always important to have goals whose attainment is measurable. It is best to have broad, general, optimistic sentiments, if necessary, expressed as mission statements and to have the concrete goals of the program expressed as behavioral objectives.

A behavioral objective is a statement of what the program should achieve, expressed in such a way that progress and attainment can be objectively measured. For instance, if the mission statement is to lead Mill Grove County into a golden age of literary enlightenment, the following might be possible behavioral objectives:

- to add 75 new trainees to the program by the end of the year.
- to double the number of volunteer tutoring hours available by the end of the quarter.
- to reduce the drop-out rate by 25 percent by the end of next month.
- to raise the average graded reading level of trainees by 2 years for every calendar year they spend in the program.

Notice that these behavioral objectives are clear and specific. They specify some measurable quantity that should be assessed within a given period of time. Whether or not such goals are realistic depends on past success, the size of the program, and so forth. Adding 75 new trainees, for example, may be easy in a large urban program but nearly impossible in a new and small program with little publicity.

GATHERING DATA FOR THE EVALUATION

After the goals are clearly in mind, the evaluator must gather data on the program's progress toward the goals. There are many ways to do this, and if there is time, all should be used.

Interviews

Interviews with program managers, tutors, and trainees do not have to rely on planned questions, as a questionnaire generally must. This is a great advantage. The interview may begin with a list of planned topic areas or even questions, but if issues that were not anticipated arise in the course of the interview, it is relatively easy to respond to them. The evaluator can shift focus and probe into areas not planned.

Good Interviewing Style

The interviewer must appear warm and friendly to set interviewees at ease and encourage them to answer honestly. Assure them their comments are important, but will not be written down with their names attached. In other words, interviewees will remain anonymous and nothing they say can be traced directly back to them later. Furthermore, do not argue with what interviewees say or try to talk them into saying what you want to hear. On the other hand, do not let interviewees waste endless time on discursive tangents. Stay on track by repeating the questions, perhaps in slightly different words.

Good Interviewing Questions

Do not load questions in such a way that the response is biased. The following are loaded questions:

- You would agree that this is a good literacy program, wouldn't you?
- Most people here think the program hours should be extended—what do you say?
- I can see that there are a lot of problems with this program. Can you enlighten me on some of them?

In contrast to these poor questions, a good question does not bias the interviewee or attempt to lead to a foregone conclusion. A good interview question is not too specific, either. Highly specific questions requiring only a yes-no response or a choice among a small set of alternatives belong on written questionnaires. The following questions, if used at all, should be used on questionnaires rather than in interviews:

Is this a good or a bad literacy program? Choose one.

Should the program's hours be extended? Yes or No.

What is the main problem with this literacy program?
a. No pay for tutors.
b. Unmotivated trainees.
c. Not enough space for training.
d. Not enough support from management.

Easy-to-answer questions such as these do not belong in an interview, no matter how well written. Interview questions should be broad enough to motivate the interviewee to provide insights that might not occur to the interviewer. The following questions, based on the same concerns expressed in the poorly worded questions, are suitable for interviews:

What do you think are the strong points of this literacy program? What are its weak points?

Do you think the program hours are adequate or not? If not, what changes would you recommend?

Do you think there are any problems with this program? If so, what are they?

Taking Notes on Interviews

Writing good questions is just the beginning of a successful interview. Making proper notes about responses is equally important but far more difficult. People use language in unique ways, with distinct styles. Some may hesitate while others may ramble. Maintain an appearance of patience and interest throughout the interview and steer the interviewee back on track whenever necessary. Write down what the interviewee actually says—rephrasing too much may cause the interviewer's biases to appear in the notes. Of course, there is no point in writing down everything the interviewee says; only the important things need be scripted. The key is not to let personal prejudices determine what you consider important. In other words, do not write down something you want to hear and ignore things that conflict with your opinions. Leave out tangents the interviewee strays into, but include everything that directly answers the question asked.

Questionnaires

Almost all program evaluations should use questionnaires. They provide the quickest way to get the most information. One interviewer can get interviews sequentially, one at a time. That interviewer can obtain any number of questionnaires in a large group all at once. For the program staff and trainees, questionnaires are the least threatening mode to provide information. If staff and trainees are reassured that no names need be included on the form and that they will remain anonymous, they will feel relatively free to express their true feelings and thoughts. Furthermore, if the questions are structured well, they automatically keep people on track. Analyzing the data is simple. Depending on the type of response scale used, the responses can be summed up and divided by the number of respondents to provide an average response for the entire sample or group. To obtain one advantage of the interview method, include one or two open-ended questions at the end of the structured portion of the questionnaire. An open-ended question might be, Are there any other good or bad points about the program that we have not covered in the questionnaire? If so, please list and describe briefly below.

There are some pitfalls to avoid even with questionnaires:

Keep questions simple. Each question should deal with only one thought. Otherwise, the reader has no way to differentiate the response. Do not ask a question like, "Do you think the program's tutors are dedicated and effective?" If the respondent thinks they are dedicated but not effective, or vice versa, then the question cannot be answered. Break the thought into two questions. More questions can be added to cover all the areas that the evaluation is to cover.

Avoiding bias. As with interviews, the questions on survey forms must avoid bias. Avoid questions like, "Wouldn't you agree that the literacy program is in trouble? Yes or no." Instead, try, "Please rate the overall quality of this program on a seven-point scale."

Types of questions. The most common and useful questions ask respondents to answer using various numerical scales. In most cases, these scales are anchored at each end with opposite adjectives. For example,

How would you rate the overall quality of this program?
Please circle one number below:

1	2	3	4	5	6	7
very poor			unsure			very good

Would you say the number of tutoring hours offered in this program is not enough, too much, or just about right?

1	2	3	4	5	6	7
not enough			about right			too much

Another type of question makes a statement and then asks the respondent how much he or she agrees with it.

Most tutors in this program are highly effective teachers.

1	2	3	4	5	6	7
strongly agree			unsure			strongly disagree

Answer codes. With questions that use numerical scales, avoid always putting the more positive response with the higher number. In other words, avoid the good adjective or the *agree* response always being at the upper end of the scale. Some people tend to circle all high numbers or all low numbers without thinking much. Having half the questions with the low numbers most positive and half with high numbers most positive forces the respondent to think and mark carefully. If all high or low numbers are circled the respondent probably did not take the questionnaire seriously, and the form can be discarded.

Personal Observation

Depending upon the results of interviews and questionnaires, the evaluator may wish to observe parts of the program in action. This is, without a doubt, the most threatening type of evaluation, and it should not be resorted to lightly. Some people get very nervous when being watched, and this tension could ruin a performance that would otherwise be adequate. For example, a tutor who normally does an excellent job may be rattled knowing that the evaluator is observing and thus perform poorly just when it counts the most. Avoid direct observation when possible.

If observation is required, try to seem as unintimidating as possible. Let the instructor know in advance what you are doing. Be inconspicuous during the event and do not intervene in any way; throughout the observation session, appear friendly and supportive. By all means avoid frowns, an uncomfortable or inscrutable look, or taking notes in an urgent or other negative manner. Afterwards, be sure to thank the tutor and students for allowing you to observe.

Tracking Program Statistics

The least intrusive way to gather evaluation data on the program is to gain access to the files and simply note statistics on various elements of the program, such as the number of trained tutors, the number of trainees, progress reports, and so on. The program manager should be notified of this in advance. Tell the program manager what data is needed, and let the manager or a designated aide help you find what you need.

INTERPRETING EVALUATION DATA

After you have gathered data from the many sources, the next step is to make some sense of it. There are various ways to do this, depending on the type of measure used to gather the data.

Interview Data

Information from interviews is almost impossible to collate unless the data is first coded. For example, if an interview question asked the respondent to name the problems with the program, start a master list of problems mentioned. Assign each problem a code number. When another interview mentions the same problem, write the code number down again (to enter the data into a computer program later) or add a tick mark beside the problem on the master list (to tally data by hand). Problems arise when the same or similar problems are phrased in slightly different ways. For example, should "Trainees often unmotivated" and "Poor quality trainees" be counted as slight variations of the same problem or as two different problems? In such cases, the evaluator must make a subjective judgment about how to code the material.

Questionnaire Data

If the questionnaire was written properly, basic analysis of the data is simple: just average the numerical responses to each question. It is easy to compose a table with an abbreviated form of each question to the left and the average response to it on the right. Be sure to include the answer scale at the top or bottom of the table so that the numbers make sense to someone reading the report. Open-ended questions pose more difficulty – they must be coded like interview questions.

Observation Data

Observation data could be coded in a way similar to that for interview data. Or the evaluator could subjectively combine personal impressions to produce an overall sense of the quality of the program. This type of section in a report should be clearly labeled as a subjective, overall impression. It might make a good opening or closing section of the report but should be clearly distinguished from the more objective data.

Program Statistics

Statistics should be organized and tallied in a way that makes their import clear. For example,

- a summary table citing averages or percent improvements,
- graphs plotting changes in various parameters over time, or
- bar charts showing where the program stood last year and where it stands now on each of several measures. The height of each bar corresponds to a statistic, such as the number of trainees.

RECOMMENDATIONS FOR REFINING THE LITERACY PROGRAM

The evaluation should link the goals of the program and the success achieved with specific recommendations targeting areas for improvement. For example, if the program shows strong growth in recruitment of trainees and tutors, the evaluation report might conclude that little improvement is required in those areas. But if program statistics reveal that tutor drop-out rates seem high, the questionnaire and interview data reveal that tutor drop-out rates are perceived as a problem, and in the course of observation and interviews two or three suggestions for improvement emerge, then the final report would mention the problem, the statistics indicating its severity, and the recommendations that might improve the situation.

Recommendations for improvement are the capstone of a good evaluation report. There is little value to a report that merely evaluates things as they exist; this, in effect, assigns grades to the program. The purpose of an evaluation is not merely to state where the program stands but to point out where it could go and how it could get there. Evaluation reports should always end with some good and practical recommendations for refining the program.

ADDITIONAL READINGS ON PROGRAM EVALUATION

Cook, T. D., and Campbell, D. T. 1979. *Quasi-experimentation: Design and analysis issues for field settings.* Boston: Houghton Mifflin.

DuMont, R. R., and DuMont, P. F. 1979. Measuring library effectiveness: A review and assessment. In *Advances in Librarianship*, edited by M. H. Harris, vol. 9, 111. New York: Academic Press.

Grotelueschen, A.; Gooler, D.; and Knox, A. 1976. *Evaluation in adult basic education: How and why.* Urbana, Ill.: University of Illinois at Urbana-Champaign.

Johnson, Debra W. 1986. Evaluation of library literacy projects. *Library Trends* 35 (Fall): 311-326.

Johnson, Debra W., and Soule, Jennifer A. 1987. *Libraries and literacy: A planning manual.* Chicago: American Library Association.

Koberg, D., and Bagnall, J. 1976. *The universal traveler. A soft-systems guide to: Creativity, problem-solving and the process of reaching goals.* Los Altos, Calif.: William Kaufmann, Inc.

Schulberg, H. C., and Baker, F. 1968. Program evaluation models and the implementation of research findings. *Journal of Public Health* 58 (July): 1248-1255.

Warwick, D. P., and Lininger, C. W. 1975. *The sample survey: Theory and practice.* New York: McGraw-Hill.

Weiss, C. H. 1972. *Evaluation research: Methods for assessing program effectiveness.* Englewood Cliffs, N.J.: Prentice-Hall.

9

LIBRARY LITERACY PROGRAM

A Case Study

This chapter features an actual library literacy program, which was financed by a federal grant. This program was developed for a public library, but similar activities could be fostered by libraries in schools, colleges, businesses, or institutions. The case is presented in detail in the hope that readers will more fully appreciate its strengths and weaknesses. To emphasize the project and its development, the name of the library system has been omitted and names of the participants have been changed.

Because this program was funded by the federal government, the timetable is given in terms of federal fiscal years beginning each October. Year one saw the writing of the first grant application, which was not funded. Year two saw the writing of the second application, the notification of funding, and preparation for the project. In year three began the actual project, as well as the writing of the third grant application. The same project activities could have been accomplished in much less time with an internal budget allocation or with external funding from a nongovernmental source.

INTRODUCTION

The public library system serves a county with about 275,000 residents in a state whose illiteracy rate is among the 10 highest in the nation. A river separates this county from a neighboring county of about 90,000, which shares its socioeconomic base. However, the political jurisdiction, tax base, school system, and library system of each county are self-contained.

The local literacy coalition encompasses both counties, whose combined census figures indicate 10,000 citizens over age 25 (about 5 percent of that group) had completed fewer than five years of school and an additional 25,000 (about 13 percent of adults over 25) never entered high school. While both of these groups certainly are at risk for illiteracy, most of the 10,000 probably lack basic literacy skills, while the remaining 25,000 possibly lack coping skills.

At about the time *Alliance for Excellence* was published (Center for Libraries and Education Improvement, 1984), the county library system director began the first stages of involvement with literacy. This included purchasing a small core of circulating materials (mostly instructional and coping skills), encouraging staff to become literacy tutors, and supporting employee attendance at literacy workshops.

New Position

A couple of years later, at the request of the library administration, the board of trustees approved creation of a new professional position that incorporated publicity, promotion, programs, and adult services. Among many other responsibilities of this new position, one function was the coordination of the library's literacy efforts. The coordinator's first literacy activity was preparing an application for a LSCA Title VI library literacy program grant.

YEAR ONE: FIRST TIME OUT

Henry Hollis, the librarian hired for the newly created adult services position, had not yet reported for duty when year one started because he was working on a special project in another department. By arrangement with the supervisor, Hollis was able to spend small blocks of time over several weeks to develop the grant application with assistance from the library's assistant director, Jane Stevens. This was the first attempt at a federal grant for both Hollis and Stevens, although Stevens had previously written an application for a state grant unrelated to literacy.

Title VI Grant Guidelines

The LSCA grant application package featured a booklet with eight sections, including general instructions and mailing information, addresses for single points of contact, copies of the applicable law, and pages from the *Federal Register*. Buried in tiny print in a section subpart was an outline of the guidelines by which the grant application would be evaluated. Evaluation was based on a point system, with the selection criteria totaling 100 points as follows:

- plan of operation, 20 points;
- quality of key personnel, 20 points;
- budget and cost effectiveness, 10 points;
- evaluation plan, 20 points;
- adequacy of responses, 10 points; and
- cooperation and coordination, 20 points.

To Hollis and Stevens, the relative weights of these categories seemed out of kilter. The emphasis seemed to be on whether a library had the wherewithal to carry out the proposed program and whether the program was structured in such a way that it could be objectively evaluated rather than whether the project had merit. Hollis and Stevens had little experience thinking of library activities in terms of those categories.

Putting It Together

Writing the grant application was a daunting task. In order to match explanations to the guideline categories, a great deal of duplicate wording was required. Stevens began drafting responses to each evaluation category while Hollis solicited input from the local LVA chapter coordinator and another key member of the literacy coalition. Hollis and Stevens had met several times to discuss the library's role in literacy efforts and quickly realized they had different perspectives. They agreed the library did have a role in literacy, but Hollis was more encompassing in his approach while Stevens believed the library should limit its activity. They hammered out a compromise plan that included the following activities:

- purchase 1,300 titles written specifically for adult new readers; purchase about 65 titles (books, films, and videos) as the start of a professional collection for tutors, trainers, program providers, and librarians;

- provide a central phone number with recorded information on local tutoring programs, computer-assisted learning labs, and the library's collection of literacy materials;

- contract for professional productions of TV, radio, and billboard advertisements to promote awareness of illiteracy and use of the central phone number; and

- print 50,000 brochures to distribute throughout the two-county area, primarily in neighborhoods with high illiteracy rates.

The library's director indicated a commitment to assume the operating costs of the central clearinghouse phone line after the grant period was over. The team believed that commitment would be regarded highly by the Title VI evaluators. A final step in completing the application was contacting the state's single point of contact for an authorization number, which was required for the cover sheet.

The magnitude of the grant application task and the qualifications necessary are exemplified by this true story.

On the very day the application was required to be in Washington, D.C., a person not affiliated with the library came to ask the library for help in applying for a Title VI grant. Stevens could not learn how the money was to be spent, nor whether the visitor was affiliated with a literacy program. Stevens and another colleague gently explained the program was for libraries, the library had already submitted an application, the application was extremely detailed and required much work, and it was due in Washington, D.C. on that very day. The visitor did not seem to comprehend any problems and again requested the library's help in submitting the package.

The encounter was faintly humorous in the retelling, but it pointed out how little the general public may know about federal grants, governmental programs, and eligibility criteria.

Then came the waiting period of almost eight months to find out whether the grant was approved. It was not.

Rejection and Evaluation

This project was not the only one turned down by the Title VI evaluators: Only 224 out of 490 applications were approved that year. The library's application was basically sound and would have done a great deal to help the local literacy efforts, but Stevens and Hollis realized it had several weaknesses. Hollis requested the Title VI evaluation forms and received them at the end of September. The two reviewers were harsh: Out of a possible 100 points, one assigned 60 and the other allowed only 55. It seemed to Hollis and Stevens that if the reviewers did not like how the application addressed a category, they automatically deducted half the points. For example, in a category with 20 possible points, the reviewers seemed not to assign relative values, but gave either 20 points for "pass" or 10 for "fail."

After reviewing the evaluations and studying the application again Stevens and Hollis arrived at the following conclusions:

> *Equipment*—About 20 percent of the grant would have paid for computer equipment and software for Hollis to use in composing brochures, flyers, bookmarks, and other literature and for compiling information on literacy programs. While it was a valid expenditure—he needed the equipment and software for literacy involvement—it was clearly not going to be used exclusively for literacy.
>
> *Contracts*—The evaluators seemed unsure whether the library team should or could enter into contractual arrangements for the professional production of TV, radio, and billboard advertisements. This might have been a matter of semantics; the evaluators possibly stumbled over the word *contract*. What Hollis and Stevens meant was the library would use grant money to pay for the production of these advertisements.
>
> *Collection locations*—Purchasing the adult new reader materials was an appropriate use of the funding, but the library did not make clear where the materials would be housed. Hollis and Stevens believed it appropriate for some literacy materials to be in the library, but they would be accessible to many more people if they were placed in other facilities that at-risk adults were already using.
>
> *Cooperation*—While the application assured the government that the library would cooperate fully with other literacy program providers, the team neglected to supply evidence of such cooperation. This could take the form of endorsements from other agencies or letters stating the kind of interaction that would occur.

Rejection of the first application was a demoralizing setback, particularly with respect to the overall timetable, but it allowed Hollis and Stevens time to reflect on the responses of the Title VI evaluators and to rethink the library's role in literacy.

YEAR TWO: PICKING UP THE PIECES

There were only about four months between the rejection of the first application and the deadline for the second. After evaluating the application and having further discussions with Stevens, Hollis went into action to correct the weaknesses of the first attempt. He had begun meeting with the local literacy coalition and had done some basic research into the literature. This gave him a better grasp of how the library could meet the needs in some key areas of the local efforts. Through conferences with Hollis, Stevens gained a clearer understanding of the importance of the library to literacy and she broadened the limits of library involvement.

Doing Some Homework

Hollis had recently attended a workshop that dealt with another part of his overall job unrelated to literacy. A portion of the workshop dealt with grant applications and Hollis learned what most grant agencies like and do not like to fund and better ways to present the relationship of each activity to the overall purpose of the project.

Another major development was a phone conversation between Hollis and a key local literacy figure who worked with the county education system and who had been a pioneer in the area's literacy coalition. She helped bring into sharp focus the problems with well-intentioned but misguided literacy programs and she identified some of the areas that were not being handled locally by any agency. After that call, Hollis and Stevens reconfigured the project to address those needs in a better framework than their first effort.

Hollis also secured letters of endorsement from the county school superintendent, the head of the local LVA chapter, and others involved in literacy or education. Using the input from the phone call and the format from the workshop, Hollis completely rewrote the program part of the grant application and attached letters that verified the library's cooperation with other agencies.

Getting on Track

If grant applications were automobiles, you could say Hollis and Stevens's new one ran better, carried more, and had a smoother finish; it was more powerful and got better mileage. Hollis and Stevens kept the good parts of the first project—the materials for new adult readers, the phone line supplying information from the literacy data base, the professional collection materials, and the promotion and advertising. But they eliminated the equipment request and the need for contractual services; they increased the number of new reader volumes; and they indicated the types of accessible, nonlibrary locations where the satellite collections would be housed.

The new application had a clearer statement of purpose and it broke the project down into objectives and activities. The application clearly indicated how each objective was related to the purpose and how it affected the budget. The statement of the library's cooperation and coordination was reworked to reflect Hollis's recent interaction. The portions dealing with quality of key personnel, budget and cost effectiveness, evaluation plan, and adequacy of resources received only minor revisions.

Once again, the waiting period began.

Bad News and Good News

In March of year two, Hollis announced his transfer to a job with a different library system. That bad news dampened Stevens's reception of the good news in April: a phone call from a Title VI official who said the project would be approved. The official requested some additional paperwork related to drug-free workplace certification and other matters.

Without Hollis, Stevens had to make several adjustments. First, she had to remind herself that literacy was just one of Hollis's former responsibilities, which were now back in her own lap. Next, Stevens had to assume the role of library liaison to the literacy coalition. Finally, she had to locate a suitable replacement to handle the literacy project as well as Hollis's other responsibilities in publicity, promotion, programs, and adult services.

Preliminary Activity

Even with several months before the grant funding began, there were a number of things that had to be done. The official notification of the grant's approval arrived in May, followed by packets of material related to governmental regulations and finances. One item was an entire manual: the Education Department General Administrative Regulations (EDGAR). There were forms, instructions, rules, schedules, and addresses of contact people in Washington, D.C.

Stevens began searching the literature for articles that would form the basis of the literacy resource center when the office reopened. She was already swamped, and, without Hollis, the situation looked almost hopeless.

In the Market

Stevens went to the annual ALA conference with a handful of job descriptions, hoping to net an enthusiastic new MLS graduate whose zeal for literacy was surpassed only by work ethic, organizational skills, and personality. The job placement service yielded unsatisfactory results that year for public libraries ("Placement stats: Steady state," 1989) and similar results for Stevens. Although the library had raised its starting MLS salary significantly during the previous few years, there was no interest in the vacant position—at that salary.

The position remained unfilled throughout the summer. With only two months left before the start of the grant, Stevens had to take drastic measures. If the position and its salary would not attract any qualified MLS candidates, she would have to formulate an alternative plan. Stevens reasoned that as long as she remained close to the project, it was not absolutely essential for its coordinator to be fully trained in librarianship. She met with the library director, who agreed to temporarily abandon the MLS search for filling the vacancy as announced. They advertised a half-time literacy position at a level that did not require the MLS.

After interviewing several candidates, Stevens selected Stanley Garner, who was special projects coordinator for the local LVA chapter and had several years' experience as a literacy tutor. Garner's coordinating experience seemed particularly helpful, and the understanding he had gained from tutoring would give the library's project valuable perspective. He also had some accounting background, which would be useful in keeping the books for the literacy project.

The Money Hassle

Getting the grant approved was the hard part, Stevens reasoned; once the grant was awarded, obtaining the funds would be relatively easy. That assumption was grossly incorrect.

Obtaining the money that had been approved was one of the most complicated and frustrating aspects of the whole year. Stevens thought the entire grant amount would be awarded on October 1 and would be expended, as needed, over the project year. She and the director had planned to deposit the single check into the library's operating account and set up a mechanism to have grant expenditures charged against that account. The worst-case scenario involved quarterly checks from the government. To Stevens's shock, she learned the money would be disbursed by the government *weekly*!

Tied to the county government's budgeting and disbursement system, the library routinely experienced delays of two or three weeks between sending a check request and having an invoice paid. Furthermore, the county's computer system frequently showed different balances in various accounts within the library's $3.5 million budget. With the kind of penny-by-penny accounting the government seemed to expect for the grant funds, and with the precise timing required by their weekly disbursement method, it was clearly not practical to use the regular county financial channels.

Government Options

The options outlined by the U.S. Department of Education Fiscal Management Service (FMS) did not leave many choices in how the money could be handled. If the FEDWIRE method (which involved the Federal Reserve Bank, the county accounting department, and the library) would not work, the only choices were a clumsy manual method, which relied heavily on mail, or the automated clearinghouse/electronic funds transfer (ACH/EFT). Stevens selected the ACH/EFT, which used a separate bank account for the library's grant and direct deposits from the government. This method seemed smooth enough: The account is assigned a Project Identification Number (PIN), which is used over the phone with an access code to request a specific amount for the next week's expenses. The amount is wired directly to the account within a few working days and is available to pay for the specific invoices covered by that week's request.

Catch-555

But then there was "Catch-555." During one of the phone calls to Washington, D.C., Stevens learned the rules of five: You may request funds no more frequently than every five days (that is, once each work week), and should allow up to five days for the deposit to be received by the bank, and you must disburse the funds within five days of receiving the deposit. The education department apparently wanted the account to restabilize at a balance of one dollar or less after each deposit was received. Stevens feared that if the account ever showed a balance in excess of one dollar, the government might delay the next deposit request. That suggested that timing was absolutely critical.

Then came another surprise: The government would not send advance funds so the library could open the separate account, even though the account had to be established before the funding process could begin. Education department officials could not check any details or answer any specific questions about the grant because the project did not exist until October 1. The project would not show up on the federal computers until it was funded, and no one knew exactly when that would be because funding depended partly upon Congress voting on the budget. The timing was also affected by the library's first deposit request, which required a manual form, since the account was not yet established.

Looking for a Dollar

Confused, Stevens phoned a public library that was already administering a Title VI grant to find out how it solved the financial start-up problems. The other library system was using the FEDWIRE method, which worked satisfactorily with one major exception: As a trial run of the accounting process, the Department of Education sent a deposit of one dollar to the library literacy program fund. When the dollar deposit appeared, the library was to notify the department, which would then turn on the faucet so the other deposits could be sent weekly as requested. However, the dollar never showed up! The library could not find it, the county could not find it, and education department officials could not find it. Fortunately, the government did allow the process to continue and the regular deposits appeared in the proper places at the correct times. But almost monthly, the library received a note from Washington, D.C., inquiring "where's the dollar?"

In a subsequent call to the education department, Stevens learned that the ACH/EFT method also required a trial dollar to test the mechanism. Following specific advice, Garner sent the manual form to request the trial dollar about two weeks before October 1. The form bounced around the department's FMS section (and was eventually sent by mistake to a beauty school in Connecticut) because the project did not yet show up on the education department's computers.

Budget and Reports

The total grant was for $20,000 and covered five categories, including:

- satellite collection materials for adult new readers and titles for the resource center—$9,000 (about 45 percent);
- wages and related payroll expenses for the literacy clerk—$6,000 (about 30 percent);
- printing and advertising—$2,000 (about 10 percent);
- telephone lines, equipment, and related charges—$1,500 (about 8 percent); and
- book racks, processing supplies, and office supplies—$1,500 (about 8 percent).

The federal reports for the grant itself were relatively straightforward: a quarterly financial report and a final project summary with evaluation. But the quarterly payroll reports were considerably more complicated.

Stevens and Hollis had used the Employer Identification Number (EIN) of the county government's payroll department for the first grant application. At that time, and for the second application, it was not known that Catch-555 would require a separate bank account. Since payroll reports require an EIN and since the library's grant account was in fact separate from the county, the library had to secure its own EIN for the grant's payroll requirements. After the new EIN was obtained, the library changed that number on the bank account and notified the Department of Education so the grant records could be corrected.

Believing the grant would be handled through the regular library-county channels (which were exempt from Social Security and which paid unemployment on a claim-reimbursement basis), Stevens and Hollis had figured the entire $6,000 allocated for a part-time clerk would be salary. It turned out, however, that the $6,000 would have to include the Social Security deduction and matching contribution, plus the federal unemployment tax (FUTA). In order to stay on budget, Garner had to reduce the number of hours the clerk could work each week.

Much later, after all of the EIN changes and the adjustments to the payroll, Garner learned of a different interpretation that overturned some of the changes the library had made.

Staffing and Starting

Garner began work about three weeks before the grant started. During that time he and Stevens interviewed and selected a part-time clerk, hired with grant funds, to conduct some of the activities of the project. He ordered the phone equipment and set up the office area. Stevens turned over Hollis's files and explained what had been learned about financial interaction with the government. Garner set up the bank account and made all the final contacts with the Department of Education, then reissued the manual check request that had been lost.

Fortunately, he was able to report successful receipt of the trial dollar but still had to wait another two weeks before the project could be funded. So year three began with the literacy program already behind in clerical salary and bills for the phone equipment.

Stevens held several conferences with Garner to acquaint him with the library's role in literacy, the specifics of the literacy project, and the financial matters. During the summer, the literacy coalition had formulated goals and objectives in an attempt to focus its efforts and gain momentum. One of its foremost objectives was to have a central office with a single phone number that could serve as a clearinghouse for all information related to literacy. That perfectly matched a major portion of the library's literacy program.

YEAR THREE: THE GRANT BEGINS

After hiring Ginny Betts as the literacy clerk and settling the matter of the dollar, Garner turned his attention to prioritizing the activities for the grant year. There was a great deal to be done, and much of it depended upon something else being done first. For example, he could not start promotional efforts until the information clearinghouse was established and the project logo was designed. He could not place the satellite collection materials until the site coordination was complete and the books were ordered and processed.

The library had already hosted one literacy coalition meeting in the month before Garner arrived, and it hosted another meeting in late October. The coalition had decided to hold meetings in as many locations as possible in order to acquaint its members with the individual literacy programs and their environments. Garner and Betts began attending these meetings along with Stevens.

In preparation for the new grant application, Stevens set up a meeting with the literacy coalition president, who also served on a state literacy task force, and the county education individual who had been so helpful previously. The purpose of Stevens's meeting was to establish how the library's program could benefit the composite local literacy effort, how the library could assist with the workings of the coalition, what could be done to reduce or eliminate duplication of effort, and what were appropriate and inappropriate areas of library involvement.

Another Grant Application

Looming over all those early activities was the grant application for year four, which had a November deadline just six weeks after the beginning of year three. Garner had never written a grant. Stevens quickly taught him the most basic operations of word processing software for the grant application and spreadsheet software for the clearinghouse data base. Then they began a series of conferences to formulate a project that would continue building on the foundation of the year three grant but that was clearly more than maintenance and operational activities.

The year four grant called for additional satellite sites for adult new reader material collections; these would be locations that had high concentrations of citizens at risk for illiteracy. The new grant would fund a significant advertising campaign to target individuals who lacked literacy skills and to promote literacy involvement for citizens at large (tutors, donors, and so forth). The new project would establish the library literacy office as a resource center that collected material on every aspect of illiteracy, literacy, programs, and funding. The resource center would be promoted among program providers, tutors, churches, schools, agencies, political and community leaders, and libraries. The information clearinghouse phone line and data base would be enhanced with additional listings of new programs and with updated information on the existing agencies.

The Program Logo

Garner and Stevens worked together to design the library's literacy program logo. It had to be visually striking, communicate clearly without words, and be suitable to serve as the central part of the advertising and promotion of the clearinghouse phone number. The library printed several thousand, in color, on vinyl stickers 3 inches square; these were distributed at meetings and placed on glass doors at library outlets. Larger versions were laminated and distributed to satellite sites and other locations.

The Satellite Collections

Garner selected several general adult literacy titles from the specialty catalogs, but he quickly realized the satellite collections would be more effective if the host site's coordinator participated in the selection process. Stevens and Garner had previously identified several potential sites, and Garner booked other locations as he came into contact with additional program providers. Garner and Betts visited each site to talk with the host coordinator and to assess the environment and clientele.

The only processing that was done was to affix a vinyl logo sticker to the back of each book to identify it as belonging to the satellite collection. The only paperwork for the satellite sites was a receipt (showing each title), which was signed by the coordinator at each location. Stevens was certain the government would want a paper trail to establish where the books were placed. While the library team wanted circulation figures and other use statistics for the satellite collections, it was decided in the early stages not to impose a rigid transaction system. A highly structured circulation system could hinder the use of the materials; the team was willing to accept the coordinators' estimates of use and circulation on a monthly or quarterly basis.

The first satellite collection put into service was placed in an empty school complex through a program started by the local Catholic diocese. The program trained tutors, had space for tutoring sessions, and featured many other services for the community. The diocese had chosen the Laubach instructional method, so Garner worked with the program coordinator to order appropriate materials. With its new collection of materials from the library's grant, that literacy center opened in early January with excellent attendance and media coverage.

The second satellite collection opened in the county jail complex where LVA trainers educated selected prisoners as tutors for other inmates. To select the materials, Garner coordinated with one of the jail administrators, who was also on the literacy coalition. Other satellite sites opened in a YWCA family crisis center, a church-sponsored family enrichment center, a city-funded community recreation center, a housing project community center, a Christian Services program center, and a halfway house. Each site had a social service program and staff, or volunteers who could assist with the collections. Most of the sites did not have literacy programs in place when Garner first contacted them. The literacy collection placed by the library served as a catalyst for establishment of literacy programs at those sites.

Promotional Efforts

Only one-tenth of the grant budget was allocated for printing and advertising, so the library had to marshal other resources to help with its promotional efforts. The literacy coalition meetings began to draw a wider attendance, including representatives of a local cable TV company and a public radio station. Both of them pledged their support to Garner for PSAs and other coverage.

The cable TV representative set up a meeting with the library and the production department to discuss literacy PSAs. Prior to the meeting Stevens and Garner developed and sketched ideas for several approaches to the public awareness PSAs. The production team members were glad to have that raw material in hand as they discussed the possibilities for developing the PSAs. The result was an agreement to develop and air a series of four PSAs, the first of which began production in April. The airing of these PSAs began in June.

The public radio representative continued to meet with the coalition and spearheaded the production of call-in radio shows, forums, and coverage of the library's "Night of 1000 Stars" event during National Library Week.

Stevens and Garner met with the director of community projects for the local ABC-TV affiliate to develop a promotional campaign featuring local literacy efforts. The station had designated two focal points for community projects in that calendar year: education and geriatrics. The library believed both of those had a natural tie-in with literacy.

The library's grant promotion budget was spent on posters and brochures, since the cost of advertising on bus sideboards was prohibitive. The plans featured a large multicolor poster aimed at potential pupils, which conveyed its message by illustration rather than words. However, the team encountered a great deal of difficulty in developing material that was both appealing and understandable to nonliterates, so they bought newspaper advertising space which was very effective in recruiting tutors.

Other efforts included flyers promoting the library's literacy information clearinghouse for program information and referrals, the resource center materials for tutors, trainers, program coordinators, and educators, and special literacy events.

Other Activities

Other promotional activities included PSAs that were sent to all radio and TV stations, news releases highlighting the library literacy program in conjunction with the opening of each new satellite collection, an interview with Garner on the state's public TV network about the library's grant and literacy involvement, flyers distributed at a local movie theater showing *Stanley and Iris*, a film about a tutor and an illiterate student, and miscellaneous flyers produced for distribution at specific events. Networking and personal contacts at the coalition meetings also were valuable sources of promotion.

Garner presented workshops on the library's literacy-related materials for various groups, including an LVA tutor-training session. Stevens and a branch librarian attended a literacy forum sponsored by the state endowment for the humanities with funding from National Endowment for the Humanities. Garner attended a conference on Workplace Literacy, which was sponsored by the governor.

The monthly meetings of the literacy coalition were attended by Garner, Stevens, or Betts, with all three present when schedules permitted. Stevens had been named to the coalition's executive board, and Garner served on the nominating committee to select a slate of new officers. Garner also worked closely with the editor of the daily newspaper's education section to help develop a commercially sponsored literacy supplement.

Serendipity

With greater exposure, the library's literacy office began to gain ground in public awareness. Occasionally, serendipitous events validated and revitalized the library's literacy mission. A retailer called Garner and offered several sections of used magazine display shelving; these were utilized in some of the satellite sites. A tutor and her student dropped in for a visit; Garner gave a brief tour of the library, assisted the student in registering for a library card, and showed them the new adult literacy collection. The student was so delighted with the materials he checked out on his new library card that he was already reading them as he walked out the door.

Garner received a call one day from a woman with a problem she could not handle: her child could not read. Garner offered to call the child's teacher and provided suggestions for the parent as follow-up. The parent and teacher got together on the problem as a result of Garner's assistance.

There were many other instances of people who called the literacy office because they needed assistance and did not know who to contact. Whether it was coordinating with the driver's license bureau for a verbal test or contacting the bank for assistance with an account, Garner helped the caller reach a destination. In most of these cases, the callers said they did not "know what to say" or "who to call" or "how to do it" themselves. But once Garner paved with way with initial contact, the callers were able to follow through and solve their problems.

Internal Communication

Stevens had already written, at the director's request, several memos for the board of trustees regarding the literacy grant's program and budget. She also had reported on literacy regularly in the monthly meetings of library department heads. At the end of the first quarter, she prepared a detailed update that was sent to each branch and department and to the board members. Garner followed up with additional periodic updates, and he also attended a meeting of the branch managers to explain the literacy efforts. Betts assembled into a binder examples of the most common types of adult literacy material in the library's collection and in the satellite collections. Each branch library received a copy of the binder to examine and to share with tutors and other patrons interested in literacy efforts.

Good News for Year Four

At the end of April, Stevens received a call from the LSCA Title VI representative that the year four grant had been approved. A minor adjustment in the paperwork was needed before the library could receive written confirmation. She faxed the changes that afternoon and mailed an original with two copies the next day. Official written approval of the grant application was not received until the end of August, after repeated queries from Garner.

Before Garner and Stevens could think about the year four grant, there was still a lot of work to do on the initial project. And six weeks after the year three program ended, the year five application was due in Washington, D.C.!

SUMMARY AND CRITIQUE

Although the library was relatively late in becoming involved in literacy, its effort was well structured, generally effective, and well received. The information clearinghouse data base and telephone number and the resource center materials fulfilled two of the major objectives of the literacy coalition. The satellite collections were well placed and customized to fit the needs of each site; it was very beneficial for the library team to visit each site during the coordination phase. The program made good use of the library's areas of involvement: materials, information, and promotion. The activities were appropriate extensions of functions in which the library was already engaged, e.g., collecting and indexing information.

The library team reacted properly to the disappointing rejection of its first grant application: Team members studied the evaluation, sought greater local input, and made dramatic changes for the second try. But they wasted a full year by relying upon LSCA Title VI as the only funding source. That year would have been better spent looking for other external funds rather than waiting, without action, until the next federal cycle. The library did allocate several hundred dollars, which Stevens used to start building the in-house adult literacy collection. But with its relatively strong budget, the library should have purchased additional adult literacy materials ($500 would buy a good variety) to set up a pilot satellite collection and get the external program rolling.

The library team reacted well to disappointments and adapted nicely to changing circumstances. When they discovered the grant budget had grossly underestimated the cost of bus sideboard ads, they used the promotional funds for flyers and ads. When they realized it was beyond their ability to create a multicolor poster (with no text) aimed at potential literacy pupils, they channeled their efforts into other areas of promotion.

Losing Hollis in midstream obviously had a significant effect on the library's momentum. Much of the time Stevens spent handling Hollis's nonliteracy duties and looking for a replacement could have been used on literacy efforts if Hollis had remained. Selecting Garner, a LVA projects coordinator and tutor, was an excellent choice because it gave the library a more complete perspective on the illiteracy problem. While the director and Stevens both supported literacy in a general sense and understood the broad scope of the problem, neither had a very clear grasp of the needs and difficulties of individual illiterates. Garner's LVA experience provided a valuable catalyst to the library administration's literacy commitment.

Final Note

It should be clear from examining this public library literacy program that there is no single scope, direction, or configuration that works in every environment. Each library should create its own response to the illiteracy problem. This case study emphasizes several important aspects of a library literacy effort.

- A literacy program requires quite a bit more time and effort than most people think it will.
- You cannot let surprises or obstacles throw you off course or cause you to cancel your program.
- Do not zero in on a single possibility (e.g., a particular funding agency) and ignore others.
- Take advantage of the local literacy network members for whatever services they are equipped to provide (e.g., publicity, printing, meeting space, equipment, or labor).
- Formulate a program that features activities that will be genuinely useful to students, tutors, and other program providers.
- Allow flexibility, in the program and its participants, to respond to new opportunities as they develop (e.g., customizing the satellite collections instead of ordering six duplicate sets of a generic list).
- Get started, no matter how small your first effort.

REFERENCES

"More jobs than seekers." 1988. *American Libraries* 19 (March): 181.

"Placement stats: Steady state." 1989. *American Libraries* 20 (September): 806.

Appendix A

NONLIBRARY LITERACY ORGANIZATIONS AND PROGRAMS

Organizations and agencies listed in this appendix have one thing in common: programs that support the literacy effort. The entries are organized by the type of group (that is, nonprofit, government, business-related). Within each group entries are organized alphabetically.

Listing here does not necessarily imply endorsement of the group or all of its activities. Chapter 7 gives more information on some of these organizations.

NONPROFIT AND VOLUNTEER AGENCIES

American Reading Council (ARC)
45 John St., Suite 811
New York, NY 10038
(212) 619-6044

Christian Literacy Associates (CLA)
541 Perry Highway
Pittsburgh, PA 15229
(412) 364-3777

Coalition for Literacy
50 E. Huron St.
Chicago, IL 60611
(312) 944-6710
Literacy Hotline: (800) 228-8813

Contact, Inc.
P.O. Box 81826
Lincoln, NE 68501
(402) 464-0602

English Family Literacy Project
Bilingual/ESL Studies Program
University of Massachusetts at Boston
Boston, MA 02125-3393
(617) 287 5760

International Reading Association (IRA)
800 Barksdale Rd.
P.O. Box 8139
Newark, DE 19714
(302) 731-1600

Kenan Trust Family Literacy Project
National Center for Family Literacy
One Riverfront Plaza
Suite 608
Louisville, KY 40202
(502) 584-1133

Laubach Literacy International
1320 Jamesville Ave.
P.O. Box 131
Syracuse, NY 13210
(315) 422-9121

Literacy Volunteers of America
Widewaters 1 Office Building
5795 S. Widewaters Parkway
Syracuse, NY 13214
(315) 445-8000

Mothers' Reading Program
c/o University Settlement
184 Eldridge St.
New York, NY 10002
(212) 674-9120, ext. 176

Parent and Child Education (PACE) Program
Division of Community Instruction
Kentucky Department of Education
Capital Plaza Tower
Frankfort, KY 40601
(502) 564-4770

Parent Readers Program
New York City Technical College
300 Jay St.
Brooklyn, NY 11201
(718) 643-5723

Parents as Partners in Reading
College of Education, Erickson Hall
Michigan State University
East Lansing, MI 48823
(517) 355-9628

Push Literacy Action Now, Inc.
1332 G St. NW
Washington, DC 20003
(202) 547-8903

GOVERNMENT AGENCIES

Clearinghouse on Adult Education
U.S. Department of Education
Division of Adult Education
Mary E. Switzer Building
400 Maryland Ave. SW
Washington, DC 20202
(202) 732-2270

Head Start Bureau
P.O. Box 1182
Washington, DC 20013
(202) 755-7782

Library Literacy Program
Office of Library Programs
U.S. Department of Education
555 New Jersey Ave. NW
Suite 400
Washington, DC 20208
(202) 357-6292

National Advisory Council on Adult Education (NACAE)
300 7th St. SW
Washington, DC 20202
(202) 634-6300

National Commission on Libraries and Information Science (NCLIS)
1111 18th St. NW
Washington, DC 20036
(202) 382-0840

PROGRAMS RELATED TO BUSINESS

American Association of Advertising Agencies (AAAA)
666 Third Ave.
New York, NY 10017
(212) 682-2500

Business Council for Effective Literacy (BCEL)
1221 Avenue of the Americas
New York, NY 10020
(212) 512-2412

B. Dalton Bookseller
122 Fifth Ave.
New York, NY 10011
(212) 633-3311

Appendix B

SAMPLES OF ADULT LITERACY ENRICHMENT MATERIAL

Although several publishers offer a wide range of specialized reading material for basic skills instruction and coping skills (chapter 5), relatively little is available for new adult readers who have attained basic skills and need to reinforce them. New readers need enrichment material written on lower reading levels with subjects of interest to adults. Reading for pleasure, recreation, and leisure may be a lifelong dream for an adult who has finally made the significant effort to become literate.

Unfortunately, many new literates must either look for their enrichment reading among childrens' story books or be frustrated by attempting to read newsstand magazines and paperbacks. Struggling new readers need all types of enrichment material but there is a particular lack of humorous material on lower reading levels.

Until a greater variety of enrichment material becomes available, libraries can contribute greatly to filling this "gap" by producing its own enrichment material for the literacy collection. Stories such as the ones in this appendix can be collected and "published" in looseleaf binders, plastic binders, report folders, or with staples and tape. It would be a good idea to have a reading instruction specialist examine them first to determine grade levels. If that is not possible, one of the library staff can quickly learn how to assign approximate grade levels using either Fry's Readability Graph or the Gunning Fog Index.

There are probably several possible sources right in your community. Local tutors may be delighted to provide copies of stories they have already written for use in their own classes. Education department faculty at nearby colleges may be willing to "assign" a story to their students each term as a practical exercise. In fact, students in education or English classes may volunteer to write stories on their own. Also, many libraries will have staff members with the ability and interest in composing stories.

Below are two locally-written stories which can serve as examples of new adult reader enrichment material in the humorous vein. The author of "Skating I" and "Skating II" is a tutor with LVA; "Pam's Errand" was written by a former public library employee. Each story is presented on a different reading level, two to three grades apart. Comparing the two versions of the same story will point out some of the elements which must be considered in writing for new adult readers.

* * *

SKATING I
by Sharyn M. Gilsoul

When I was a child I wanted to learn to roller skate.
All the other kids could skate.

One day my dad bought me a brand new pair of skates.
My mom thought that they would help make my feet turn
out instead of in.
The skates were bright and shiny and came with a key.
I loved them!

Mom put a ribbon through the key.
Dad buckled the skates onto my shoes and tightened the
clamps with the key.
Then he put the key around my neck and let me go.

I did not go very far because I was a new skater.
Also, my feet would slowly move together as I skated.
My skates would crash into each other and I would fall
into a heap on the sidewalk.

After many falls I had two pretty awful looking skinned knees.
So I took off my skates and started for home.
I felt like a failure.
I sat on the porch holding the tears back.
I was thinking about what a "klutz" I was when suddenly
I had an idea.
I could practice on my porch.

Our porch was slightly higher on one end than the
other.
If I started at the high end I could roll to the other
end and maybe train my feet to go out instead of in.

I sat down at the higher end of the porch and put my
skates back on.
I held on to the railing and pulled myself up.
I pointed myself toward the other end of the porch and
let go.
I was skating!

I was skating faster and faster.
Much faster than I thought I would go.
The other end of the porch was getting closer.
My feet were coming together again.

My skates crashed together.
I hit the railing.
I did a flip over the railing into the bushes below.

(Story continues on page 138.)

When I opened my eyes I saw my two brothers and their creepy friends staring at me.
All I could think of was that they had seen the whole thing.
I would never live this down.

I was amazed to find out that they thought it was a neat trick.
They thought I had done it on purpose!
From then on I got a lot more respect from the boys in the neighborhood.
I was sometimes allowed to hang out with them even though I was a girl.

COMMENT: This original story depicts an adult recalling a juvenile experience that had an unexpectedly humorous ending. It is written at a grade level of between 3.5 (Fry's) and 4.5 (Gunning-Fog). Notice that each sentence begins a new line and an extra space is inserted between each paragraph. If published, the type size would be 12 point and the page size probably would be 5 by 7 inches. Some of the words are long (e.g., *neighborhood*) but are probably recognizable to adults reading at this level.

SKATING II
by Sharyn M. Gilsoul

When I was a child, one of my greatest ambitions was to learn to roller skate. Every other kid in my neighborhood seemed to be an expert at it, and they would go whizzing by me as I sat on the porch. I dreamed of becoming one of those lady roller skaters in a short skating skirt and fancy skates with beautiful white shoes attached to them. I wanted to be the Skate Queen.

One day my dad bought me a brand new pair of skates. Mom had suggested that skating might help me to walk more like a lady. What she meant was that skating might help make my feet start turning out rather than in (I was horribly pigeon-toed). I had been wearing corrective shoes for years and I think she was dreaming of buying me some of those beautiful Mary Jane shoes instead of the clunky brown ones I was used to wearing.

I didn't care what the reason. I loved my skates. They were shiny and new and came with a key. My mom put a pretty pink silk ribbon through the key and told me I could wear it as a necklace and that way I would always have the key when I needed it. I could hardly believe my luck! I had gotten new skates and jewelry all in the same day and it wasn't even my birthday!

I put my new key necklace on, picked up my shiny new skates and went outside to begin my career as the Skate Queen. Dad buckled the skates onto my shoes and tightened the clamps with the key. Then he put the key around my neck and I took off.

Needless to say, I did not go very far. My problem was not only that I did not know how to skate, but my awful, pigeon-toed feet would slowly move toward one another, causing the skates to crash and making me fall in a heap on the sidewalk.

After many falls, my knees were pretty banged up and my dreams of being the Skate Queen were shattered. I took off my skates and started for home. I was defeated. I sat on the porch holding back the tears. I was thinking about what a klutz I was when suddenly I had an idea. I could teach myself to skate on the porch. When I got good enough on the porch I would move to the sidewalk and then move on to become the Skate Queen.

Our porch was slightly tilted, and I could start out at the high end and roll down toward the lower end. I would first learn to keep my toes pointing outward. What a great idea! I sat on the higher end of the porch and put my skates back on. I held onto the railing, pulled myself up, pointed myself to the opposite end of the porch, and took off. It was great. I was skating!

(Story continues on page 140.)

The problem was that I was skating much faster than I ever imagined I would. The other end of the porch was getting too close too soon. I could feel my feet closing in on one another, and before I could do anything about it my skates crashed together. I thought I would fall but instead I hit the railing and flipped over into the bushes below.

When I opened my eyes I saw my two brothers and their creepy friends peering down at me. All I could think of was that they had seen the whole thing and I would never ever live this down. I would be teased forever until I died ... or they died. Maybe that could be arranged. I had thought of it often before. This might be just the thing that would push me to action.

Then I noticed that they were not acting like they usually did. They were saying things like "wow," "cool," and "neat trick," and my brothers actually looked proud of me. They thought I had done it on purpose! They thought it was some kind of neat trick!

From then on I got a lot more respect from all of the neighborhood boys. Although I never did become the Skate Queen, I became something of a neighborhood legend and was sometimes allowed to hang out with the boys even though I was *just* a girl.

COMMENT: This version is written at a grade level of between 6.0 (Fry's) and 7.5 (Gunning Fog). Enhancements over the lower version include daydreaming about becoming Skate Queen, more insight into the sibling relationship, and additional dialogue. The ending is still humorous, but has more punch due to the broader vocabulary.

Notice the paragraphs are fully formed but still quite short and not separated by blank lines. At this level are words (*usually, actually, ambitious, horribly,* and *corrective*) that probably could not be used in the first version because of the number of syllables. Other words (*although, somewhat,* and *needless*), while shorter, may have been confusing in the level 1 version of the story.

PAM'S ERRAND I
by Denise W. Salter

Pam drove her car through the gates of the railroad yard. She parked at the end of the lot. She looked up at the dark sky and hoped it would not rain.

She read the directions to the lab. They said, "Go to the end of the middle building. Turn and go up the ramp. Enter the door at the top of the ramp. Give the papers to Mr. Lee."

Pam walked toward the buildings. The drops began to fall from the sky. Pam put the papers inside her coat to keep them dry. The sprinkle changed to rain as Pam got to the middle building.

She looked for a ramp at the end of the building. There was no ramp! There were many giant doors that were open, and she could see train engines inside. But she could not find the ramp!

Pam read the directions again. Maybe the ramp was *behind* the middle building. She ran to the end of the building.

Great! There was a ramp! Pam was soaking wet by now. She ran up the ramp to a door. Then she grabbed the doorknob and opened the door. Pam quickly stepped inside out of the rain.

Pam wiped the rain from her eyes. Something was wrong. This was not the lab. There was no lab equipment. But there were a number of men standing in front of lockers. Some of them did not have all their clothes on! She could see steam from a shower. This was the men's locker room!

Pam covered her eyes. One man was wrapped in a towel. He asked Pam, "Can I help you?"

Pam said, "Yes. I am looking for the lab." Pam backed up to the door. "I need to see Mr. Lee. I have some papers for him." Her eyes were still closed.

The man said, "Aren't you lucky? I am Mr. Lee. You have just *seen* me!"

COMMENT: This version is written at a grade level of between 2.0 (Fry's) and 3.5 (Gunning Fog). While it is one-third shorter than the more advanced version (see pages 143-144), it includes every action and most of the dialogue included in the longer version. The story depicts an adult in a confusing situation, in which an everyday work errand has a surprising and humorous ending.

(Comment continues on page 142.)

While the simpler version of the skating story placed each sentence on a separate line, this one uses standard paragraph form but adds an extra space between the paragraphs. Most of the paragraphs have only three sentences. The print would probably be 14 point type for a published version.

Note: One of the shortest words, "lab," may be more difficult to understand than some of the longer words. An adult reading at this level may stumble over the contextual problem of a laboratory in a railroad yard.

PAM'S ERRAND II

by Denise W. Salter

As Pam drove through the gates of the railroad yard, she looked for a parking space. The only space empty was at the end of the lot. She looked up at the sky again. Maybe it won't rain yet, she thought.

Pam locked her car door and read the instructions her boss had given her. The directions said, "Go to the end of the middle building. Turn and go up the ramp. Enter the door at the top of the ramp. Give the envelope to Mr. Lee in the lab." Her boss had also told her, "I think there are only three buildings. If you get lost, look for the building that has train engines inside."

Pam started walking toward the buildings. So far, so good. There were only three buildings. She reached the end of one building. Drops of rain began to fall from the sky. When she turned to go between the first and second buildings, it began to rain harder. Pam tucked the envelope inside her coat. It would be better for the rain to wet her hair rather than the papers. She didn't want to have to type those pages again.

Pam reached the end of the middle building. Where was the ramp? She was sure this was the correct building. There were several giant doors open, and she could see locomotive engines inside. The problem was she still had not found the ramp!

Pam reached into her pocket and got the directions out again. Maybe when her boss said, "Turn and go up the ramp," he meant turn *behind* the building. Pam stuffed the paper back into her pocket and jogged to the end of the building.

Great! There was the ramp! The rain was coming down harder now. Pam's hair was soaking wet, but her envelope was dry! She glanced through the windows as she ran up the ramp. There were counters full of lab equipment, so that had to be the lab. But there was no door there.

Near the other end of the ramp was a door. Pam went to it, opened the door, and quickly stepped in out of the rain. After she wiped the water from her eyes, she realized something was wrong. This was not the lab! She saw steam coming from a shower. There were several men standing in front of lockers, and some of them did not have all their clothes on! This was the men's locker room!

(Story continues on page 144.)

Pam quickly covered her eyes. A man wrapped in a towel asked, "Can I help you find something?"

"Yes. I need to see Mr. Lee," Pam answered as she edged back toward the door. "I have to deliver some papers to him."

"Aren't you lucky?" the man chuckled. "I am Mr. Lee, and you've just *seen* me!"

COMMENT: This story takes the same everyday, work-related errand and humorous ending but presents it about two grade levels higher. It is at a grade level of between 4.0 (Fry's) and 5.0 (Gunning Fog). Although some of the words (*instructions, envelope, locomotive,* and *equipment*) are somewhat long, they are probably common enough that they would not present problems for adult readers at this level. This version is almost 50 percent longer than the simpler text. It includes more detail about Pam's instructions, the rain, the difficulty locating the correct building, and the locker room. In print, this story probably would be set in 12 point type. Notice that the paragraphs are separated by an extra space, unlike the skating story, which is at a higher level.

Notice that (in these samples) there is usually a full grade level or more between the estimates using Fry's Readability Graph and the Gunning Fog Index. Both systems examine three or more 100-word samples to determine averages that represent the entire text.

Fry's process uses the average number of syllables in relation to the average number of sentences. Where these converge on the graph is the indicator of the approximate reading level. Since this method counts each syllable, even a handful of two-syllable words tends to inflate the grade level rating. A passage with many two-syllable words would be rated at a high level even if there were no long (i.e., difficult) words.

The Gunning Fog method has no graph. It uses the average sentence length (number of words) plus the number of words having more than two syllables. The sum is then multiplied by a factor of .4 to arrive at the approximate grade level. Even if practically every word had two syllables, it would not increase the Fog rating; a passage with short sentences and no three-syllable words would get a low rating.

Librarians are encouraged to consult local reading instruction specialists for assistance with determining grade levels of material.

BIBLIOGRAPHY

It would not be practical or particularly useful to list every item that relates to literacy. Due to the large number of applicable citations, this bibliography is, for the most part, limited to the past 10 years, except as noted. The list is arranged by the following categories for easier access:

1. Books in print, published since 1980, pertaining to the United States and of probable interest to librarians or general audiences.

2. Book reviews, which focus on a few mainstream, contemporary books with wide appeal.

3. Manuals, handbooks, and guides.

4. Government documents of specific interest to librarians.

5. Theme issues and special sections.

6. Articles published since 1980, except for those specific to libraries. Article topics include libraries and materials; programs and funding; statistics, surveys, and economic impact; international literacy; city, state, and federal levels; workplace, business, industry, and employment; society and culture; education, school, and reading instruction; family literacy, reading at home, and children; literacy cases and personal narratives; and general interest.

BOOKS

Most of the books listed here are still in print and have been published since 1980. They pertain to the United States and are of probable interest to librarians or general audiences.

Adult basic education collection: An annotated list of titles. 1990. Washington, D.C.: Martin Luther King Memorial Library.

Anzalone, Stephen, and McLaughlin, Stephen. 1983. *Making literacy work: The specific library approach.* Amherst, Mass.: University of Massachusetts, Center for International Education.

Arnove, Robert F., and Graff, H. J., eds. 1987. *National literacy campaigns: Historical and comparative perspectives.* New York: Plenum Publishing Corp.

Balmuth, Miriam. 1987. *Essential characteristics of effective adult literacy programs: A review and analysis of the research.* New York: City University of New York.

Bertelson, Paul. 1987. *The onset of literacy: Cognitive processes in reading acquisition.* Cambridge, Mass.: MIT Press.

Bibliography of basic materials: Reading, English as a second language, humanities. 1980. Syracuse, N.Y.: Literacy Volunteers of America.

Bleich, David. 1988. *The double perspective: Language, literacy, and social relations.* New York: Oxford University Press.

Bloome, David, ed. 1987. *Literacy and schooling.* Norwood, N.J.: Ablex Publishing Corporation.

Brown, Eleanor F. 1971. *Library service to the disadvantaged.* Metuchen, N.J.: Scarecrow.

Buckingham, Melissa F. 1982. *Reader development bibliography.* Syracuse, N.Y.: New Readers Press.

Cahen, Robert. 1986. *Illiteracy as an economic development issue.* Youngstown, Ohio: Youngstown State University, Center for Urban Studies.

Campbell, Robert E., and Sechler, Judith A. 1987. *Adult literacy: Programs and practices.* Columbus, Ohio: Ohio State University, National Center for Research in Vocational Education.

Carnevale, Anthony P. et al. 1988. *Workplace basics: The skills employers want.* Washington, D.C.: The American Society for Training and Development.

Carroll, John B., and Chall, Jeanne S., eds. 1975. *Toward a literate society: A report from the National Academy of Education.* New York: McGraw-Hill.

Cashdan, Asher. 1985. *Literacy.* Cambridge, Mass.: Basil Blackwell, Inc.

Chisman, Forrest P. et al. 1990. *Leadership for literacy: The agenda for the 1990s.* San Francisco: Jossey-Bass.

Cook, Wanda D. 1977. *Adult literacy education in the United States.* Newark, Del.: International Reading Association.

Cressy, David. 1980. *Literacy and the social order.* New York: Cambridge University Press.

Davidson, Judith, and Koppenhaver, David, eds. 1988. *Adolescent literacy: What works and why.* New York: Garland Publishing.

De Castell, Suzanne et al., eds. 1986. *Literacy, society, and schooling.* New York: Cambridge University Press.

Duggins, Lydia et al. 1988. *Literacy: Ten steps away.* Redding Ridge, Conn.: Black Swan Books Ltd.

Eberle, Anne, and Robinson, Sandra. 1980. *The adult illiterate speaks out: Personal perspectives on learning to read and write.* Washington, D.C.: National Institute of Education.

Fields, Marjorie. 1988. *Literacy begins at birth.* Tucson, Ariz.: Fisher Books.

Final report: The adult performance level study. 1977. Austin, Texas: University of Texas at Austin.

Fingeret, Arlene, and Jurmo, Paul, eds. 1989. *Participatory literacy education.* San Francisco: Jossey-Bass.

First steps to literacy: Library programs for parents, teachers, and caregivers. 1990. Chicago: American Library Association.

First teachers: A family literacy handbook for parents, policy-makers, and literacy providers. 1989. Washington, D.C.: Barbara Bush Foundation for Family Literacy.

Fleming, Lois D. 1974. *Adult basic education and public library service.* Tallahassee, Fla.: State Library of Florida.

French, J. N. 1987. *Adult literacy: A source book and guide.* New York: Garland Publishing.

Gamliel, Amram. 1985. *Educational imperatives in adult literacy.* Newton Center, Mass.: Gamliels Publishing.

Goelman, Hillel et al., eds. 1984. *Awakening to literacy.* Portsmouth, N.H.: Heinemann Educational Books Inc.

Graff, Harvey J. 1981. *Literacy in history: An interdisciplinary research bibliography.* New York: Garland Publishing.

______. 1987. *The legacies of literacy: Continuities and contradictions in Western culture and society.* Bloomington, Ind.: Indiana University Press.

Gray, B. et al. 1977. *Literacy programs and public libraries.* rev. ed. Santa Clara, Calif.: South Bay Cooperative Library System.

Harman, David. 1987. *Illiteracy: A national dilemma.* New York: Cambridge Book Company.

Heiser, Jane-Carol. 1983. *Literacy resources: An annotated checklist for tutors and librarians.* Baltimore: Enoch Pratt Free Library.

Hirsch, E. D., Jr. 1987. *Cultural literacy: What every American needs to know.* Boston: Houghton Mifflin.

Hirsch, E. D., Jr., et al. 1988. *The dictionary of cultural literacy: What every American needs to know.* Boston: Houghton Mifflin.

Hladczuk, John et al., eds. 1990. *General issues in literacy/illiteracy: A bibliography.* Westport, Conn.: Greenwood.

______. 1990. *Literacy/illiteracy in the world: A bibliography.* Westport, Conn.: Greenwood.

Holdaway, Don. 1984. *Stability and change in literacy learning.* Portsmouth, N.H.: Heinemann Educational Books Inc.

Holmes, Barbara J. et al. 1988. *Solutions in progress: Results from a survey of literacy programs and activities.* Denver, Colo.: Education Commission of the States.

Hoyles, Martin, ed. 1980. *The politics of literacy.* New York: Writers & Readers Publishing, Inc.

Hunter, Carman, and Harman, David. 1985. *Adult illiteracy in the United States: A report to the Ford Foundation.* 2d ed. New York: McGraw-Hill.

Johnson, Laura S. 1980. *Reading and the adult learner.* Newark, Del.: International Reading Association.

Johnson, Terry D., and Louis, Daphne R. 1988. *Literacy through literature.* Portsmouth, N.H.: Heinemann Educational Books Inc.

Jones, Edward V. 1981. *Reading instruction for the adult illiterate.* Chicago: American Library Association.

Judy, Stephen N. 1980. *The ABC's of literacy: A guide for parents and educators.* New York: Oxford University Press.

Kazemak, Francis E., and Rigg, Pat, eds. 1984. *Adult literacy.* Newark, Del.: International Reading Association.

Kintgen, Eugene R. et al., eds. 1988. *Perspectives on literacy.* Champaign, Ill.: University of Illinois Press.

Kozol, Jonathan. 1980. *Prisoners of silence: Breaking the bonds of adult illiteracy in the U.S.* New York: Continuum Publishing Corporation.

______. 1985. *Illiterate America.* Garden City, N.J.: Doubleday.

Langer, Judith, ed. 1987. *Language, literacy and culture: Issues of society and schooling.* Norwood, N.J.: Ablex Publishing Corp.

Lanham, Richard A. 1983. *Literacy and the survival of humanism.* New Haven, Conn.: Yale University Press.

Lankshear, Colin, and Lawler, Moira. 1987. *Literacy, schooling and revolution.* New York: Taylor & Francis.

Laubach, Frank C., and Laubach, Robert S. 1960. *Toward world literacy: The each one teach one way.* Syracuse, N.Y.: Syracuse University Press.

Laurita, Raymond E. 1983. *Solving the literacy mystery.* Yorktown Heights, N.Y.: Leonardo Press.

Lerche, Renee S. 1985. *Effective adult literacy programs.* New York: Cambridge Book Company.

Levine, Kenneth. 1987. *The social context of literacy.* New York: Routledge, Chapman & Hall.

Long, Lynellyn D., and Podnecky-Spiegel, Janet. 1987. *In print: Beginning literacy through cultural awareness.* Reading, Mass.: Addison-Wesley Publishing Co.

Luke, Allan. 1988. *Literacy, textbooks and ideology: Postwar literacy instruction and the mythology of Dick and Jane.* New York: Taylor & Francis.

Lyman, Helen H. 1973. *Library materials in service to the adult new reader.* Chicago: American Library Association.

______. 1976. *Reading and the adult new reader.* Chicago: American Library Association.

______. 1977. *Literacy and the nation's libraries.* Chicago: American Library Association.

McCracken, R. A., and McCracken, M. J. 1986. *Stories, songs, and poetry to teach reading and writing: Literacy through language.* Chicago: American Library Association.

McCuen, Gary E., ed. 1988. *Illiteracy in America.* [s.l.], G. E. McCuen Publications.

MacDonald, Bernice. 1966. *Literacy activities in public libraries: A report of a study of service to adult illiterates.* Chicago: American Library Association.

Mackie, Robert. 1981. *Literacy and revolution: The pedagogy of Paulo Freire.* New York: Continuum Publishing Company.

Malone, Cheryl K. 1987. *Gender, unpaid labor, and the promotion of literacy: A selected, annotated bibliography.* New York: Garland Publishing.

Meacham, Louisa, and Schwartzberg, Beverly. 1987. *Literacy action: A resource book for colleges and universities.* Washington, D.C.: ACTION.

Meek, Margaret, and Mills, Colin, eds. 1988. *Language and literacy in the primary school.* New York: Taylor & Francis.

Mercer, Neil, ed. 1987. *Language and literacy from an educational perspective,* vol. 1. New York: Taylor & Francis.

______. 1987. *Language and literacy from an educational perspective: In school,* vol. 2. New York: Taylor & Francis.

Mikulecky, Larry et al. 1987. *Training for job-literacy demands: What research applies to practice.* University Park, Penn.: Pennsylvania State University, Institute for the Study of Adult Literacy.

Nolan, Susanne, and Hawkins, Nan. 1981. *The VITAL bibliography: A basic collection of books and learning materials for an adult literacy program.* Bloomington, Ind.: Monroe County Public Library.

Olson, David R., and Torrance, Nancy, eds. 1984. *Literacy, language and learning: The nature and consequences of reading and writing.* New York: Cambridge University Press.

Olsen, Harry, ed. 1978. *An annotated bibliography of books and materials for adult basic education classes with deaf students.* Washington, D.C.: Gallaudet College.

Omerod, Jan. 1985. *Reading.* New York: Lothrop.

Orpwood, Jean. 1980. *Bibliography for adult literacy.* Willowdale, Ontario: North York Public Library.

Pattison, Robert. 1982. *On literacy: The politics of the word from Homer to the age of rock.* New York: Oxford University Press.

Porter, Thomas E. 1987. *The literate mind.* Dubuque, Iowa: Kendall-Hunt.

Pursell, Frances J., ed. 1989. *Books for adult new readers: A bibliography developed by Project: LEARN.* Syracuse, N.Y.: New Readers Press.

Raymond, James C., ed. 1982. *Literacy as a human problem.* Tuscaloosa, Ala.: University of Alabama Press.

Richardson, Richard C., Jr., et al. 1983. *Literacy in the open-access college.* San Francisco: Jossey-Bass.

Salinger, Terry. 1988. *Language arts and literacy for young children.* Columbus, Ohio: Merrill Publishing Co.

Schieffelin, Bambi, and Gilmore, Perry. 1986. *The acquisition of literacy: Ethnographic perspectives.* Norwood, N.J.: Ablex Publishing Corporation.

Schumacher, Edward D. 1973. *The struggle against adult functional illiteracy in Louisiana: A historical analysis.* Sulphur, La.: Maplewood Books.

Scribner, Sylvia, and Cole, Michael. 1986. *The psychology of literacy.* Cambridge, Mass.: Harvard University Press.

Smith, Frank. 1983. *Essays into literacy.* Portsmouth, N.H.: Heinemann Educational Books Inc.

Stein, Nancy L., ed. 1986. *Literacy in American schools: Learning to read and write.* Chicago: University of Chicago Press.

Stevens, Edward W., Jr. 1988. *Literacy, law, and social order.* Chicago: Northeastern Illinois University Press.

Sussman, Henry. 1988. *High resolution: Critical theory and the problem of literacy.* New York: Oxford University Press.

Taylor, Denny, and Dorsey-Gaines, Catherine. 1988. *Growing up literate: Learning from inner-city families.* Portsmouth, N.H.: Heinemann Educational Books Inc.

Tuman, Myron C. 1987. *Preface to literacy: An inquiry into pedagogy, practice and progress.* Tuscaloosa, Ala.: University of Alabama Press.

Vaughan, Elinor F. 1986. *An examination of library involvement in the literacy education programs of the North Carolina community college system: A perceptual analysis.* Greensboro, N.C.: University of North Carolina.

Wagner, D. A., ed. 1987. *The future of literacy in a changing world.* Elmsford, N.Y.: Pergamon Press.

Wesner, Maralene, and Wesner, Miles E. 1986. *Johnny can read!* Idabel, Okla.: Diversity Oklahoma.

Westbury, Ian, and Purves, Alan C., eds. 1988. *Cultural literacy and the idea of general education.* Chicago: University of Chicago Press.

Wheeler, Thomas C. 1979. *The great American writing block: Causes and cures of the new illiteracy.* New York: Viking.

Young, Peter, and Tyre, Colin. 1983. *Dyslexia or illiteracy?* New York: Taylor & Francis.

BOOK REVIEWS

This section includes reviews of three mainstream, contemporary books on illiteracy with wide appeal.

Illiterate America (Kozol 1985)

Brown, Laurence D. 1985. *Phi Delta Kappan* 67 (October): 161.

Business Week. 1985. 2893 (6 May): 22.

Chance, Paul. 1986. *Psychology Today* 20 (March): 75.

Cole, Diana. 1985. *Savvy* 6 (April): 101.

Condie, Betty. 1985. *NEA Today* 3 (June): 16.

Education Digest. 1985. 50 (May): 60.

Ehrenreich, Barbara. 1985. *Mother Jones* 10 (April): 54.

Frommer, Harvey. 1985. *Library Journal* 110 (1 March): 79.

Hacker, Andrew. 1985. *The Nation* 240 (25 May): 643.

Harman, David. 1985. *The New Republic* 192 (27 May): 36.

Kleiner, Art. 1985. *Whole Earth Review* (Winter): 118.

Library Journal. 1986. 111 (January): 48.

Murphy, Joseph S. 1985. *The New York Times Book Review* 90 (14 April): 36.

The New Yorker. 1985. 61 (1 April): 113.

The New York Times Book Review. 1986. 91 (20 April): 38.

O'Conner, Patricia T. 1986. *The New York Times Book Review* 91 (7 December): 84.

Prescott, Peter. 1985. *Newsweek* 105 (11 March): 73.

Illiteracy: A National Dilemma (Harman 1987)

The Economist. 1987. 303 (16 May): 94.

Gebhardt, Richard C. 1988. *Phi Delta Kappan* 69 (February): 458.

Hopkinson, Shirley L. 1987. *Library Journal* 112 (January): 80.

Weisman, Adam Paul. 1987. *The New Republic* 196 (20 April): 47.

Cultural Literacy: What Every American Needs to Know (Hirsch 1987)

Gray, Donald J. 1988. *Phi Delta Kappan* 69 (January): 386.

Kanfer, Stefan. 1987. *Time* 130 (20 July): 72.

Postman, Neil. 1989. *The Atlantic* 264 (December): 119.

Urban, Wayne J. 1988. *Journal of American History* 75 (December): 871.

MANUALS, HANDBOOKS, AND GUIDES

Most of the publications included here are of specific interest to librarians. The numerous tutor-related publications of LLI, LVA, or the National Center for Research in Vocational Education are not included.

Bayley, Linda. 1977. *ABE: Guide to library materials.* Austin, Texas: University of Texas at Austin.

______. 1984. *Opening doors for adult new readers.* Syracuse, N.Y.: New Readers Press.

Berlin, Gordon, and Sum, Andrew. 1988. *Toward a more perfect union: Basic skills, poor families, and our economic future.* New York: Ford Foundation.

Breivik, Patricia S. et al. 1989. *American Library Association Presidential Committee on Information Literacy: Final report.* Washington, D.C.: ALA Presidential Committee.

Chisman, Forrest P. 1989. *Jump start: The federal role in adult literacy.* Southport, Conn.: Southport Institute for Policy Analysis.

Collino, Gladys E. et al. 1988. *Literacy and job performance: A perspective.* University Park, Penn.: Pennsylvania State University, Institute for the Study of Adult Literacy.

Conklin, Nancy F., and Hurtig, Janise. 1986. *Making the connection: A report for literary volunteers working with out-of-school youth.* Portland, Ore.: Northwest Regional Educational Laboratory.

Costa, Marie. 1989. *Adult literacy/illiteracy in the United States.* Santa Barbara, Calif.: ABC-Clio.

DiPerna, Paula. 1982. *Functional literacy: Knowledge for living*, pamphlet 607. New York: Public Affairs Pamphlets.

Foundation Center. 1990. *Grants for libraries and information services.* New York: The Foundation Center.

Harman, David. 1985. *Turning literacy around: An agenda for national action.* New York: Business Council for Effective Literacy.

Information and resources for task forces. n.d. Pittsburgh, Penn.: Project Literacy U.S.

Johnson, Debra W., and Soule, Jennifer A. 1987. *Libraries and literacy: A planning manual.* Chicago: American Library Association.

Kadavy, Rhonda et al. 1983. *Reducing functional illiteracy: A national guide to facilities and services.* Lincoln, Neb.: Contact Literacy Center.

Kirsch, Irwin S., and Jungeblut, Ann. 1986. *Literacy: Profiles of America's young adults.* Princeton, N.J.: Educational Testing Service.

Kulleseid, Eleanor, and Strickland, Dorothy. 1990. *Literature, literacy and learning: Classroom teachers, library media specialists, and the literature-based curriculum.* Chicago: American Library Association.

McCune, Donald, and Alamparese, Judith. 1985. *Turning literacy around: An agenda for action.* New York: Business Council for Effective Literacy.

McIvor, M. Conlon, ed. 1990. *A survey of successful programs.* Syracuse, N.Y.: New Readers Press.

Mayer, Stephen E. 1985. *Guidelines for effective adult literacy programs.* Minneapolis, Minn.: B. Dalton Bookseller.

Mendel, Richard A. 1988. *Meeting the economic challenge of the 1990's: Workforce literacy in the South.* Washington, D.C.: The Sunbelt Institute.

National Center for Service Learning. 1983. *Literacy forum resource package: A resource handbook.* Washington, D.C.: ACTION.

Opening doors: How to help an adult learn to read. n.d. Knoxville, Tenn.: University of Tennessee.

Reder, Stephen et al. 1979. *A bibliographic guide to functional literacy.* Portland, Ore.: Northwest Regional Educational Laboratory.

Rosenthal, Nadine. 1987. *Teach some to read: A step-by-step guide for literacy tutors.* Belmont, Calif.: David S. Lake Publishers.

Ryan, Jenny L. 1990. *Literacy collection development in libraries: A bibliography*, updated ed. Syracuse, N.Y.: New Readers Press.

Tutor support systems 1986-87. 1987. Pittsburgh, Penn.: Greater Pittsburgh Literacy Council.

Upgrading basic skills for the workplace. 1989. University Park, Penn.: Pennsylvania State University, Institute for the Study of Adult Literacy.

Weibel, Marguerite. 1984. *The library literacy connection: Using library resources with adult basic education students.* Columbus, Ohio: State Library of Ohio.

U.S. GOVERNMENT DOCUMENTS

Binkley, Marilyn R. 1986. *Becoming a nation of readers: Implications for teachers.* Washington, D.C.: U.S. Department of Education.

Center for Libraries and Education Improvement. 1984. *Alliance for excellence: Librfarians respond to* A Nation at Risk. Washington, D.C.: U.S. Department of Education.

Chute, Adrienne. 1987. *Meeting the literacy challenge.* Washington, D.C.: U.S. Department of Education.

Gunderson, Doris V., ed. 1986. *Blueprint for tutoring adult readers.* Washington, D.C.: U.S. Department of Education.

Harman, David. 1984. *Functional illiteracy in the United States: Issues, experiences, and dilemmas.* San Francisco: National Institute of Education, National Adult Literacy Project.

Lang, Patricia A. 1986. *Bibliography of the clearinghouse on adult education resource materials.* Washington, D.C.: U.S. Department of Education.

The nation responds: Recent efforts to improve education. 1984. Washington, D.C.: U.S. Department of Education.

National Advisory Council on Adult Education. 1986. *Illiteracy in America: Extent, causes, and suggested solutions.* Washington, D.C.: U.S. Government Printing Office.

National Commission on Excellence in Education. 1983. *A nation at risk: The imperative for educational reform.* Washington, D.C.: U.S. Department of Education.

Office of Educational Research and Improvement. 1987. *Library programs: Library literacy program abstracts of funded projects, 1986.* Washington, D.C.: U.S. Department of Education.

______. 1988. *Library programs: LSCA VI library literacy program analysis of funded projects, 1987.* Washington, D.C.: U.S. Department of Education.

______. 1989. *Library programs: LSCA VI library literacy program analysis of funded projects, 1988.* Washington, D.C.: U.S. Department of Education.

Resnick, Daniel. 1983. *Literacy in historical perspective.* Washington, D.C.: Library of Congress.

Robinson, Margaret J. 1985. *National adult literacy project 1983-1985: Final report.* Washington, D.C.: National Institute of Education.

Sarmiento, Anthony R. 1990. *Worker-centered learning: A union guide to workplace literacy.* Washington, D.C.: U.S. Department of Labor.

Zweizig, Douglas et al. 1989. *Libraries and literacy education: Comprehensive survey report.* Washington, D.C.: U.S. Government Printing Office.

THEME ISSUES AND SPECIAL SECTIONS

Publications in this list are issues of library and education periodicals in which most or all of the contents are devoted to literacy.

Forinash, M. R., ed. 1978. Public library and adult basic education. *Drexel Library Quarterly* 13 (October).

Heiser, J. C. 1984. The public library in the coalition against illiteracy. *Public Libraries* 23 (Winter): 107-123.

Illiteracy and libraries. 1983. *Catholic Library World* 56 (October).

Literacy and libraries. 1985. *Bookmark* 43 (Summer): 163-200.

Literacy: Gateway to fulfillment. 1980. *Unesco Courier* [33] (June).

Literacy: The ladder of achievement. 1984. *Unesco Courier* [37] (February).

Orpwood, J., ed. 1980. Libraries and illiteracy. *Canadian Library Journal* 37 (August).

Perritt, Patsy H., ed. 1982. Libraries and literacy in Louisiana: A theme issue. *Louisiana Library Association Bulletin* 45 (Summer): 3-25.

Seamon, J. 1985. The Illinois literacy effort. *Illinois Libraries* 67 (September): 571-644.

Seamon, J., and Miller, C. R. 1987. Illinois literacy effort. *Illinois Libraries* 69 (June): 353-442.

Weingand, Darlene E., ed. 1986. Adult education, literacy, and libraries. *Library Trends* 35 (Fall): 183-345.

ARTICLES

Most of these articles were published since 1980, except for some articles from the 1970s that are related to libraries.

Libraries and Materials

Aboyade, B. O. 1984. Communications potentials of the library for non-literates. *Libri* 34 (September): 243-262.

Adult learning services in libraries: The California literacy campaign. 1989. *California State Library Foundation Bulletin* 26 (January): 5-15.

ALA and National Public Radio launch author radio show. 1982. *Library Journal* 107 (1 February): 216.

ALA and other members of Coalition for Literacy announce $1.7 million goal. 1982. *American Libraries* 13 (July-August): 481.

ALA Public Information Office. 1984. Libraries tackling illiteracy in America. *Public Libraries* 23 (Spring): 11.

Alford, T. E. 1985. There is a need for a larger adult literacy effort. *Catholic Library World* 56 (April): 379-381.

ALTA's Short urges trustees to combat U.S. illiteracy. 1976. *Library Journal* 101 (1 May): 1069.

Baker, A. 1987. Libraries: The front line. *Library Association Record* 89 (August): 387.

Baker, Shay et al. 1982. Ohio libraries fight illiteracy. *Ohio Library Association Bulletin* 52 (October): 4-8.

Barbara Bush on the road for literacy. 1990. *Library Journal* 115 (15 April): 18.

Barbara Bush visits Peoria Public Library. 1985. *Wilson Library Bulletin* 60 (September): 13.

Beizaei, W. 1988. A look at Alice Public Library's program. *Texas Libraries* 49 (Spring): 7.

Bibliography for adult literacy. 1980. *American Libraries* 11 (March): 171.

Blumenthal, Howard. 1988. Books on audiotape provide good tool for persons learning to read. *Shreveport Journal* 94 (6 September): 2B.

Brady, Ben. 1988. Literacy status report: Louisiana public libraries. *Louisiana Library Association Bulletin* 50 (Spring): 177-178.

Brawer, Jennifer. 1989. Reading magic library. *A+* 7 (February): 93.

Breting, E. 1986. Kansas City Public Library's activities for literacy. *Show-Me Libraries* 37 (March): 16-18.

Brooklyn PL opens centers to combat illiteracy. 1986. *Library Journal* 111 (January): 22.

Buckingham, Melissa Forinash. 1978. Materials selection for ABE collections. *Drexel Library Quarterly* 13 (October): 14-32.

Burns, Mary Florence. 1989. Libraries can counteract adult illiteracy, but they need help. *The New York Times*, national ed. 139 (26 October): A22 (N).

Butler, Dorothy. 1989. Saying it louder. *School Library Journal* 35 (September): 155.

Carr, David. 1986. The meanings of the adult independent library learning project. *Library Trends* 35 (Fall): 327-345.

Casey, D. W. 1978. John T. Short enlists trustees in war against illiteracy. *Public Library Trustee* 68 (September): 10.

Cheatham, Bertha M. 1988. Literacy. *In* News of '88: A recap of events and happenings. *School Library Journal* 35 (December): 32.

Cheatham, Bertha M., and Cohen, Andrew. 1990. LC symposium strikes at the cycle of illiteracy. *School Library Journal* 36 (January): 9.

Cherry, S. S. 1979. Special report: Conference urges libraries to lead literacy activities. *American Libraries* 10 (May): 230-231.

Chester County lauded for programs for illiterates and mentally ill. 1982. *Library Journal* 107 (15 December): 2298.

Childhood literacy project launched by Cleveland Public. 1982. *Library Journal* 107 (15 March): 584.

Coleman, Jean Ellen. 1976. Library literacy programs. *ALA Yearbook:* American Library Association, 219-223.

______. 1986. ALA's role in adult and literacy education. *Library Trends* 35 (Fall): 207-217.

Columbus literacy project to enlist computer aid. 1982. *Library Journal* 107 (15 November): 2134.

Considine, D. M. 1986. Visual literacy and children's books: An integrated approach. *School Library Journal* 33 (September): 38-42.

Cooking up a blow against illiteracy. 1990. *Woman's Day* 53 (22 May): 24.

Copeland, Jeffrey S. 1987. Multiple-storyline books for young adults: Why? *English Journal* 76 (December): 52.

Dahlin, R. 1976. Libraries and the problem of literacy. *Publishers Weekly* 209 (10 May): 48-49.

Dale, J. 1980. Libraries and literacy. *Nebraska Library Association Quarterly* 11 (Summer): 34-35.

Darling, M. J. 1979. Trenton PL literacy project. *New Jersey Libraries* 12 (March): 10-11.

Davidson, Judith. 1988. Meeting young adolescents' literacy needs: What librarians can do. *VOYA* 11 (December): 229-230.

Davis, Nancy, and Fitzgerald, Pam. Literacy clearinghouse (column) *Library Journal.*

July 1989. 114: 37.

August 1989. 114: 45.

September 1, 1989. 114: 145.

September 15, 1989. 114: 34.

October 1, 1989. 114: 37.

October 15, 1989. 114: 35.

November 1, 1989. 114: 43.

November 15, 1989. 114: 33.

December 1989. 114: 47.

January 1990. 115: 45.

February 1, 1990. 115: 39.

February 15, 1990. 115: 135.

March 1, 1990. 115: 33.

March 15, 1990. 115: 33.

April 1, 1990. 115: 45.

April 15, 1990. 115: 31.

May 1, 1990. 115:25.

May 15, 1990. 115: 25.

June 1, 1990. 115: 57.

June 15, 1990. 115: 31.

August 1, 1990. 115: 33.

Dealing with illiteracy. *In* Pursuing happiness in the Golden State: ALA conference report. 1981. *Wilson Library Bulletin* 56 (September): 23-24.

DeCandido, Graceanne A., and Rogers, Michael. 1989. Senator Simon champions libraries for literacy. *Library Journal* 114 (15 September): 17-18.

______. 1990. White House conference on libraries: 1991 and beyond. *Library Journal* 115 (15 March): 14-15.

Devereaux, W. A. 1975. Adult literacy and the public library service. *Library Association Record* 77 (Spring): 209.

Drennan, H. T. 1981. Libraries and literacy education. *Catholic Library World* 52 (April): 376-385.

Eberhart, W. Lyle. 1976. A closer look: Gallup survey of American adults assesses the role of libraries in America. *American Libraries* 7 (April): 206-209.

Eiselstein, J., and Makricosta, P. 1986. Lifelong learning at Mary H. Weir Public Library. *West Virginia Libraries* 39 (Summer): 24-25.

Elliott, D. S. 1988. Libraries and literacy. *Show-Me Libraries* 40 (Fall): 26-29.

The Erase Illiteracy campaign. 1989. *American Libraries* 20 (September): 755.

Esperanza, M. 1986. Role of public libraries in socio-economic development. *Herald of Library Science* 25 (July-October): 189-194.

Fields, Howard. 1983. House asks $50-million for literacy work. *Publishers Weekly* 223 (15 April): 14.

______. 1984a. Four new groups aid ALA's literacy push. *Publishers Weekly* 225 (27 January): 30.

______. 1984b. Library of Congress report: Abolish illiteracy in five years. *Publishers Weekly* 226 (14 December): 11-12.

______. 1987. White House library conference to emphasize literacy services. *Publishers Weekly* 231 (24 April): 15.

Fillion, R. 1977. Editor's point of view: Illiteracy. *PNLA Quarterly* 41 (Summer): 18-19.

Fischer, D. R. 1986. Help! I can't read: One librarian's response. *Texas Library Journal* 62 (Fall): 161-163.

______. 1987. How to find literacy project information. *Texas Library Journal* 63 (Winter): 118-119.

______. 1988. Libraries and literacy: A partnership whose time is now. *Texas Libraries* 49 (Spring): 6-7.

Fleming, J. E. 1982. Adult illiteracy in the United States during the 20th century. *Public Libraries* 21 (Summer): 54-56.

Fleming, Lois D. 1983. Internal considerations in support of library adult learners' services. *Library Trends* 32 (Spring): 639-654.

Fogg, E. C. 1987-88. Establishing literacy training in Salem County. *New Jersey Libraries* 20 (Winter): 14-18.

Francois, H. L. 1984. Public libraries must combat illiteracy. *Catholic Library World* 56 (September): 85-87.

Gaughan, Karen K. 1986. Literacy projects in libraries. *Library Trends* 35 (Fall): 277-291.

Gehlen, Ann R. 1986. Libraries and employability. *Library Trends* 35 (Fall): 303-309.

Gerhardt, Lillian N. et al. 1989. Presidential focus. *In* Deja vu in Dallas: ALA's 108th annual conference. *School Library Journal* 35 (August): 39.

Gleason, M. L. 1988. Library literacy programs in Rochester—a cooperative approach. *Bookmark* 46 (Summer): 236-238.

Grant to help literacy in Queens Borough, N.Y. 1985. *Library Journal* 110 (1 March): 24.

Griggs, H. K. 1982. Should public libraries help to improve literacy in North Carolina? *North Carolina Library Journal* 40 (Fall-Winter): 259-265.

Heiser, J. C. 1988. Libraries and literacy. *The ALA Yearbook of Library and Information Services* 13: 182-186.

______. 1989. Libraries and literacy. *The ALA Yearbook of Library and Information Services* 14: 138-140.

Hemmett, P. 1987. A community college interacts with area public libraries. *Illinois Libraries* 69 (June): 405-406.

Hintner, J., and Goldberg, R. 1989. Family literacy at the High Meadows branch library. *Texas Library Journal* 65 (Summer): 52-53.

Hobbs, Lenora et al. 1988. Reading motivation: A library mission. *Book Report* 6 (January-February): 13-25.

Holten, Kathryn I. 1989. Louisiana literacy initiatives. *Chronicle, Louisiana Endowment for the Humanities* 11 (September): 1.

Humes, Barbara. 1990. Thanks for literacy column. *Library Journal* 115 (15 April): 8.

The Illinois adult literacy/volunteer initiative 1984-1986. 1987. *Illinois Libraries* 69 (June): 395-399.

Johnson, Debra W. 1986a. Evaluation of library literacy projects. *Library Trends* 35 (Fall): 311-326.

______. 1986b. Libraries and adult literacy education. *RQ* 26 (Fall): 5-7.

______. 1988. Libraries and adult literacy. *ALA Yearbook of Library and Information Services* 13: 1-7.

Johnson, Debra W., and Soule, Jennifer A. 1987. Library literacy planning guide. *Illinois Libraries* 69 (June): 409-429.

Josey, E. J. 1984. The role of trustees in helping eradicate illiteracy. *Bookmark* 43 (Fall): 41-43.

Kaula, P. M. 1983. Role of public libraries in promoting literacy. *Herald of Library Science* 22 (July-October): 226-227.

The key to literacy—unlocking library doors. 1986. *School Library Journal* 32 (January): 19-21.

Klevar, G., and Smith, M. A. 1988. Rural campaign on illiteracy: The region, the technical institutes and the libraries. *Rural Libraries* 8(1): 33-38.

LaCaff, L. 1984. The library and adult literacy: A bibliography. *Unabashed Librarian* (50): 23-24.

Lancy, David, and Hayes, Bernard. 1988. Interactive fiction and the reluctant reader. *English Journal* 77 (November): 42.

Landers, Ann. 1989. Husband ashamed of illiteracy. *The [Shreveport] Times* 119 (5 October): 3C.

Lassise, Joyce. 1982. School librarians teach reading. *School Library Journal* 29 (November): 42.

Libraries and literacy. 1983. *American Libraries* 14 (February): 74.

Libraries and literacy conference held in Washington. 1979. *Public Library Trustee* 70 (June): 7-8.

Libraries and literacy—a national overview. 1987. *Illinois Libraries* 69 (June): 400-403.

Libraries and literacy: A selected bibliography. 1988. *Texas Libraries* 49 (Spring): 10.

Libraries and literacy: A workshop. 1984. *Texas Libraries* 45 (Fall): 105.

Libraries and needs for literacy: A statement. 1975. *Library Association Record* 77 (August): 184.

Library pulling the plug on illiteracy in Flushing. 1983. *Library Journal* 108 (1 October): 1832.

Literacy grant report. 1988. *Louisiana State Library Communiqué* 4 (30 April): 2.

Literacy services in New York City. *In* ALA meets at ground-zero, New York City. 1986. *Wilson Library Bulletin* 61 (September): 31-32.

Literacy statistics. 1988. *Library Administrator's Digest* 23 (May): 35.

Literacy tutors. 1986. *Library Administrator's Digest* 21 (May): 37.

Lora, Pat. 1987. Multi-media attack on illiteracy. *Wilson Library Bulletin* 62 (December): 12-14.

______. 1989. Literacy videotapes: A selected list. *Booklist* 85 (1 March): 1206-1208.

Lyman, Helen H. Library literacy programs. *ALA Yearbook.*

1977. 198-200.

1978. 181-182.

1979. 163-167.

1980. 196-200.

1981. 182-187.

1982. 171-173.

1983. 8: 173-175.

1984. 9: 191-195.

1985. 10: 185-189.

______. 1979. Literacy education as library community service. *Library Trends* 28 (Fall): 193-217.

______. 1984. Libraries and adult literacy education in Wisconsin: 1965-1984. *Wisconsin Library Bulletin* 79 (Winter): 134-137.

Lyons, A. J. 1986. Libraries and literacy. *Show-Me Libraries* 37 (March): 7-10.

McCallan, Norma J. 1978. Organizing ABE materials in libraries. *Drexel Library Quarterly* 13 (October): 33-42.

______. 1980. What state libraries can do to eliminate illiteracy. *Catholic Library World* 52 (September): 71-74.

McClendon, P. 1989. The literacy imperative for Idaho: What libraries can do and are doing. *Idaho Libraries* 41 (April): 34-35.

Madden, D. R. 1987-88. Literacy in New Jersey. *New Jersey Libraries* 20 (Winter): 2-18.

Magill, D. 1987. A rural public library oversees a countywide project. *Illinois Libraries* 69 (June): 406-408.

Malus, S. 1987. The logical place to attain literacy. *Library Journal* 112 (July): 38-40.

Manley, Will. 1988. Facing the public. *Wilson Library Bulletin* 62 (February): 64-65.

Margaret Monsour to head literacy project. 1989. *American Libraries* 20 (December): 1134.

Marshall, P. 1982. Our role as rescue-educators in an age of basic needs information. *Library Association Record* 84 (February): 57-58.

Melton, Emily, ed. 1989. Literacy collections. *American Libraries* 20 (November): 998.

Miller, B. 1986. Literacy or "ill"-literacy. *Show-Me Libraries* 37 (March): 11-15.

Miller, B., and Smith, R. 1988. Literacy update—Springfield-Greene County Library District. *Show-Me Libraries* 40 (Fall): 30.

Monroe, Margaret E. 1986. The evolution of literacy programs in the context of library adult education. *Library Trends* 35 (Fall): 197-205.

Morris, P. 1987. The public library as a partner in a metropolitan literacy coalition. *Illinois Libraries* 69 (June): 408-409.

Morrow, A. 1987. Cole County's literacy project. *Show-Me Libraries* 38 (March-April): 29-30.

Munisi, S. E. 1976. Illiteracy: The hard choice. *Library Association Record* 78 (January): 38.

NCLIS and the U.S. Army co-sponsor literacy project. 1984. *Bulletin of the American Society for Information* 11 (October): 5-6.

NOPL literacy center. 1990. *Library Journal* 115 (15 February): 124.

Nee, P. 1987-88. Planning for a cooperative literacy project. *New Jersey Libraries* 20 (Winter): 4-6.

New check series furthers adult literacy. 1990. *For Our Customers* 4 (January): 2.

1984 ALA awards winners. 1984. *Library Journal* 109 (August): 1405.

1985 ALA awards winners. 1985. *American Libraries* 16 (September): 589.

1986 ALA awards winners. 1986. *American Libraries* 17 (September): 632.

1987 ALA awards winners. 1987. *American Libraries* 18 (September): 703.

1988 ALA awards winners. 1988. *Library Journal* 113 (August): 36.

1989 ALA awards winners. 1989. *Library Journal* 114 (August): 54.

North York library uses Apple II to develop literacy program. 1983. *Library Journal* 108 (15 April): 786.

Nunn, H. 1981. Literacy education becomes a viable part of First Regional Library. *Mississippi Librarian* 45 (Fall): 74.

Ohanian, Susan. 1989. Creating a generation of 'aliterates.' *Education Digest* 54 (February): 29.

Oliver, M. 1979. Libraries and literacy. *Publishers Weekly* 215 (16 April): 27.

O'Brien, Roberta Luther. 1983. Libraries and literacy education in the '80s. *RQ* 22 (Summer): 349-353.

Parent, R. H. 1986. Literacy and libraries. *ALA Yearbook of Library and Information Services* 11: 198-202.

______.1987. Literacy and libraries. *ALA Yearbook of Library and Information Services* 12: 195-198.

Pelzman, Frankie. 1989. Washington observer. *Wilson Library Bulletin* 63 (March): 64.

Person, R. J., and Phifer, K. O. 1985. Support for literacy education in academic libraries. *College & Research Library News* 46 (March): 147-152.

President's programs: Passionate about preservation and literacy. 1990. *American Libraries* 21 (March): 252-253.

Prete, Barbara. 1990. What new readers want to read: Possibilities for publishers. *Publishers Weekly* 237 (9 February): 40.

Project literacy. 1988. *Library Administrator's Digest* 23 (May): 35.

Quezada, S. S., and Soolman, R. 1986. Establishing and evaluating library literacy programs. *Catholic Library World* 57 (May-June): 267-270.

Quezada, Shelley. 1990. Strengthening the library network for literacy. *Wilson Library Bulletin* 64 (February): 26.

Reichel, Mary. 1989. Library literacy. *RQ* 28 (Winter): 189-196.

Role for libraries in literacy backed. 1980. *Library Journal* 105 (1 January): 12.

Romisher, S., and Farmer, M. L. 1987-88. Urban/suburban cooperation in a literacy program. *New Jersey Libraries* 20 (Winter): 3-4.

Rural persuasion. 1985. *Blair & Ketchum's Country Journal* 12 (July): 12.

San Bernardino to use literacy software. 1988. *Wilson Library Bulletin* 62 (April): 10.

S.F. library/school districts join war on illiteracy. 1976. *School Library Journal* 22 (May): 16.

Sanders, K. 1988. Literacy is our business: Arkansas Library Association's 65th annual conference. *Arkansas Libraries* 45 (December): 12-14.

Scales, A. 1986. Manual on literacy programs for public libraries. *Rural Libraries* 6(1): 41-52.

Scilken, Marvin H. 1989. Preventers of illiteracy. *Library Journal* 114 (September): 8.

Searles, F. 1979. Lifting the lid off illiteracy: What libraries can do. *Connecticut Libraries* 21 (Winter): 18-21.

Short, J. T. 1976. Facing the problem: America's millions who can't read. *Public Library Trustee* 60 (March): 8.

Smith, E. G. 1984. Literacy education gap: The involvement of public libraries in literacy education. *Library and Information Science Research* 6 (January): 75-94.

Smith, E. T. 1979. Report on the national libraries and literacy conference. *Catholic Library World* 51 (September): 86-87.

______. 1980. Advocates for literacy? The library situation. *Catholic Library World* 52 (September): 65-70.

Soloman, R. C. 1980. New illiteracy. *Show-Me Libraries* 31 (September): 27-28.

______. 1981. New illiteracy. *Texas Libraries* 43 (Spring): 26-29.

The source: Literacy. 1983. *American Libraries* 14 (December): 751.

Strong, Gary E. 1984. Public libraries and literacy: A new role to play. *Wilson Library Bulletin* 59 (November): 179-182.

Sullivan, Peggy. 1982. Reading and successful living. *School Library Journal* 28 (February): 21-27.

Symington, L. 1984. Library services to adult new readers. *New Zealand Libraries* 44 (December): 145-147.

Taskforce gears up for 2nd WHCLIS in '91. 1989. *American Libraries* 20 (October): 845.

Thresher, J., and Shields, J. 1978. Adult independent learner project of the Westchester Library System. *Bookmark* 37 (Spring): 74-79.

Two Maryland counties link for literacy drive. 1986. *Library Journal* 111 (15 November): 22.

Vaughan, E. 1986. Library involvement in literacy education programs of the N.C. communities. *North Carolina Libraries* 44 (Spring): 33-43.

Volunteer recruiting video. 1989. *American Libraries* 20 (September): 755.

Waddle, Linda. 1987. School media matters. *Wilson Library Bulletin* 61 (June): 44-45.

Weibel, M. C. 1983. Use the public library with adult literacy students. *Journal of Reading* 27 (October): 62-65.

______. 1985. The library literacy connection: Using library resources with adult basic education students. *Illinois Libraries* 67 (September): 616-644.

Weiner, P. B. 1983. On literacy and librarians. *Catholic Library World* 54 (March): 303-304.

Weingand, Darlene E. 1986a. Introduction to "Adult education, literacy, and libraries". *Library Trends* 35 (Fall): 183-186.

______. 1986b. The library-learner dynamic in a changing world. *Library Trends* 35 (Fall): 187-195.

Weiss, D. A. 1980. Reversing the illiteracy trend: Challenges of librarians and library binders. *Library Scene* 9 (September): 8.

WHCLIST annual meeting focuses on literacy. 1984. *School Library Journal* 31 (November): 12.

WHCLIST pledges to aid adult literacy initiative. 1983. *American Libraries* 14 (November): 636.

WHCLIST veterans plan White House Conference II for autumn 1990. 1988. *American Libraries* 19 (October): 750.

White House conference vets gear up for a second round. 1984. *American Libraries* 15 (October): 617-619.

Williams, L., and Meyers, G. B. 1987. Libraries and literacy: Getting started. 1987. *Ohio Library Association Bulletin* 57 (April): 20-21.

Wisconsin receives literacy grant. 1986. *Wilson Library Bulletin* 60 (May): 12.

Workshop 2: Literacy programs that work. 1978. *Public Library Trustee* 68 (September): 6.

Yates, M. W. 1978a. ALTA's crusade against illiteracy. *Public Libraries* 17 (Summer): 10.

______. 1978b. ALTA task force on literacy. *Public Library Trustee* 67 (March): 8-10.

______. 1980. America's millions who can't read. *Public Library Trustee* 72 (April): 6-7.

Young, Christina Carr. 1988. Literacy comes of age in 1987. *Bowker Annual* 33: 82-87.

Literacy Programs and Funding

American literacy crisis stirs developers; shopping centers provide classrooms for adult education programs. 1989. *Chain Store Age Executive* 65 (November): 143.

Anthony, Carolyn. 1985. Literacy programs in action. *Publishers Weekly* 227 (24 May): 39-41.

Arlington Heights continues literacy program via grant. 1988. *Library Journal* 113 (December): 30.

Arnove, Robert, and Graff, Harvey. 1987. National literacy campaigns: Historical and comparative lessons. *Phi Delta Kappan* 69 (November): 202-206.

ASNE committee begins campaign to combat illiteracy. 1987. *Editor & Publisher* 120 (31 January): 42.

Carnegie launches book program. 1986. *School Library Journal* 32 (August): 16.

Cherry, S. S. 1979. Literacy projects blossom from Florida to Colorado. *American Libraries* 10 (April): 165.

Coleman, J. E. 1985. Coalition for literacy: Mobilizing for action. *Bowker Annual* 30: 106-110.

Cullinan, Bernice E. 1989. Latching on to literature: Reading initiatives take hold. *School Library Journal* 35 (April): 27-31.

Curing the 'ill' in illiteracy: Read to succeed. 1989. *Stores* 71 (March): 71.

Dallas Public receives literacy grant from Dalton. 1984. *Wilson Library Bulletin* 59 (December): 252.

Dawkins, Wayne J. 1985. Fighting illiteracy. *Black Enterprise* 15 (July): 25.

Feinberg, Samuel. 1982. DH widens literacy, Hispanic programs. *Women's Wear Daily* 144 (23 November): 8.

Fields, Howard. 1982. Business groups to be asked for literacy funding. *Publishers Weekly* 221 (5 March): 18.

______. 1983. B. Dalton launches $3 million literacy campaign. *Publishers Weekly* 224 (30 September): 390.

______. 1984a. McGraw funds literacy council. *Publishers Weekly* 225 (3 February): 291.

______. 1984b. Reagan budget ignores literacy, libraries. *Publishers Weekly* 225 (10 February): 15.

______. 1985a. Kozol: U.S. should pay $1 billion for literacy. *Publishers Weekly* 228 (5 July): 24.

______. 1985b. The view from Washington. *Publishers Weekly* 227 (24 May): 31-34.

______. 1986. Gannett begins $2 million literacy drive. *Publishers Weekly* 230 (26 September): 19.

______. 1987. Pell and McGraw ask for more money to fight illiteracy. *Publishers Weekly* 232 (28 August): 18.

______. 1988. Senate approves funds for literacy and gifted children programs. *Publishers Weekly* 234 (12 August): 320.

______. 1989. Defensive end Manley in poignant plea for federal literacy aid. *Publishers Weekly* 235 (9 June): 10.

Fineman, Marcia Pollack. 1987. Project: LEARN—adults become readers. *Library Journal* 112 (1 March): 45-46.

Fischer, Marge. 1988. Local groups join fight for literacy. *Shreveport Journal* 94 (6 September): 1B.

______. 1989. The fight for literacy: Local groups join effort to promote ability to read. *Shreveport Journal* 95 (31 August): 1B.

Frank, Jerome P. 1984. "Help save the book" is publishers' plea to BMI. *Publishers Weekly* 225 (3 February): 380-382.

Gannett Foundation increases literacy funding. 1985. *Wilson Library Bulletin* 60 (November): 13.

Garry, Michael. 1988. Publishers fighting illiteracy: Time Inc. takes lead in battling a projected $225 billion problem. *Folio: The Magazine for Magazine Management* 17 (October): 39.

"Give the Gift of Literacy" dissolves, asks retailers to aid local efforts. 1988. *Publishers Weekly* 233 (8 April): 11.

Grimm, Matthew. 1989. Learning to read at Waldenbooks. *Adweek's Marketing Week* 30 (19 June): 17.

Hajek, Ellen. 1982. "Hey, look at me!" gets kids reading. *American Libraries* 13 (May): 334.

Kozol, Jonathan. 1980. How we can win: A plan to reach and teach 25 million illiterate adults. *Wilson Library Bulletin* 54 (June): 640-644.

Leatherneck + book = "Renaissance Warrior." 1989. *Library Journal* 114 (1 September): 128.

Lilly endowment has granted ALA $132,000 for a one-year project. 1979. *Wilson Library Bulletin* 53 (February): 424.

Literacy hotline. 1983. *American Libraries* 14 (November): 638.

Literacy programs and projects reflect diversity of effort. 1987. *Library Journal* 112 (15 November): 17.

Literacy project grants go to 26 Mid-Atlantic libraries. 1990. *American Libraries* 21 (May): 470.

Literacy workshop held. 1989. *Wilson Library Bulletin* 63 (May): 12.

Loftus, Jack. 1988. Project Literacy: Duffy's quest. *Television-Radio Age* 36 (22 August): 18.

Matthews, Anne J. et al. 1986. Meeting the literacy challenge: A federal perspective. *Library Trends* 35 (Fall): 219-241.

Miller, Holly G. 1986. Heads up for literacy: A unique educational program for teaching children and adults to read and write is getting good marks in tests around the country. *Saturday Evening Post* 258 (September): 50.

National groups form Coalition for Literacy. 1982. *Publishers Weekly* 222 (24 September): 16.

New York literacy volunteers to publish books. 1988. *Publishers Weekly* 233 (19 February): 18.

Radolf, Andrew. 1988. SNPA launches three-year literacy program. *Editor & Publisher* 121 (22 October): 39.

Reagan and LC endorse ABC/PBS literacy project. 1986. *American Libraries* 17 (February): 94.

Reynolds, Brian, and Reynolds, Wendy. 1988. The Siskiyou County READ project: A success story in rural adult literacy. *Library Journal* 113 (15 November): 43.

Ringling Brothers and RIF launch readers program. 1986. *School Library Journal* 32 (August): 16.

Rotherberg, Randall. 1989. BBDO Atlanta. *The New York Times*, national ed., 138 (16 August): C17 (N).

Rutkowski, Thaddeus. 1988. Adult literacy programs. *Adweek's Marketing Week* 29, HP26.

Schwabach, Deborah. 1980. The Gilbertsville book scuffle. *American Education* 16 (April): 17.

States fight illiteracy in prisons. 1990. *The [Shreveport] Times* 119 (25 February): 14A.

Stein, M. L. 1986. Year of the reader: *San Francisco Chronicle* undertakes ambitious project to raise literacy. *Editor & Publisher* 119 (25 October): 46.

______. 1987. Literacy projects grow: More and more newspapers are sponsoring programs. *Editor & Publisher* 120 (14 November): 28.

______. 1988. Combining literacy and computer training. *Editor & Publisher* 121 (24 December): 28.

Strong, Gary E. 1986. Adult illiteracy: State library responses. *Library Trends* 35 (Fall): 243-261.

Texas Literacy Council activates hotline. 1988. *Texas Libraries* 49 (Summer): 50.

VISTA looks at literacy; plus programs in Calif., N.C., N.J. 1988. *Library Journal* 113 (1 May): 18.

Volunteers for literacy focus of new ad campaign. 1985. *School Library Journal* 31 (February): 10.

Wagner, S. 1978. To wipe out illiteracy, publisher urges nothing less than a reassessment of national priorities. *Publishers Weekly* 214 (25 September): 47.

With Barbara Bush present, literacy event raises $215,000. 1989. *Publishers Weekly* 235 (9 June): 10.

WYFF-TV produces on-air lessons to boost area's literacy rate. 1989. *Television-Radio Age* 37 (7 August): 58.

Young, Christina Carr. 1986. Anatomy of a technology transfer: The NCLIS literacy project. *Library Trends* 35 (Fall): 263-275.

Literacy Statistics, Surveys, and Economic Impact

Barbara Bush warns of "epidemic of illiteracy." 1982. *Publishers Weekly* 222 (24 September): 16.

Bowen, Ezra. 1986. Losing the war of letters: A government study finds that one of eight Americans cannot read. *Time* 127 (5 May): 68.

Bracey, Gerald W. 1989. Learning to read and write. *Phi Delta Kappan* 70 (March): 559.

Dealing with adult illiteracy: Study commissioned by the Ford Foundation. 1979. *USA Today* 108 (December): 8-9.

Edmondson, Brad. 1987. Read before buying. *American Demographics* 9 (December): 23.

Fields, Howard. 1985. New study expands illiteracy estimates. *Publishers Weekly* 228 (30 August): 308-309.

Gintis, Herbert. 1984. The political economy of literacy training. *Unesco Courier* [37] (February): 15-16.

Hale, Robert D. 1986. Musings. *Horn Book Magazine* 62 (May-June): 352-353.

I need to see your children. 1986. *American Demographics* 8 (October): 77.

"Illiterate" car owners bypass recall warnings. 1983. *Moneysworth* 12 (Winter): 3.

Jaben, Jan. 1989. Illiteracy: Who pays when Johnny can't read? *Folio: The Magazine for Magazine Management* 18 (April): 107.

Kozol, Jonathan. 1985. A nation's wealth. *Publishers Weekly* 227 (24 May): 28-30.

Lin, Lisa. 1988. Illiteracy in America. *Seventeen* 47 (April): 98.

McGovern, George. 1980. Illiteracy in America. *USA Today* 108 (May): 24.

Micklos, John, Jr. 1982. Reading achievement in the United States. *Education Digest* 48 (November): 22.

Nelson, W. Dale. 1986. Differing figures. *In* Dateline: Washington. *Wilson Library Bulletin* 60 (February): 34.

Pett, Joel. 1988. Reading the writing on the wall. *Phi Delta Kappan* 69 (March): 468.

Piastro, Dianne B. 1988. High price of illiteracy costs more than dollars. *Shreveport Journal* 94 (6 September): 2B.

Pipho, Chris. 1988. Sorting out the data on adult literacy. *Phi Delta Kappan* 69 (May): 630-631.

Riley, Susan. 1983. Teaching illiterates to succeed. *Maclean's* 96 (19 September): 48.

Ruffin, David C. 1986. A look at tomorrow's issues today. *Black Enterprise* 16 (February): 35.

Schoultz, C. O. 1986. Reading between the lines: The high cost of ignorance. *Training & Development Journal* 40 (September): 44.

Smith, James P. 1984. Race and human capital. *American Economic Review* 74 (September): 685.

Stone, Marvin. 1983. Plague of illiteracy. *U.S. News & World Report* 94 (21 February): 90.

Study: Most illiterate U.S. adults are white. 1988. *Jet* 73 (18 January): 30.

Viedma, Christiane. 1988. A health and nutrition atlas: Food for thought. *World Health* 31 (May): 2-31.

When mom and dad can't read: Illiteracy survey. 1986. *U.S. News & World Report* 100 (5 May): 9.

International Literacy and Illiteracy

Anuar, H. 1987. Women, illiteracy and reading: The library's role. *Singapore Libraries* 17: 13-24.

Arnove, Robert F. 1981. The Nicaraguan national literacy crusade of 1980. *Phi Delta Kappan* 62 (June): 702.

Atlas of the Caribbean Basin: Literacy. 1982. *Department of State Bulletin* 82 (September): S11.

Barndt, Deborah. 1984. Nicaragua: The war comes to Managua ministries. *Canadian Dimension* 18 (May): 33.

Bethell, Tom. 1983. But can Juanito really read? *National Review* 35 (30 September): 1196-1199.

Butler, S. 1986. Fighting illiteracy: The role of library technicians. *Canadian Library Journal* 43 (December): 419-422.

Cannon, Margaret. 1980. A revolution to read, a future to spell out. *Maclean's* 93 (9 June): 60.

Cortazar, Julio. 1980. Literacy and the liberation of a people. *Unesco Courier* [33] (June): 12-13.

Daniels, Rudolph. 1987. The structure of the South African labor market, 1970-83. *Review of Black Political Economy* 15 (Spring): 63.

DeClerck, Marcel. 1984. Where there's a will ... changing societies and motivation to learn. *Unesco Courier* [37] (February): 9-11.

Dingwall, James. 1986. Debate heats up on issues. *D & B Reports* 34 (November-December): 52.

Dismuke, Diane. 1989. Illiteracy: A worldwide problem. *NEA Today* 7 (May-June): 3.

Duras, Marguerite. 1986. An illiterate in Paris. *Unesco Courier* [39] (May-June): 32.

Editorial to literacy theme issue. 1984. *Unesco Courier* [37] (February): 3.

Education. *In* Perspective section. 1985. *UN Chronicle* 22 (May): ix-x.

Equal chance for everyone: Illiteracy and the problems of youth. 1977. *Unesco Courier* 30 (March): 26-27.

Eskola, K. 1989. Literacy and the reading of books: The Nordic countries, Europe, the world. *Scandinavian Public Library Quarterly* 22(2): 3-8.

Feridun, Hussein Husnu. 1980. UNRWA and UNESCO: A thirty-year partnership. *Unesco Courier* [33]: 31-33.

Ficek, R. 1981. Literacy news. *Ontario Library Record* 65 (March): 56-58.

Fox, Geoffrey. 1983. Literacy race. *The Nation* 236 (7 May): 562.

Freire, Paulo. 1980. Letters for a young nation. *Unesco Courier* [33] (June): 27-30.

______. 1984. Word within world: A critical reading of the universe. *Unesco Courier* [37] (February): 29-31.

Galenson, D. W. 1981. Literacy and age in preindustrial England. *Economic Development & Culture* 29 (July): 813.

Gillette, Arthur, and Ryan, John. 1986. Literacy and well-being. *World Health* 29 (March): 6.

Hamadache, Ali. 1984. Illiteracy in the "fourth world." *Unesco Courier* [37] (February): 22-25.

Hendrikse, Dick. 1986. Illiteracy: Threat to European magazines? *Folio: The Magazine for Magazine Management* 15 (September): 169.

Husen, Torsten. 1983. Milestones to the learning society. *Unesco Courier* [36] (May): 13-14.

Infant mortality in Third World is linked to literacy. 1986. *World Health* 29 (January-February): 30.

International literacy day celebrated at LC. 1982. *Library of Congress Information Bulletin* 41 (24 September): 297-298.

International literacy day is celebrated at Library. 1989. *Library of Congress Information Bulletin* 48 (30 October): 382.

International Literacy Year. 1988. *IFLA Journal* 14(4): 384-385.

International Literacy Year. 1989. *Bookbird* 27 (May): 22-23.

Jabir, Rafique. 1988. Illiteracy: Pakistan's Achille's heel. *Economic Review* 19 (October): 7.

Jelloun, Tahar Ben. 1986. Writer between two worlds. *Unesco Courier* [39] (May-June): 59.

Kearns, L. J. 1989. Librarians and literacy programs: Get educated before getting involved. *Canadian Library Journal* 46 (June): 141-142.

Khoi, Le Thanh. 1983. Stemming the tide of illiteracy. *Unesco Courier* [36] (May): 9-12.

Kibirige, H. M. 1977. Libraries and illiteracy in developing countries: A critical assessment. *Libri* 27 (March): 54-67.

Kleinbach, Russell. 1985. Nicaraguan literacy campaign: Its democratic essence. *Monthly Review* 37 (July-August): 75.

Kozol, Jonathan. 1978. New look at the Cuban literacy campaign. *Education Digest* 44 (December): 29-33.

Literacy awards for 1983. 1984. *Unesco Courier* [37] (February): 34.

Literacy news. 1979. *Ontario Library Record* 63 (June): 165-166.

Literacy news. 1980. *Ontario Library Record* 64 (June): 130-133.

Literacy programmes and the public library service in Jamaica. 1981. *Unesco Journal of Information Science* 3 (October): 235-240.

Literacy: A right denied to 800 million. 1980. *Unesco Courier* [33] (June): 4-9.

Liu, G. 1979. Literacy news. *Ontario Library Record* 63 (September): 214-218.

McKenzie, D. F. 1984. The sociology of a text: Orality, literacy and print in early New Zealand. *The Library* (6th Series) 6 (December): 333-365.

Makletzoff, A. 1978. Literacy in Ontario. *Ontario Library Record* 62 (June): 119-123.

Malya, S. 1977. After literacy, what next? Tanzanian folk tales in readers. *Unesco Courier* 30 (February): 23-27.

Mirsky, Jonathan. 1983. 235,820,002 cannot read. *New Statesman* 105 (15 April): 16.

M'Bow, Amadou-Mahtar. 1980. Nicaragua's nation-wide literacy campaign. *Unesco Courier* [33] (June): 10-11.

______. 1984. A moral imperative. *Unesco Courier* [37] (February): 4-5.

The national literacy crusade. 1981. *New Catholic World* 224 (September-October): 212.

Nine award-winning campaigns. 1980. *Unesco Courier* [33] (June): 14-17.

The 1983 literacy awards. 1984. *Unesco Courier* [37] (February): 34.

Orpwood, Jean. 1988. Literacy should be a priority. *Canadian Library Journal* 45 (April): 69.

Ouane, Adama. 1984. What next? A world panorama of back-up materials for new literates. *Unesco Courier* [37] (February): 12-14.

Peck, S. D. 1986. Functional literacy in developing countries. *Leads* 28 (Fall): 1-2.

Perissinotto, Giorgio. 1983. Educational reform in Mexico. *Current History* 82 (December): 425.

Perspective: 1983 state of the world's children: Report from UNICEF. 1983. *UN Chronicle* 20 (February): 57.

Petersen, J. 1989. The International Literacy Year and public libraries. *Scandinavian Library Quarterly* 22(2): 9-12.

Psacharopoulos, G., and Arriagada, A. 1989. Determinants of early age human capital formation. *Economic Development & Culture* 37 (July): 683.

Ramzi, Sonia Abadir. 1984. Children in nomansland: The dilemma of second-generation immigrants. *Unesco Courier* [37] (February): 26-28.

Reports from around the world: Alfa '84. 1984. *Unesco Courier* [37] (February): 17-21.

Richards, M. 1978. Britain tackles illiteracy. *Change* 10 (September): 16-19.

Richardson, J. 1983. Libraries and the neoliterate. *International Library Review* 15 (January): 9-13.

______. 1983. The public library and the neoliterate in India: A literature survey. *Herald of Library Science* 22 (July-October): 163-173.

Ryan, John W. 1980. Secrets of the written code: Mother tongues and access to literacy. *Unesco Courier* [33] (June): 22-23.

Sancton, Thomas A. 1980. The land of the smoking gun. *Time* 116 (18 August): 34-35.

Schreiner, Samuel A., Jr. 1980. Going strong at 101. *Reader's Digest* 117 (December): 139.

Shepherd, P. 1984. Literacy and numeracy and their implications for survey research—Evidence from the National Child Development Study. *Journal of the Market Research Society* 26 (April): 147.

Steacy, Anne. 1988. The high cost of not reading. *Maclean's* 101 (29 February): 44-45.

Straiger, Ralph C. 1980. The reading habit. *Unesco Courier* [33] (June): 34.

Taylor, Greg W. 1987. Adults who can't read: The enormous cost affects us all. *Reader's Digest* (Canadian ed.) 130 (March): 111.

The 3 "R's"—An open book. 1980. *Unesco Courier* [33] (June): 24-25.

Thomas, A. M. 1978. Adult illiteracy: A concern for librarians? *Ontario Library Record* 62 (June): 159-161.

Tilley, C. M. 1984. Australian public libraries, the Library Association of Australia and literacy. *International Library Review* 16 (April): 143-156.

Tsang, K. C. 1985. China's classroom revolution. *World Press Review* 32 (September): 54.

U.N. begins literacy year with celebration. 1989. *The New York Times*, national ed. 138 (9 September): 2.

UN names 1990 "International Literacy Year." 1989. *Stores* 71 (March): 68.

Unesco and the struggle against illiteracy. 1984. *Unesco Courier* [37] (February): 32-33.

Unwritten wisdom. 1980. *Unesco Courier* [33] (June): 18-21.

U.S. international literacy day observance held September 8. 1983. *Library of Congress Information Bulletin* 42 (10 October): 349.

Wagner, Lloyd A. 1989. Education in revolutionary Nicaragua. *Canadian Dimension* 23 (April-May): 25.

Walberg, Herbert J. 1983. Scientific literacy and economic productivity in international perspective. *Daedalus* 112 (Spring): 1.

Wallace, B., and Moore, C. 1979. Literacy news. *Ontario Library Record* 63 (December): 336-337.

War on illiteracy wins applause for Ethiopia. 1981. *Jet* 59 (8 January): 14.

Women around the world. 1987. *Scholastic Update* 119 (18 May): 26.

Wood, Richard H., Jr. 1988. Literacy and basic needs satisfaction in Mexico. World Development 16 (March): 405.

World in focus. 1984. *Scholastic Update* 117 (19 October): 15.

Wright, Tennant C. 1981. Education as an act of love. *National Catholic Reporter* 17 (14 August): 9.

Youssef, C. 1979. Literacy update. *Ontario Library Record* 63 (March): 49-51.

Literacy at City, State, and Federal Levels

Adult literacy programs: Services, persons served, and volunteers. 1987. *Bowker Annual* 32: 396-410.

Alabama fights illiteracy. 1981. *American Libraries* 12 (January): 46.

Alabama literacy project. 1980. *American Libraries* 11 (April): 239.

Alabama undertakes crusade against illiteracy. 1981. *Wilson Library Bulletin* 55 (January): 332.

Baltimore Mayor Schmoke cites city's read-a-thon. 1989. *Jet* 76 (28 August): 23.

Barreto, Julio. 1989. Urban literacy problem demands cooperative efforts. *Nation's Cities Weekly* 12 (13 February): 2.

Bolick, Nancy O'Keefe. 1987. The shame: One in 10 Bostonians cannot read this. *Boston Magazine* 79 (November): 212.

California awards $2.5 million to combat illiteracy. 1984. *Wilson Library Bulletin* 58 (February): 393.

California budget approves $2.6 million for literacy. 1984. *American Libraries* 15 (July): 476.

California Department of Education launches major reading effort. 1986. *Publishers Weekly* 229 (27 June): 44.

California funds state literacy program. 1984. *Wilson Library Bulletin* 59 (November): 167-168.

Castelli, Jim. 1989. How to close tomorrow's literacy gap. *Safety & Health* 140 (December): 54.

Colorado sounds alarm on adult illiteracy. 1985. *Library Journal* 110 (1 April): 25.

Computer tie-in makes program in Lincoln City, Nebraska, a success. 1983. *Library Journal* 108 (1 January): 12.

DiPrete, Edward D. 1989. Government must enlist business in the fight against illiteracy. *Governing* 2 (April): 74.

Fields, Howard. 1980. Eleven groups urge coordinated federal literacy action. *Publishers Weekly* 217 (14 March): 16.

______. 1985. Congress debates role in fighting illiteracy. *Publishers Weekly* 228 (18 October): 20.

______. 1987. House votes 401-1 to extend education programs through 1989. *Publishers Weekly* 231 (19 June): 26.

______. 1989. Capitol Hill heeds illiteracy. *Publishers Weekly* 235 (3 March): 30.

______. 1989. Senators sponsor major 'assault' on illiteracy, increase funding. *Publishers Weekly* 236 (28 July): 128.

Fischer, Marge. 1990. State literacy official outlines agency's policies. *Shreveport Journal* 96 (16 February): 7A.

$4 million for Illinois for adult literacy programs. 1987. *Library Journal* 112 (1 November): 20.

Freeland, Sherry. 1983. Literacy. *Education Digest* 49 (November): 60.

Hirsch, E. D., Jr. 1988. A postscript. *Change* 20 (July-August): 22.

Holt, Patricia. 1978. Knowlton proposes tax incentive for corporations that teach literacy. *Publishers Weekly* 214 (20 November): 19.

House approves funding for American reading council's inner-city literacy. 1978. *Publishers Weekly* 213 (17 April): 26.

House approves library funding with emphasis on literacy. 1989. *Publishers Weekly* 236 (6 October): 12.

Illinois Funds library literacy programs. 1985. *Wilson Library Bulletin* 59 (June): 651.

Kentucky forms literacy commission. 1985. *Wilson Library Bulletin* 59 (April): 521-522.

Literacy gets big boosts in California and Texas. 1985. *Library Journal* 110 (1 March): 24.

Mahoney, John. 1986. People plenary hears of need to fight illiteracy. *Nation's Cities Weekly* 9 (15 December): 8.

Mallows, Mike, and Wells, David. 1986. Notes from the new white ghetto. *Philadelphia Magazine* 77 (December): 165.

The Mayor's Commission on Literacy in Philadelphia. 1985. *Wilson Library Bulletin* 59 (April): 521.

Nelson, W. Dale. 1983. Federal approach to literacy problem. *Wilson Library Bulletin* 57 (January): 408-409.

______. 1987. OMB halts literacy survey. *In* Dateline Washington. *Wilson Library Bulletin* 61 (February): 29.

Nickelsburg, M. 1987. Literacy in Iowa. *Iowa Library Quarterly* 24 (Spring): 34-51.

Nussbaum, Bruce. 1988. Needed: Human capital. *Business Week* 3070 (19 September): 100-103.

Pelzman, Frankie. 1989. Simon says. *Wilson Library Bulletin* 64 (October): 14-16.

______. 1990. Literacy's voice in the Senate: Speaking with Senator Paul Simon. *Wilson Library Bulletin* 64 (February): 24-25.

Prete, Barbara. 1989. Baltimore, the city that reads. *Publishers Weekly* 236 (4 August): 71-72.

Reading initiative program focuses on literacy in Arizona. 1988. *School Library Journal* 34 (March): 90.

Reading program lauded: Governor proposes Writing to Read for all schools. 1990. *The [Shreveport] Times* 119 (23 April): 2A.

Reagan kicks off literacy program. 1983. *Publishers Weekly* 224 (23 September): 18.

Reagan spotlights literacy: Hearing aid grabs headlines. 1983. *American Libraries* 14 (October): 578.

Remedial programs will help inner-city youth. 1981. *Jet* 60 (6 August): 15.

Rudd, Amanda. 1984. What to do when 20 percent can't read. *Chicago* 33 (January): 164.

San Antonio approves $46.5 million bond issue. 1989. *Wilson Library Bulletin* 64 (September): 19.

Senate passes literacy bill. 1990. *American Libraries* 21 (April): 281.

Silvey, Anita. 1986. California Reading Initiative. *The Horn Book Magazine* 62 (September-October): 549.

State of California institutes reading initiative program. 1986. *School Library Journal* 32 (August): 9.

Stingley, Alisa. 1990. New literacy office to call for financing. *The [Shreveport] Times* 119 (25 February): 14A.

U.S. agency to coordinate attack on illiteracy. 1982. *Publishers Weekly* 222 (22 October): 14.

Literacy in the Workplace: Business, Industry, and Employment

Anderson, Alden M. 1988. Illiteracy is the business of business. *American Banker* 153 (15 April): 4.

Baxter, Milton B. et al. 1982. Reading: A vocational skill. *The Clearing House* 56 (November): 115.

Bernardon, Nancy L. 1989. Let's erase illiteracy from the workplace. *Personnel* 66 (January): 29-32.

Berney, Karen. 1988. Can your workers read? *Nation's Business* 76 (October): 26-28.

Booke, Ellis. 1990. Company school days. *Computerworld* 24 (15 January): 77.

Business fights illiteracy. 1988. *The Futurist* 22 (May-June): 50.

Carter, Robert A. 1985. Mobilizing business for literacy. *Publishers Weekly* 227 (24 May): 35-38.

Catterton, Mike. 1989. Literacy remains important workplace issue: Meeting topic. *IAPES News* 49 (December): 21.

Child, Charles. 1989. Biz grapples with undereducated. *Crain's Detroit Business* 5 (27 February): 1.

Christiansen, Laurence A., Jr. 1989. Can we read and write? *Textile World* 139 (June): 15.

Ehrlich, Elizabeth. 1988. Business is becoming a substitute teacher. *Business Week* 3070 (19 September): 134-135.

Eubanks, Paula. 1990. Literacy crisis threatens hospital workforce. *Hospitals* 64 (20 January): 50.

Feldman, Diane. 1989. Companies buzz about corporate spelling bee. *Management Review* 78 (August): 7.

Feuer, Dale. 1987. Skill gap: America's crisis of competence. *Training: The Magazine of Human Resources* 24 (December): 27.

Finkel, James I. 1985. Low-level jobs for machine operators will soon vanish. *School Product News* 24 (June): 14.

Foegen, J. H. 1984. Let's develop Employee Assistance Programs to teach reading and writing. *Personnel Journal* 63 (March): 83.

Functional illiteracy: It's your problem, too. 1989. *Supervisory Management* 34 (June): 22.

Fusco, Mary Ann Castronovo. 1989. Employment relations programs: At Polaroid, the Technology Readiness program provides the company with skilled, literate workers while providing workers with the means for advancement. *Employment Relations Today* 16 (Spring): 89.

Goddard, Robert W. 1987. The crisis in workplace literacy. *Personnel Journal* 66 (December): 73.

______. 1989. Combating illiteracy in the workplace. *Management World* 18 (March-April): 8.

Gorman, Christine. 1988. The literacy gap. *Time* 132 (19 December): 56-57.

Greenberg, Eric Rolfe. 1989. Corporate testing for the three "Rs." *Management Review* 78 (April): 56.

Haseltine, Robert W. 1988. High-tech illiteracy. *USA Today* 116 (May): 29.

Horton, Thomas R. 1988. A national crisis: Illiteracy in the workplace. *Business Credit* 90 (March): 14.

How business is joining the fight against functional illiteracy. *Business Week* 2838 (16 April): 94.

Jakubovics, Jerry. 1986. Coping with illiteracy in the workplace. *Management Solutions* 31 (November): 5.

Jurmo, Paul et al. 1989. How can businesses fight workplace illiteracy? *Training & Development Journal* 43 (January): 18.

Koehn, Hank E. 1983. Remedial education—on company. *American Banker* 148 (20 January): 4.

Lahey, James W. 1988. Tomorrow's workplace. *Safety & Health* 137 (June): 46.

______. 1988. Will today's workers work tomorrow? *Safety & Health* 138 (October): 70.

Lee, Chris. 1986. Literacy training: A hidden need. *Training: The Magazine of Human Resources* 23 (September): 64.

______. 1988. Basic training in the corporate schoolhouse. *Training: The Magazine of Human Resources* 25 (April): 27.

Lutz, Raymond P. 1986. For lack of an education. *Industrial Management* 28 (September-October): 1.

McGowan, William. 1983. Corporations aim to wipe out illiteracy. *Business & Society Review* (Winter): 37-40.

McGraw, Harold W., Jr. 1987. Adult functional illiteracy: What to do about it. *Personnel* 64 (October): 38-42.

McKenna, Joseph F. 1990. A little learning is a dangerous thing. *Industry Week* 239 (8 January): 74.

McLaughlin, Mark. 1987. If you can read this, you've got a jump on many workers. *New England Business* 9 (2 February): 21.

Miller, Annetta. 1988. Spelling bees for business: Battling the memo crisis. *Newsweek* 112 (4 July): 29.

Nelson, W. Dale. 1985. Illiteracy in the workplace. *In* Dateline: Washington. *Wilson Library Bulletin* 60 (October): 39.

O'Toole, Patricia. 1985. I can't read: The illiteracy epidemic. *Glamour* 83 (September): 368.

Newman, Melinda. 1985. 6 Flags supporting education with "Read to Succeed" program. *Amusement Business* 97 (16 November): 17.

Park, R. J. 1984. Overcoming the illiteracy barrier. *Training & Development Journal* 38 (March): 76.

Pascarella, Perry. 1987. Skills gap threatens our competitiveness. *Industry Week* 235 (19 October): 7.

Plawin, Paul, and Kainen, Bertha. 1988. Educating our work force. *Changing Times* 42 (April): 107.

Polychron, John P. 1989. Many workers can't read these words. *Business Month* 133 (January): 71.

Prete, Barbara. 1989. Business defines its role. *Publishers Weekly* 235 (26 May): 20.

______. 1989. What companies can do. *Publishers Weekly* 236 (27 October): 47.

Ritts, Morton. 1986. What if Johnny still can't read? *Canadian Business* 59 (May): 54.

Ross, Irwin. 1986. Corporations take aim at illiteracy. *Fortune* 114 (29 September): 48-50.

Sarmiento, Anthony R. 1989. Workplace literacy and workplace politics. *Work-America* 6 (September): 1-2.

Shaw, Gary, and Weber, Jack. 1989. The basic business vocabulary. *Across the Board* 26 (December): 15.

Torrence, David, and Torrence, Jo A. 1987. Training in the face of illiteracy. *Training & Development Journal* 41 (August): 44.

Walter, Albert. 1989. Illiteracy in the workplace. *Communication World* 6 (June): 18.

Wantuck, Mary-Margaret. 1984. Can your employees read this? *Nation's Business* 72 (June): 34.

Weinstein, Jeff. 1988. Literacy problems threaten revenues: Domino's Pizza steps to the forefront of work-place literacy training. *Restaurants & Institutions* 98 (2 September): 23.

Zemke, Ron. 1989. Workplace illiteracy: Shall we overcome? *Training: The Magazine of Human Resources* 26 (June): 33.

Literacy in Society and Culture

Adams, Katherine H., and Cotton, William T. 1989. The questions of cultural literacy. *The Clearing House* 62 (March): 285.

Ahead: A nation of illiterates? 1982. *U.S. News & World Report* 92 (17 May): 53.

Alexander, Benjamin H. 1982. Reading—the key to preserving our liberty: No room for compromise. *Vital Speeches* 48 (1 September): 699.

Arons, A. B. 1983. Achieving wider scientific literacy. *Daedalus* 112 (Spring): 91.

Arzoumanian, Mark. 1988. Keeping a big secret. *Paperboard Packaging* 73 (November): 4.

Asimov, Isaac. 1980. A cult of ignorance. *Newsweek* 95 (21 January): 19.

Bell, Terrel H. 1984. Illiteracy: Our national shame. *American Legion Magazine* 117 (December): 20.

Bernick, Michael. 1986. Illiteracy and inner-city unemployment. *Phi Delta Kappan* 67 (January): 364.

Booth, Wayne C. 1988. Cultural literacy and liberal learning. *Change* 20 (July-August): 10.

Brandt, Anthony. 1980. Do we care if Johnny can read? *American Heritage* 31 (August-September): 4-13.

Calloway, D. Wayne. 1987. The Noah principle and the public sector: We all must get involved. *Vital Speeches* 53 (1 April): 357.

Chall, Jeanne, and Snow, Catherine. 1988. Influences on reading in low-income students. *Education Digest* 54 (September): 53.

Christenbury, Leila. 1989. Cultural literacy: A terrible idea whose time has come. *English Journal* 78 (January): 14.

Cramer, Jerome. 1987. If you can read this, says E. D. Hirsch, you may still be illiterate. *People Weekly* 28 (10 August): 69.

Dykeman, John B. 1988. Read it and weep. *Modern Office Technology* 33 (February): 14.

D'Aniello, Charles A. 1989. Cultural literacy and reference service. *RQ* 28 (Spring): 370.

Edwards, Audrey T. 1984. Cultural literacy: What are our goals? *English Journal* 73 (April): 71.

Everyday reading. 1981. *Instructor* 90 (May): 44.

Fields, Howard. 1982. "A-literacy," Hoopes warns perils democratic system. *Publishers Weekly* 222 (1 October): 34.

Fight on illiteracy is urged. 1989. *The New York Times*, national ed. 138 (25 April): C18.

Flesch, Rudolf. 1986. Why millions can't read. *American Legion Magazine* 124 (October): 26.

Friedland, C. 1979. Common enemy: Illiteracy. *Publishers Weekly* 215 (26 February): 107.

Gates, David. 1987. A dunce cap for America: What we don't know, why we don't know it. *Newsweek* 109 (20 April): 72.

Gersh, Debra. 1988. Illiteracy as a poverty issue: Reporter calls for more comprehensive approach to covering the story. *Editor & Publisher* 121 (18 June): 20.

Guerra, Marcos. 1984. The cultural roots of literacy. *Unesco Courier* [37] (February): 6-8.

Harman, David. 1986. Functional illiteracy: Keeping up in America. *Current* 285 (September): 4-9.

Hirsch, E. D., Jr. 1983. Cultural literacy. *American Scholar* 52 (Spring): 159.

______. 1985. "Cultural literacy" doesn't mean "core curriculum." *English Journal* 74 (October): 47.

______. 1988. Cultural literacy: Let's get specific. *NEA Today* 6 (January): 15-21.

Hirsch, E. D., Jr. et al. 1987. English prof calls for "cultural literacy." *NEA Today* 6 (September): 21.

Jacobs, Harvey C. 1985. Readers: An endangered species? A shamefully illiterate society. *Vital Speeches* 51 (1 May): 446.

Johnson, Curtis. 1988. Closed minds and cultural illiteracy: Higher education in democratic society. *National Forum: Phi Kappa Phi Journal* 68 (Spring): 42.

Kerewsky, Shoshana D. 1989. Playing with "Cultural Literacy." *English Journal* 78 (January): 18.

Kozol, Jonathan. 1985. The crippling inheritance. *The New York Times Book Review* 90 (3 March): 1.

______. 1987. On a one-way street. *Christian Herald* 110 (May): 24.

Lee, Barbara, and Rudman, Masha K. 1982. No-frills reading. *Parents Magazine* 57 (May): 134.

Lipson, D. Herbert. 1986. Off the cuff. *Philadelphia Magazine* 77 (November): 1.

Luckert, Laura. 1986. Illiteracy. *Women in Business* 38 (November-December): 12.

Lyles, Gray. 1988. The twin benefits of leaping into literature. *Bottomline* 5 (May): 87.

Mallardi, Vincent. 1988. A cause for concern: Literacy and the printing industry. *American Printer* 200 (March): 42.

McCabe, Stephen. 1986. Problems and solutions. *Humanist* 46 (May-June): 34.

McCarthy, Abigail. 1983. Can we rescue language? Hopefully, we can optimize things clarity-wise. *Commonweal* 110 (28 January): 37.

McLuhan, Marshall. 1986. The yestermorrow of the book. *Unesco Courier* [39] (May-June): 50.

Mooser, Etta. 1988. What they do know. *The Nation* 246 (9 January): 27.

Nelson, W. Dale. 1979. Street-wise, jail-foolish. *Wilson Library Bulletin* 54 (September): 47.

No arts, no letters—no society: Mental bankruptcy. 1980. *Vital Speeches* 46 (1 July): 562.

Oakar, M. R. 1987. Literacy and intellectual freedom. *Ohio Library Association Bulletin* 57 (October): 6-8.

Reed, Sally. 1987. What is cultural literacy? And why is everyone talking about it? *Instructor* 97 (Winter): 18.

Safran, Claire. 1986. Illiteracy: Read all about it. *Woman's Day* 49 (1 October): 86-87.

Sanoff, Alvin P. et al. 1987. What Americans should know. *U.S. News & World Report* 103 (28 September): 86-88.

Schulman, Candy. 1987. 60 million people can't read what you write: Illiteracy in America is growing alarmingly, and it hurts you. *Writer's Digest* 67 (April): 80.

Schuster, Edgar. 1989. In pursuit of cultural literacy. *Phi Delta Kappan* 70 (March): 539.

Smith, Liz. 1989. America's need to read. *Harper's Bazaar* 122 (January): 70.

Stein, Ben. 1990. Human capital: A chilling fable for America. *Business Month* 135 (January): 10-11.

Thimmesch, N., ed. 1984. *Aliteracy: People who can read but won't. AEIPPR* Conference Proceedings.

Towns, Edolphus. 1990. Adult illiteracy is as dangerous to the U.S. as substance abuse. *The New York Times* 139 (16 February): A16 (N).

Tunley, Roul. 1985. America's secret shame: One out of five adults—in the richest country on earth—cannot read or write. *Reader's Digest* 127 (September): 104.

Tuttleton, James W. 1987. Literacy at the barricades. *Commentary* 84 (July): 45.

Wagschal, Peter H. 1981. Electronics and the deschooled society. *The Clearing House* 54 (February): 245.

Literacy in Education, Schools, and Reading Instruction

Allington, Richard, and Shake, Mary. 1986. Achieving curricular congruence in remedial reading. *Education Digest* 52 (September): 54.

Andersen, Dennis, and Simons, Sandra. 1988. The seven secrets of success. *Instructor* 98 Pt. 2 (October): 15.

Applebee, Arthur N. et al. 1987. Learning to be literate: Reading, writing, reasoning. *Education Digest* 53 (December): 6.

Bang-Jenson, Valerie. 1983. Are kids who like DIRT (Daily Individual Reading Time) weird? *Instructor* 113 (September): 69.

Becoming a nation of readers: A commission's recommendations. 1985. *Education Digest* 51 (October): 12.

Bell, Terrel H. 1984a. Suggested priorities and goals for American education. *American Education* 20 (March): 30-32.

______. 1984b. Toward a learning society. *American Education* 20 (April): 2-3.

Berglund, Patricia. 1985. School library technology. *Wilson Library Bulletin* 59 (May): 606-607.

Berliner, David. 1989. Increasing scientific literacy means teaching it. *Instructor* 98 Pt. 1 (January): 14-15.

Blumenfeld, Samuel L. 1983a. The failure of whole-world reading instruction. *Education Digest* 48 (March): 36.

______. 1983b. The victims of "Dick and Jane." *American Education* 19 (January): 13-21.

______. 1984. Can phonics solve the literacy crisis? *American Legion Magazine* 116 (March): 20.

Botstein, Leon. 1983. Nine proposals to improve our schools. *The New York Times Magazine* 132 (5 June): 58.

Botstein, Leon et al. 1983. Why Jonathan can't read. *New Republic* 189 (7 November): 20.

Buckley, William F., Jr. 1987. The high-schooler's informational IQ test. *National Review* 39 (17 July): 57.

Byfield, Ted. 1987. How our schools are failing us. *Reader's Digest* (Canadian ed.) 131 (September): 163.

Carbo, Marie. 1987. Deprogramming reading failure: Giving unequal learners an equal chance. *Phi Delta Kappan* 69 (November): 197.

Carroll, John. 1987. National assessments in reading: Are we misreading the findings? *Phi Delta Kappan* 68 (February): 424.

Cassanova, Ursula. 1989. Increasing scientific literacy means teaching it. *Instructor* 98 Pt. 2 (January): 14-15.

Chall, Jeanne S. 1984. Literacy: Trends and explanations. *American Education* 20 (November): 16-22.

Cibrowski, Lee. 1980. Coping with student illiteracy. *Forecast for Home Economics* 26 (November): 29.

Cole, Tim. 1989. Science education: The bright spots. *Popular Mechanics* 166 (February): 22.

Coons, John E. 1981. Shanker vouchers—is the genie out? *Phi Delta Kappan* 63 (December): 255.

Criscuolo, Nicholas P. 1980. More miracle motivation for reluctant readers. *Instructor* 89 (March): 73.

DeBakey, Lois. 1987. Our national priority: Education or entertainment? *Vital Speeches* 53 (1 June): 496.

Dionisio, Marie. 1989. Filling empty pockets: Remedial readers make meaning. *English Journal* 78 (January): 33.

Dismuke, Diane. 1989. NEA joins national literacy drive. *NEA Today* 7 (May-June): 3.

Dunning, S. 1976. Wanted: A handful of rebels. Teachers committed to literacy programs. *Education Digest* 42 (December): 12-15.

Education department names officer to combat illiteracy. 1980. *Publishers Weekly* 217 (18 April): 24.

Ehrlich, Elizabeth. 1988. America's schools still aren't making the grade. *Business Week* 3070 (19 September): 129.

Eurich, Alvin C. 1980. Student readers: The 50 year difference. *Change* 12 (April): 13.

Feinberg, Walter. 1989. Educational misconceptions of a democratic republic. *Education Digest* 55 (October): 7.

Feldman, Ruth Duskin. 1984. How well are our schools teaching Johnny and Judy to read? *Better Homes and Gardens* 62 (September): 21.

Fields, Howard. 1986a. Education Department finds fewer illiterates. *Publishers Weekly* 229 (23 May): 30.

______. 1986b. Education Secretary disputes Kozol book. *Publishers Weekly* 229 (10 January): 22.

______. 1987. Warren Burger calls for literacy corps. *Publishers Weekly* 231 (8 May): 13.

______. 1988. Bennett calls for high reading goals in elementary schools. *Publishers Weekly* 234 (16 September): 11.

51% of New York pupils read below grade level. 1989. *The New York Times* 138 (30 June): A16.

Fiske, Edward B. 1989. The misleading concept of "average" on reading tests changes. *The New York Times* 148 (12 July): B7.

Fleder, R. 1978. What's the opposite of education? *New Times* 10 (3 April): 4.

Forbes, Roy H. 1985. Academic achievement of historically lower-achieving students during the seventies. *Phi Delta Kappan* 66 (April): 542.

Ford, Michael, and Ohlhausen, M. 1989. Helping disabled readers in the regular classroom. *Education Digest* 54 (January): 48.

Foster, H. E. 1976. Undermining literacy in schools and libraries: The educational media. *Vital Speeches* 42 (15 June): 542-544.

France, Marycarolyn, and Meeks, J. 1988. Parents who can't read: What schools can do. *Education Digest* 53 (April): 46-49.

Futrell, Mary Hatwood. 1989. Promises to keep. *NEA Today* 7 (May-June): 2.

Geller, Conrad. 1989. Classics in the remedial classroom. *English Journal* 78 (April): 25.

Gorin, A. A. 1986. The importance of visual literacy. *LLA Bulletin* 49 (Summer): 7.

Gough, Pauline B. 1989. Literacy: Use it or lose it. *Phi Delta Kappan* 70 (January): 346.

Graham, Patricia Albjerg. 1981. Literacy: A goal for secondary schools. *Daedalus* 110 (Summer): 119.

Graham, Richard T. 1987. Content reading and the recreation of meaning. *English Journal* 76 (February): 98.

Gray, Mary Jane. 1988. The reader in transition. *The Clearing House* 61 (January): 217.

Greene, Brenda M. 1988. Cross-cultural approach to literature: The immigrant experience. *English Journal* 77 (September): 45.

Greene, Maxine. 1982. Literacy for what? *Education Digest* 47 (May): 2.

______. 1985. Excellence and the basics: Making excellence a significant value. *Education Digest* 51 (September): 9.

Heath, Shirley Brice. 1987. Where is the crisis in American literacy? *Education Digest* 52 (February): 18.

Heins, Ethel L. 1980. From reading to literacy. *Today's Education* 69 (April-May): 41.

Henneberg, Susan. 1986. What do you mean, you can't read? *English Journal* 75 (January): 53.

Herber, Harold, and Nelson-Herber, J. 1987. Helping students become independent learners. *Education Digest* 53 (December): 12.

Hittleman, Daniel R. 1986. Teaching children to "read" textbook illustrations: Both learning-disabled and other students benefit. *Education Digest* 51 (April): 48.

Hoetker, James. 1989. Re-Hirsching some questions about curriculum. *The Clearing House* 62 (March): 319.

Huenergard, Celeste. 1983. Speakers urge educators to fight illiteracy. *Editor & Publisher* 116 (23 April): 68.

Improving literacy level is crucial: NAEP. 1987. *Phi Delta Kappan* 68 (May): 711.

IRA director comments on YA literacy report. 1986. *School Library Journal* 33 (December): 12.

Jenkins, Anne. 1987. Literature and reading too: The English teacher does both. *The Clearing House* 60 (April): 344.

Johnny reads better but still can't write. 1990. *Shreveport Journal* 96 (9 January): 1A.

Jones, Mary Louise. 1983. Providing reading success for academically disadvantaged secondary students. *The Clearing House* 57 (December): 167.

Kerby, Mona. 1986. Assessing student attitudes toward reading. *School Library Journal* 33 (December): 43.

Klein, Karen. 1984. Minimum competency testing: Shaping and reflecting curricula. *Phi Delta Kappan* 65 (April): 565.

KOCO-TV lines up "partners" to lend a helping hand to education. 1989. *Television-Radio Age* 37 (7 August): 57.

Kozol, Jonathan. 1985. Dehumanizing the humanities: Scholars and adult illiteracy. *Education Digest* 51 (December): 6.

LaPointe, Archie. 1986. The state of instruction in reading and writing in U.S. elementary schools. *Phi Delta Kappan* 68 (October): 135.

Lazerson, Marvin et al. 1984. Learning and citizenship: Aspirations for American education. *Daedalus* 113 (Fall): 59.

Lee, Valerie. 1987. Minorities in Catholic schools: Why do they read better? *Education Digest* 52 (February): 20.

Lerner, Barbara. 1981. Vouchers for literacy: Second chance legislation. *Phi Delta Kappan* 63 (December): 252-255.

Lipson, Eden Ross. 1989. Reading along with Barbara Bush: The endings are mostly happy. *The New York Times Book Review* 94 (21 May): 36.

Lutjeharms, Joseph E. 1987. Writing in Nebraska. *Journal of State Government* 60 (March-April): 76.

Marano, Rocco J. 1982. Educational disenfranchisement in a technological age. *Vital Speeches* 48 (15 January): 222.

Marchese, Theodore J. 1985. Bitting, bargains, seatwork, and finishers. *Change* 17 (May-June): 6.

Margo, Robert A. 1986. Educational achievement in segregated school systems. *American Economic Review* 76 (September): 794.

Maryland school district guarantees its graduates. 1989. *Jet* 77 (20 November): 37.

McHugh, Nancy et al. 1987. Where should we English teachers be heading in the next 10 years? *English Journal* 76 (April): 16.

McLean, Leslie, and Goldstein, H. 1988. U.S. national assessments in reading: Reading too much into the findings. *Phi Delta Kappan* 69 (January): 369.

Memory, David M. 1983. Preparing students in survival reading: The content area option. *The Clearing House* 56 (April): 349.

Mental deficit. 1986. *American Demographics* 8 (November): 13.

Milk vs. cream? 1980. *Time* 115 (31 March): 39.

Milner, J. O. 1987. Peripheral curriculum. *The Clearing House* 51 (September): 4.

Myers, Miles. 1984. Shifting standards of literacy: The teacher's Catch-22. *English Journal* 73 (April): 26.

Myers, Wendy S. 1989. School and industry: A partnership in education. *Women in Business* 41 (September-October): 23.

Park, Rosemarie J. et al. 1985. The selection and validation of a reading test to be used with civil service employees. *Public Personnel Management* 14 (Fall): 275.

Peck, Steven D. 1988. Teaching literacy training. *Library Journal* 113 (15 April): 56.

Perry, Nancy J. 1989. How to help America's schools. *Fortune* 120 (4 December): 137.

Petrovsky, Arthur V. 1982. Blackboard bungle? A defence of the school as the cornerstone of education. *Unesco Courier* [35] (August-September): 12-16.

Primiano, Elaine. 1989. Lauro Cavazos talks about his reading and his education goals. *Instructor* 98 (May): 34-37.

Reading, writing, and robots. 1984. *Instructor* 94 (August): 30.

Restructuring American education: A time of ferment. 1986. *Current* 286 (October): 9-22.

Reuter, Madalynne. 1987. Experiment at P.S. 192: Babar and Horton teach reading. *Publishers Weekly* 231 (27 February): 88-89.

Richardson, Richard C., Jr. 1985. How are students learning? *Change* 17 (May-June): 42.

Riley, James D., and Shapiro, John. 1987. Providing effective instruction for problem readers. *The Clearing House* 60 (March): 318.

Roberts, Francis. 1983. All about reading. *Parents Magazine* 58 (August): 36.

Roser, Nancy L. 1989. Read—and write—all about it! *Sesame Street Parents Guide* (October): 30.

Schneider, Joe. 1985. Research spawns unexpected offspring. *NEA Today* 3 (April): 17.

Schroth, Raymond A. 1987. Whether universities are closing the American mind. *National Catholic Reporter* 23 (2 October): 7.

Selsky, Deborah. 1990. The condition of education and reading proficiency. *Library Journal* 115 (1 February): 36.

Shanker, Albert. 1988-1989. Illiteracy: It's not all discouraging words. *American Teacher* (December-January).

Simons, Sandra McCandless. 1988. Beyond the spell of written words. *Instructor* 98 Pt. 2 (October): 22-24.

Smith, Ronald E. 1985. Literacy and the English teacher: Observations and suggestions. *English Journal* 74 (December): 22.

Stimpson, Catharine R. 1988. Is there a core in this curriculum? And is it really necessary? *Change* 20 (March-April): 26.

Striner, Herbert E. 1987. Education: The road to American productivity. *Management Quarterly* 28 (Fall): 39.

Taylor, Denny. 1989. Toward a unified theory of literacy learning and instructional practices. *Phi Delta Kappan* 71 (November): 184.

Thompson, C. L., and Williamson, J. 1988. Literacy musts: The jug and the wine. *The Clearing House* 62 (December): 148.

Time to call a halt to "the mutilation of English." 1983. *U.S. News & World Report* 95 (7 November): 86.

Toward tomorrow. 1985. *NEA Today* 4 (September): 25.

Troy, Helen B. 1982. Success of our public schools. *Education Digest* 47 (April): 22.

Tsurumi, Yoshi. 1983. A different perspective on U.S. education results. *Heating & Refrigeration News* 159 (16 May): 42.

Weir, Patricia A. 1986. Our faltering educational system: How technology can help. *Vital Speeches* 52 (15 June): 523.

Whimbey, Arthur. 1987. A fifteenth-grade reading level for high school seniors? *Phi Delta Kappan* 69 (November): 207.

Wilensky-Lanford, Sheila. 1989. Children's booksellers and teachers: Partners in literacy. *Publishers Weekly* 235 (20 January): 101.

Wixson, Karen et al. 1987. New directions in statewide reading assessment. *Journal of State Government* 60 (April): 73.

Zirinsky, Driek. 1987. Facing our own literacy crisis. *English Journal* 76 (December): 61.

Zuckerman, Mortimer B. 1989. Illiteracy epidemic. *U.S. News & World Report* 106 (12 June): 72.

Family Literacy, Reading in the Home, and Children

ALA and Bell Atlantic join to break cycle of illiteracy. 1989. *Library Journal* 114 (August): 28.

Bell Atlantic and ALA join literacy fight. 1989. *School Library Journal* 35 (October): 14.

Bell Atlantic to finance family literacy project. 1989. *American Libraries* 21 (July-August): 707.

Bell, Elise. 1988. An endangered species? *Instructor* 98 (November-December): 8.

Bettelheim, Bruno. 1982. How parents can help their child learn to read. *McCall's* 109 (February): V-8.

Bettelheim, Bruno, and Zelan, Karen. 1981. Why children don't like to read. *The Atlantic* 248 (November): 25.

Bjorklund, David, and Bjorklund, B. 1988. Babe Ruth is not a candy bar ... other facts children must know to boost their learning power. *Parents Magazine* 63 (September): 127.

Bloom, Allan. 1987. "A book can transform a life." *U.S. News & World Report* 103 (28 September): 95.

Broyard, Anatole. 1982. Reading to the kids. *The New York Times Book Review* 87 (3 October): 39.

Butler, Dorothy. 1983. Reading begins at home. *The Horn Book Magazine* 59 Pt. 2 (December): 742.

Colen, Kimberly. 1986. EPA panels discuss childhood literacy and the audio market. *Publishers Weekly* 229 (21 March): 70.

Don't turn kids off to reading. 1988. *USA Today* 117 (August): 4.

Elkind, David. 1988. Cuddle up with a good book. *Parents Magazine* 63 (June): 200.

Family literacy fact sheets available. 1990. *American Libraries* 21 (April): 378.

Family literacy fair. 1990. *American Libraries* 21 (March): 268.

Family literacy project funded. 1989. *Wilson Library Bulletin* 64 (September): 18.

Fields, Howard. 1989. Barbara Bush Foundation for Family Literacy launched at White House. *Publishers Weekly* 235 (24 March): 12.

Goddard, Connie Heaton. 1988. Putting reading research into practice. *Instructor* 98 Pt. 2 (October): 8-10.

Goodman, Yetta M. 1986. Developing the writing of preschoolers: Children as active learners. *Education Digest* 51 (April): 44.

How to encourage a love of reading. 1987. *Redbook* 169 (September): PTA15.

Jeffery, Debby, and Mahoney, Ellen. 1989. Sitting pretty: Infants, toddlers, and lapsits. *School Library Journal* 35 (April): 37.

Lansky, Vicki. 1984. The eager reader. *Parents Magazine* 59 (June): 66.

Locke, Jill L. 1988. Pittsburgh's "Beginning with Books" project. *School Library Journal* 34 (February): 22.

Marzollo, Jean, and Sulzby, E. 1988. See Jane read! See Jane write! *Parents Magazine* 63 (July): 80.

Monsour to direct family literacy project. 1990. *Wilson Library Bulletin* 64 (January): 11.

Oklahoma project encourages families to read together. 1981. *American Libraries* 12 (June): 383.

Owen, Roy. 1981. 50 questions parents ask about reading. *Instructor* 90 (February): 66.

O'Neill, Hugh. 1988. What literate parents should know. *Publishers Weekly* 233 (26 February): 174.

Parents as teachers: A program for mothers. 1988. *School Library Journal* 34 (February): 10.

Pelzman, Frankie. 1989. Kudos to Bell. *Wilson Library Bulletin* 64 (October): 16-17.

Ponish, Karen. 1987. "Babywise" and toys develop literacy skills. *American Libraries* 18 (September): 709.

Rohrer, Judith A. 1988. "Flintstones" help bring high marks for Old Stone's reading campaign. *Bank Marketing* 20 (February): 28.

Rossi, Mary Jane Mangini. 1982. Read to me! Teach me! *American Baby* 44 (September): 35.

Rowan, C. T., and Mazie, D. M. 1977. Johnny's parents can't read either. *Reader's Digest* 110 (January): 153-156.

Sanoff, Alvin, and Solorzano, Lucia. 1985. It's at home where our language is in distress. *U.S. News & World Report* 98 (18 February): 54.

Segal, Julius, and Segal, Zelda. 1989. The love of books. *Parents Magazine* 64 (December): 216.

Sheffer, C. L., and Simon, A. 1988. Federal funds fight family illiteracy: The family reading program. *Bookmark* 46 (Spring): 185-187.

Smith, Franklin, 1987. Old Stone Bank brings books to life with children's theater. *American Banker* 152 (2 September): 13.

Stanton, David. 1989. Give your child's reading skills a big boost: Turn on the computer. *Compute!* 11 (March): 15.

Vos, Joan. 1989. Raising a reader. *American Baby* 51 (October): 64.

Weissbourd, Bernice. 1988. The ABC's of reading readiness. *Parents Magazine* 63 (March): 160.

______. 1989. Eager readers. *Parents Magazine* 64 (March): 190.

Wells, Melanie. 1988. The roots of literacy: Think 2-year-olds know nothing about reading? *Psychology Today* 22 (June): 20.

Wilson, Mary E. 1989. Reading: A family affair. *School Library Journal* 35 (November): 48.

Literacy Cases and Personal Narratives

Alexander, Jan. 1987. The ABCs of making it. *Money* 16 (June): 47-50.

Balamaci, Marilyn. 1989. Until he tackled his illiteracy, the Redskins' gridiron terror lived in fear of the ABC's. *People Weekly* 32 (25 September): 49.

Borris, Rose, and Jiles, Paulette. 1988. At a loss for words. *Saturday Night* 103 (June): 30.

Bragg, Forrestine A. 1989. I read and write. *Essence Magazine* 20 (May): 148.

Budz, Sherry, and Sullivan, Deidre. 1987. I've kept my secret for too long. *Redbook* 169 (October): 61.

Buttler, F. 1978. Illiterate cornerback. *New Times* 11 (16 October): 32.

Cornman, Leta. 1987. "No, you are not stupid." *Christian Herald* 110 (May): 22.

Darrach, Brad. 1988. A success as a teacher and builder, John Corcoran had a humiliating secret. *People Weekly* 30 (5 December): 199-201.

DeBlasio, Fran, and Sugden, Jane. 1986. Read all about it: How a former illiterate overcame her fear.... *People Weekly* 26 (13 October): 101.

Fotheringham, Allan. 1983. When heroes become monsters. *Maclean's* 96 (26 September): 72.

Greene, Bob. 1984. The ABCs of courage: At day's end, one man learns that he can learn. *Esquire* 102 (August): 10.

______. 1984. "I just want to read to my granddaughter." *50 Plus* 24 (December): 36.

______. 1988. ABCs of courage. *Reader's Digest* 133 (August): 126.

Jordan, Pat. 1987. Bertha's triumph. *Reader's Digest* 131 (August): 55.

Kevin Ross' explosion ends in Chicago with new beginning in Calif. 1987. *Jet* 72 (10 August): 14-15.

Lapham, Lewis H. 1984. On reading. *Harper's* 268 (May): 6.

McGowan, Hattie. 1990. Never too late: A literacy tutor's story. *Wilson Library Bulletin* 64 (February): 26.

McLaughlin, Paul. 1988. Spelling disaster. *Canadian Business* 61 (August): 83-85.

Morales, Rosario. 1987. Of course she reads. *Ms. Magazine* 41 (December): 92.

Peters, Verne. 1981. An ambulance emergency: Learning to read. *Phi Delta Kappan* 62 (May): 668.

The Ross tales: Fact or fiction? 1983. *The Sporting News* 195 (6 June): 62.

Selemani, Yusufu. 1980. "I was made to work like a plough." *Unesco Courier* [33] (June): 21.

Stingley, Alisa. 1990. Inmates escaping prison of illiteracy. *The [Shreveport] Times* 119 (25 February): 1A.

______. 1990. Non-reading CDC inmate "was lost out there." *The [Shreveport] Times* 119 (25 February): 14A.

Terrorizing Dexter Manley tearfully testifies that he learned to read at age 28. 1989. *Jet* 76 (5 June): 50.

Turpin, Audrey. 1987. I couldn't read until I was 35. *Chatelaine* 60 (April): 54.

Verdi, Bob. 1989. Manley's plight is extreme, but not isolated. *The Sporting News* 207 (12 June): 4.

Volunteers give the gift of reading to adult students. 1990. *For Our Customers* 4 (January): 2.

What it's like when you can't read or write. 1982. *U.S. News & World Report* 92 (17 May): 57.

Worthington, C. R. 1976. My father's hands. *Reader's Digest* 108 (May): 169-172.

General Literacy Articles

Ad campaign is aimed at getting people to read. 1985. *Editor & Publisher* 118 (5 January): 57.

ALA report calls for "information literate" society. 1989. *Ohio Libraries* 2 (March-April): 17.

Allen, R. R. 1976. Do you really want to know why Johnny can't write? *Vital Speeches* 43 (15 December): 148-151.

Baker, D. Philip. 1980. Work together, not apart to promote reading. *Instructor* 89 (March): 163.

Balla, Philip. 1987. Literacy wars: A modest proposal. *Publishers Weekly* 231 (30 January): 376.

Bliss, Barbara A. 1986. Dyslexics as library users. *Library Trends* 35 (Fall): 293-302.

Bolle, Sonja. 1985. The bookseller effort. *Publishers Weekly* 227 (24 May): 42-43.

______. 1986. Tips on promoting literacy at the local level. *Publishers Weekly* 229 (20 June): 45.

Bormuth, J. R. 1979. Literate U.S. *Scientific American* 240 (March): 78.

Brown, Rexford. 1987. Literacy and accountability. *Journal of State Government* 60 (March-April): 68.

Broyard, Anatole. 1987. Down with ignorance, long live ontology. *The New York Times Book Review* 92 (26 July): 12.

Burke, Jeffrey. 1980. Literacy returns: The killer spelling bee meets the conquerer bookworm. *Harper's* 260 (March): 88.

Cairns, J. C. 1979. Is illiteracy necessary? *Atlas* 26 (February): 43.

Cartoonists fight illiteracy in display. 1989. *The New York Times*, national ed. 139 (11 October): B4.

Center for the Book symposium held. 1982. *Wilson Library Bulletin* 56 (February): 408.

Chall, Jeanne S. et al. 1987. Adult literacy: New and enduring problems. *Phi Delta Kappan* 69 (November): 190-196.

Cole, G. H. 1977. Chains of functional illiteracy. *Education Digest* 43 (December): 10-13.

Cole, Robert W., Jr. 1987. Gittin' literate. *Phi Delta Kappan* 68 (February): 418.

Cook, Bruce. 1989. He gives them lessons in reading, writing and pride. *Shreveport Journal* 95 (31 August): 4B.

Criscuolo, Nicholas P. 1982. Parents and the reading program. *English Journal* 71 (April): 42.

Current programs are inadequate. 1988. *USA Today* 117 (December): 10.

Davies, Michael J. 1988. Keeping newspapers healthy: Fighting illiteracy and giving good service. *Vital Speeches* 55 (1 December): 109.

Davis, Joann. 1986. Give the gift of literacy. *Publishers Weekly* 229 (20 June): 33.

D'Ignazio, Fred. 1987. Computers for adult literacy. *Compute!* 9 (January): 86.

Enzensberger, Hans Magnus. 1986. In praise of illiteracy. *Harper's* 273 (October): 12-14.

Fischer, Marge. 1988. Fighting illiteracy is a learning process for everyone involved. *Shreveport Journal* 94 (6 September): 1B.

______. 1989. Literacy volunteers become personally involved. *Shreveport Journal* 95 (31 August): 1B.

Fringe efforts. 1979. *Assistant Librarian* 72 (May): 69.

Gerhardt, Lillian N. 1979. Sharing the blame for literacy. *School Library Journal* 26 (September): 11.

Gersh, Debra. 1986. Battling against illiteracy. *Editor & Publisher* 119 (12 April): 17.

Getting a read on literacy. 1988. *Science News* 134 (17 September): 187.

Goldberg, B. 1989. DOE maps library inroads in war on illiteracy. *American Libraries* 20 (April): 281.

Guthrie, John, and Kirsch, Irwin. 1984. The emergent perspective on literacy. *Phi Delta Kappan* 65 (January): 351.

Harr, John Ensor. 1988. The crusade against illiteracy. *Saturday Evening Post* 260 (December): 42.

Hechlinger, F. 1977. U.S. literacy level not bad. *Intellect* 106 (September): 104-105.

Heller, Anne Conover. 1985. Literacy: Reading for the Republic. *50 Plus* 25 (March): 12.

Hersey, Brook. 1985. How to help people learn to read. *Glamour* 83 (September): 369.

Hillerich, R. L. 1976. Toward an assessable definition of literacy. *English Journal* 65 (February): 50-55.

Holt, Patricia. 1981. ALA/AAP panel assesses failures in literacy aims. *Publishers Weekly* 220 (17 July): 18.

______. 1987. What everyone should know about "The Year of the Reader." *Publishers Weekly* 231 (29 May): 36.

The Illiteracy blight. 1985. *Publishers Weekly* 227 (24 May): 27.

Illiteracy fight urged on press. 1989. *The New York Times* 138 (25 April): D22.

Illiteracy in America. 1986. *Show-Me Libraries* 37 (March): 3-6.

Information literacy is focus of ALA report. 1989. *Library Journal* 114 (1 March): 20-21.

IRA calls for national literacy policy. 1987. *Wilson Library Bulletin* 62 (September): 12.

Is reading important? 1980. *USA Today* 108 (April): 15.

Jenkins, Sarah. 1985. A look at the NIE report on "Becoming a Nation of Readers." *Publishers Weekly* 227 (24 May): 33.

Johnny can't write, either. 1987. *Consumers' Research Magazine* 70 (August): 18.

Kirkus announces its literacy award: ALTA seeks nominees. 1988. *Library Journal* 113 (1 November): 22.

Krieger, James H. 1986. Scientists seek to define, determine scientific literacy. *Chemical & Engineering News* 64 (23 June): 37.

Larsen, Michael. 1985. My say. *Publishers Weekly* 227 (24 May): 82.

Lasch, Christopher. 1979. New illiteracy: Excerpt from *The Culture of Narcissism. New Times* 12 (8 January): 30.

Laurita, Raymond E. 1987. Let's do something about literacy now! *America* 156 (6 June): 455.

Ledbetter, J. T., and Daniels, H. 1976. Is there a decline in literacy? *English Journal* 65 (September): 16-20.

LeGuin, Ursula K. 1989. Read my lips: On the joys—and the necessity—of reading aloud. *Utne Reader* (July-August): 126.

Levine, Daniel S. 1989. Building futures. *The New York Times*, national ed. 139 (5 November): ED52.

Lionni, L. 1984. Before images. *The Horn Book Magazine* 60 (November-December): 727-734.

Literacy billboards. 1990. *American Libraries* 21 (April): 286.

Lubow, A. et al. 1978. Blight of illiteracy. *Newsweek* 92 (6 November): 106.

Lusk, Toni. 1989. Promoting literacy: Newspapers urged to work for public policy. *Editor & Publisher* 122 (29 July): 16.

McCall, C. 1989. A historical quest for literacy. *Interracial Books for Children Bulletin* 19 (3-4): 3-6.

McCurdy, Patrick P. 1988. Needed: Some of that old-time literacy. *Chemical Week* 142 (16 March): 3.

Mendelsohn, V., and Sheffer, C. L. 1987. To read or not to read: Trustees and the challenge of literacy. *Bookmark* 45 (Summer): 271-272.

Mickelson, Carolyn. 1988. Unreadable pain. *Seventeen* 47 (April): 97.

Miller, George A. 1988. The challenge of universal literacy. *Science* 241 (9 September): 1293.

Miller, Jon D. 1983. Scientific literacy: A conceptual and empirical review. *Daedalus* 112 (Spring): 29.

Miller, L. W. 1985. Thoughts on visual literacy. *Choice* 22 (March): 936.

Muck, Terry C. 1989. Don't wait to see the movie. *Christianity Today* 33 (3 November): 13.

Murphy, Reg. 1988. Sounding the alarm on illiteracy. *Editor & Publisher* 121 (18 June): 80.

Need for coalitions stressed at information literacy symposium. 1989. *School Library Journal* 35 (June): 15-16.

Nelson, M. G. 1984. Sorrows of being streetwise. *Wilson Library Bulletin* 59 (November): 164.

Nelson, W. Dale. 1979. Still on the march. *Wilson Library Bulletin* 53 (June): 716.

______. 1985. Books in our future. *In* Dateline: Washington. *Wilson Library Bulletin* 59 (February): 394.

______. 1985. Sharpening reading skills. *In* Dateline: Washington. *Wilson Library Bulletin* 59 (April): 534.

______. 1988. Literacy—a campaign issue. *Wilson Library Bulletin* 62 (March): 60.

New ignorance: Scientific illiteracy in the United States. 1981. *The Futurist* 15 (August): 74.

Newspapers and illiteracy. 1988. *Editor & Publisher* 121 (25 June): 6.

No respect for words: Author James Baldwin. 1980. *Jet* 58 (29 May): 45.

Nyed, Diana. 1989. How illiteracy makes athletes run. *The New York Times*, local ed. 138 (28 May): S8 (L).

Older Americans who never learned to read. 1984. *Aging* 347 (October-November): 44-45.

Opheim, Teresa. 1987. Now read this.... *MPLS-St. Paul Magazine* 15 (June): 86-89.

Over 25 cartoonists do literacy drawings. 1989. *Editor & Publisher* 122 (2 September): 38.

Pelzman, F. 1989. Information literacy—a common ground. *Wilson Library Bulletin* 63 (June): 82-83.

Plethora of ABC illiteracy shows spurs Disney to cancel a TV pic. 1986. *Variety* 323 (25 June): 51.

Potential for progress. 1985. *World Health* 28 (April): 21.

Prewitt, Kenneth. 1983. Scientific illiteracy and democratic theory. *Daedalus* 112 (Spring): 49.

Printing = literacy = knowledge. 1989. *Graphic Arts Monthly and the Printing Industry* 61 (May): 143.

Radoff, L. 1985. Illiteracy: A solution. *Texas Library Journal* 61 (Winter): 108-109.

Radolf, Andrew. 1987. Major SNPA project: Combat illiteracy. *Editor & Publisher* 120 (10 October): 16-17.

Reading on ice. 1980. *American Libraries* 11 (March): 171.

Rodriguez, Johnetta Frick. 1987. The ABC's of literacy. *Ms. Magazine* 41 (December): 74.

Selfe, Cynthia L. 1988. The humanization of computers: Forget technology, remember literature. *English Journal* 77 (October): 69.

Shaughnessy, M. P. 1978. Literacy: Errors and expectations. *The New Yorker* 54 (6 November): 36-37.

Smith, Frank. 1989. Overselling literacy. *Phi Delta Kappan* 70 (January): 352-359.

Star, Jack. 1981. Teaching Willie to read. *Chicago* 30 (May): 180.

Steiner, George. 1985. Books in an age of post-literacy. *Publishers Weekly* 227 (24 May): 44-48.

Turock, B. J. 1987. Illiteracy. *The Bottom Line* 1 (2): 3.

TV series to help promote literacy. 1989. *Shreveport Journal* 95 (31 August): 4B.

Vrcan, Lori. 1988. Lighting the way to literacy. *School and College* 27 (August): 57.

Vulgamore, M. L. 1982. The place of the fourth miracle. *Vital Speeches* 48 (15 August): 662.

Wagner, S. 1978. Literacy crisis. *Publishers Weekly* 214 (18 September): 95.

West, Fred. 1986. Illiteracy and jargon. *U.S. News & World Report* 101 (13 October): 75.

What is the state of reading in America today? 1988. *Instructor* 98 Pt. 2 (October): 4-5.

What some publishers are doing. 1985. *Publishers Weekly* 227 (24 May): 37.

Whittemore, R. 1977. Newspeak generation. *Harper's* 254 (February): 16.

Williams, Dennis A. 1984. One-on-one against illiteracy. *Newsweek* 104 (30 July): 78.

Williams, J. 1985. The illiterate: Still not reading after all these years. *Ohio Library Association Bulletin* 55 (July): 26-27.

Zuckerman, Faye. 1988. Read all about it! Celebrities act on their literary instincts. *Shreveport Journal* 94 (6 September): 2B.

INDEX

WEST KENDALL